Warners Group Publications
The Maltings
West Street
Bourne
Lincolnshire
PE10 9PH
Tel: 01778 391000
Fax: 01778 392422
www.warnersgroup.co.uk

Publisher
Rob McDonnell
robm@warnersgroup.co.uk

Editor
Andy Saunders
andy.saunders@warnersgroup.co.uk
Tel: 01753 770712

Colourisation Artist
Richard J Molloy
@colourbyRJM

Aircraft Profile Artwork
Andy Godfrey
teaselstudio@yahoo.co.uk

DESIGN
Head of Design and Production
Lynn Wright
Designer
Mike Edwards

MARKETING
Marketing Manager
Katherine Brown
katherine.brown@warnersgroup.co.uk
Tel: 01778 395092
Marketing Executive
Luke Hider
luke.hider@warnersgroup.co.uk
Tel: 01778 395085

ADVERTISING
Sales Executive
Kristina Green
kristina.green@warnersgroup.co.uk
Tel: 01778 392096
Production Manager
Nicola Lock
nicola.lock@warnersgroup.co.uk
Tel: 01778 392420
Production Assistant
Charlotte Bamford
charlotte.bamford@warnersgroup.co.uk
Tel: 01778 395081

DISTRIBUTION
Warners Distribution
Andy Perry
Tel: 01778 391152

This publication is printed by Warners 01778 395111

Reproduction in whole or in part without written permission is prohibited. All rights reserved. Dates, information and prices quoted are believed to be correct at time of going to press but are subject to change and no responsibility is accepted for any errors or omissions. Neither the editor nor the publisher accept responsibility for any material submitted, whether photographic or otherwise. While we endeavour to ensure that firms and organisations mentioned are reputable, the Editor can give no guarantee that they will fulfil their obligations under all circumstances. Whilst every care has been taken to compile current valuations, the publishers cannot accept liability for loss, financial or otherwise, incurred by reliance placed on the information herein.

DISCLAIMER: The views expressed by contributors and advertisers are not necessarily those of the publishers. Every care is taken to ensure that the contents of the magazine are accurate but the publishers cannot accept responsibility for errors. While reasonable care is taken when accepting advertisements, the publishers cannot accept any responsibility for any resulting unsatisfactory transactions. They will however investigate any written complaints.

THE BATTLE OF BRITAIN

Welcome

The Battle of Britain will forever hold a special place in the collective memory of the peoples of Great Britain and her Commonwealth and was also a battle which saw the participation of airmen from no less than 15 nations, including the occupied countries of Europe. It was also a battle on which national survival depended if Germany was to be held at bay and prevented from launching any invasion and occupation of the British Isles. Indeed, such was its significance that it is unique in being the only battle of either of the world wars which has its special commemorative date set in the British calendar: Battle of Britain Day, the event marked on the nearest Sunday to 15 September each year with commemorative events and church services.

As a battle, it was perhaps caught up in the national psyche more than any other because it was fought out in the skies above Britain – and principally over the south east and London – and in full view of the British public. Certainly, the population had been exposed to relatively limited attacks by Zeppelin airships and aircraft during the First World War, although this was the very first occasion on which the British public were so much on the front line, bystanders to the greatest aerial assault that the world had yet seen. From their grandstand view of the battles which unfolded above their heads, so the public's admiration of the RAF's fighter pilots grew and was nurtured. In fact, it would be true to say that this admiration grew to adulation and hero worship as the battle progressed. This was, perhaps, increasingly the case as a realisation dawned that these young fighter pilots were seemingly all that stood between potential defeat and the catastrophe of invasion. Not only that, but as bombs began to fall on Britain in an increasing tonnage, so the RAF's fighter pilots were pretty much the only effective defence to counter the assault by the Luftwaffe's bombers. Thus, they were rightly perceived as the saviours of the nation and defenders of the people.

Eighty years on, and there is every reason to still remember with gratitude the sacrifices and the endeavours of the pilots of RAF Fighter Command during that momentous summer of 1940 and to honour their memory. Of course, the Battle of Britain has been remembered by a grateful nation across the decades and through all manner of commemorations, memorials, books, films and TV programmes. Frequently, photographs from the Battle of Britain will have been seen across many years and will be widely familiar. However, for the most part at least, these images will have been in black and white and it has often been said that our perception is almost that both world wars were fought in black and white. Now, in this unique publication, we bring you an entirely fresh view of that battle as its narrative is told through digitally colourised photographs from 1940. These colourisations have been professionally created by using references to known colours and markings of the period and by scientific evaluation of shades and tones on the original images.

I hope you enjoy this unique look at the Battle of Britain in its 80th anniversary year through a publication which is presented as a tribute to the young men of RAF Fighter Command, Churchill's revered 'Few'.

Andy Saunders
Editor, Battle of Britain in Colour

THE BATTLE OF BRITAIN IN COLOUR

The Battle of Britain
IN COLOUR

INSIDE THIS COMMEMORATIVE PUBLICATION

6 THE BATTLE LOOMS
We take a look at the lead-up to the Battle of Britain, including the Battle of France and the Dunkirk evacuations, and how those events impacted on the battles to come during the summer and autumn of 1940, as they were played out in the skies over the British Isles.

12 THE LEADERS
Two very different leaders were in charge of Britain's air defence and the Lutwaffe assault: the slightly dour and reserved Air Chief Marshal Hugh Dowding, leading RAF Fighter Command, and the flamboyantly extravagant and grandiose Reichsmarschall Herman Göring, the supreme commander of the Luftwaffe.

16 A DAY IN THE LIFE
What it meant to be a pilot in RAF Fighter Command during the Battle of Britain is examined in detail, including the mental and physical strain, the exhaustion, the nervous tension in waiting for the order to 'Scramble' and the adrenalin charged fear and excitement of combat.

30 ATTACKERS AND DEFENDERS
The equipment employed by both sides, including the quality and effectiveness of the aircraft and weaponry, were as much the deciding factors in the outcome of the Battle of Britain as was the calibre and the numbers of the men who operated that hardware.

48 THE SPITFIRE FUND
An innovative 'crowd funding' campaign, 1940 style, gave rise to a remarkable nationwide initiative for communities, organisations and businesses to raise funds for the purchase of Spitfire fighters to be gifted to the Royal Air Force.

52 A WEAPON FOR VICTORY
The unique command and control system operated by the RAF in 1940 was the first integrated air defence system in the world. Centred around radar and an observer-based reporting system, it was the key to ensuring that the Luftwaffe did not gain mastery of the air.

58 FIERCE DAYS OF FIGHTING
Although the Battle of Britain lasted from 10 July through to 31 October 1940, some days were much harder fought days than others. Three days in particular are singled out for a closer examination of the dramatic events that unfolded in the air war over the British Isles.

80 FAILED TO RETURN
When German aircraft were downed over the UK, both airframes and crews were a total loss to the Luftwaffe; the crews were either dead or prisoners and the aircraft they had flown were re-processed as scrap metal to feed the British aviation industry. We look at the stories behind some of the downed enemy aircraft during the Battle of Britain.

100 DOGFIGHTS TO BLITZ NIGHTS
When the Luftwaffe changed tactics, from attempting to destroy the RAF in the air and on the ground to its round-the-clock attacks on London, it relieved pressure on RAF Fighter Command. That, though, was of little consolation to those civilians on the receiving end. It was, however, a significant point in the Battle of Britain.

106 THE ITALIAN JOB
Briefly, and rather ingloriously, the Italian Air Force played a small part in the latter stages of the Battle of Britain, flying fighter and bomber sorties from bases in occupied Belgium. Things did not go well, however, and Italian participation in the Luftwaffe's air campaign against the British Isles was gradually drawn down.

110 THE FEARSOME CHANNEL
German fighter pilots and bomber crews not only faced the RAF after crossing the English Channel or North Sea, but then had to endure return flights, over water, possibly wounded, perhaps with damaged aircraft and sometimes running low on fuel. The Luftwaffe airman's day was just as dangerous and demanding as for their opponents.

CONTENTS

CONTRIBUTORS

Richard J Molloy
The colourisation artist for this project was Richard J Molloy who specialises in the digital colourisation of historic images. His particular interest is with military subjects and he is a regular art contributor to Iron Cross magazine, also published by Warners Group Publications Plc.

Using research based on known colours, and sometimes using period colour charts, Richard constructs accurate representations of period images. His evaluation of those images is often carried out through forensic research, requiring background investigation to properly represent the image being coloured.

This piece of work on the Battle of Britain is Richard's largest single project to date, and is work of which he is justifiably proud. Samples of Richard J Molloy's work may be viewed by searching:- @colourbyRJM

Andy Godfrey
The aircraft colour profile artwork for this publication was by Andy Godfrey of the Teasel Studio.

Andy specialises in bespoke profile artworks for publication and commission.

Working from his studio near Hastings, East Sussex, his work draws on an extensive reference collection, gathered over five decades, a deep fascination with aircraft and specialist knowledge of colours and markings. For enquiries:- teaselstudio@yahoo.co.uk

Acknowledgements

A number of individuals have helped in the production of this commemorative publication. In no particular order of merit, they are: Chris Goss, Rob Pritchard, Col Pope, Simon Parry, Winston Ramsey, Sarah Warren, Kate Pierce, Nicholas Pierce, Mark Fisher, Mike Fisher and Richard Paver.

118 URSULA'S DEMISE
The Battle of Britain captured in what was then the relatively new technology of colour photography by a Messerschmitt 110 pilot using a Leica camera and Agfa film, providing us with unique insights into the air campaign which was largely photographed, by both sides, in monochrome.

126 MEN OF THE BATTLE
The stories of those who served in the air, the 'Few', and the men and women who served and often gave all on the ground, the unsung 'many', are central to the RAF's narrative of the Battle of Britain. We pay tribute to all who served, their role in securing victory and spotlight gallantry in the air, along with the Battle of Britain's Victoria Cross action.

156 THEIR FINEST HOUR
Prime Minister Winston Churchill was the nation's inspirational and 'bulldog' leader during the Battle of Britain, spurring on both the people and the combatants with words and rhetoric in what was a battle to the death for survival, as well as a fight for the greater good of humanity and civilisation.

159 THE BALANCE SHEET
Air fighting during the Battle of Britain exacted a grievous toll on friend and foe alike, both in terms of men and of machinery. Tallying up the casualties, and the losses suffered by both sides in 1940, presents us with sobering figures. The stark numbers of the bottom line reveal the true cost to the Luftwaffe and the RAF and the scale of loss suffered by friend and foe.

THE BATTLE OF BRITAIN IN COLOUR

The Battle Looms

The Battle of Britain was one of the most iconic battles of the Second World War, embedding itself indelibly into the nation's consciousness. Earlier, the Battle of France could easily have spelled defeat before the air battles got underway in July 1940.

After the outbreak of war in September 1939, there followed eight months of what became known as the 'Phoney War'. However, it was clear that large-scale fighting would ultimately follow, and a British Expeditionary Force was sent to France before the end of that year. As part of that BEF, a large Air Component was supplemented by an Advanced Air Striking Force. In total, these air forces amounted to 25 squadrons, six of which were Hawker Hurricane-equipped fighter squadrons. The remainder of the RAF force in France comprised largely light bombers and Army Co-Operation squadrons. Eventually, however, the 'Sitzkrieg' became the 'Blitzkrieg'.

On 10 May 1940, German forces launched their all-out assault on France and the Low Countries and what followed in Belgium, the Netherlands etc. was the complete collapse of those countries under the overwhelming might of German military power. Across France, German forces rolled inexorably onwards towards the English Channel and while the French and British tried desperately to stem the advance, so the situation became ever more hopeless.

Predicted Catastrophe

When the fighting had broken out in earnest on 10 May 1940, aircraft of the Air Component were in almost constant combat, and losses had to continually be made good from squadrons based in Britain. The Commander-in-Chief of RAF Fighter Command, Air Chief Marshal Hugh Dowding, had already stated as early as September 1939, that if he was expected to defend Britain's skies, then he would need 52 fighter squadrons. At that time, he had only 32 under his command and was told it would be impossible to produce the number he required. However, efforts would be made to provide him with a further eight.

During the fighting in France, increasing numbers of fighter squadrons were sent across the Channel, urged on by desperate appeals from the French Prime Minister, Paul Reynaud. Dowding saw his resources 'slipping away like

— 6 —

BACKGROUND TO BATTLE

Left A Hurricane of 501 Squadron starts-up for an operational sortie at Betheniville, France, May 1940. Air Chief Marshal Hugh Dowding argued successfully against further wastage of the home-based RAF fighter force by sending yet more fighters to France to bolster a futile defence.

Right As the unstoppable juggernaut of German military might advanced across Europe, the deadly Junkers 87 Stuka dive-bomber came into its own. However, the RAF quickly learned how to deal with the aircraft, and this stood them in good stead when facing the Stuka during the Battle of Britain.

Below right Panzer IV tanks roll across France in May 1940. The German advance was rapid and overwhelming, and within six weeks France had collapsed and the BEF were evacuating from Dunkirk.

sand in an hour-glass' and he predicted catastrophe if Churchill continued to help the failing ally. Thus, he sent a letter to the Air Minister on 16 May 1940, which may well have saved Fighter Command, and ultimately Britain, in the nation's darkest hour. He wrote:

"I have the honour to refer to the very serious calls which have recently been made upon the Home Defence Fighter Units in an attempt to stem the German invasion on the Continent ... I would remind the Air Council that ... my strength has now been reduced to the equivalent of 36 Squadrons ... I must therefore request that as a matter of paramount urgency the Air Ministry will consider and decide what level of strength is to be left to the Fighter Command for the defence of this country, and will assure me that when this level has been reached, not one fighter will be sent across the Channel however insistent the appeals for help may be.

"I believe that, if an adequate fighter force is kept in this country, if the fleet remains in being, and if the Home Forces are suitably organised to resist invasion, we should be able to carry on the war single handed for some time, if not indefinitely. But, if the Home Defence Force is drained away in desperate attempts to remedy the situation in France, defeat in France will involve the complete and irremediable defeat of this country."

It was a hard-hitting letter, but Dowding's words had their effect and while the French still asked for more fighter squadrons to be sent to France, such appeals were rejected. However, further squadrons of Hurricanes were deployed over France, but they remained based in the UK.

Losses Mounted

At around the same time, another momentous decision was undertaken by making Lord Beaverbrook Minister of Aircraft Production. Aircraft production had in fact kept pace with fighter losses incurred during the Battle of France. Soon, production would outstrip losses. Thus, the availability of fighters would not become a limiting factor in the air defence of Britain.

However, by 1 June 1940, the RAF had lost 436 fighter aircraft and almost all its light bomber force of Fairey Battles, along with a considerable number of its Bristol Blenheims. However, RAF Fighter Command at home continued to operate over France as the situation worsened.

In a matter of six weeks, France collapsed entirely. Now, it only remained for British forces, and some units of the French army, to evacuate via Dunkirk in what was Operation 'Dynamo'. RAF Fighter Command at home continued to be called into action, covering the evacuation from Dunkirk and other French ports. Inevitably, their losses mounted. Meanwhile, the battered and depleted RAF units that had been based in France were withdrawn to Britain. Here, they were re-equipped where necessary, and manpower shortages made good so far as possible. Meanwhile, RAF Fighter Command readied for what was to come. Certainly, the Battle of France was over. The Battle of Britain was about to begin.

Immensely Powerful

Dowding had mentioned the possibility of invasion as early as the middle of May 1940, but by the end of that month the possibility had been turned into what appeared to be probability. If Hitler was to impose his will on the British people, then he could apparently only do so by crossing the English Channel and dictating his terms from Westminster. To

THE BATTLE OF BRITAIN IN COLOUR

Above The air war in France prompted huge public interest in the RAF's fighter pilots who were perceived as 'glamour boys' and already earning a kudos that only strengthened during the Battle of Britain. On the left is Flying Officer Newell 'Fanny' Orton, on the right, Flying Officer Edgar 'Cobber' Kain DFC, of New Zealand. Kain became the first Allied 'ace' of the war and was awarded the DFC in January 1940. He was killed in a flying accident on 6 June 1940. Orton was shot down on 15 May 1940 and baled out with burns. He was then shot at and wounded by French soldiers and took no part in the Battle of Britain but returned to operations in 1941, being killed in action on 17 September 1941.

Below This photograph of 'B' Flight, 56 Squadron, was taken on 3 September 1939 – the day war was declared. Within three days, two of these men had been shot down by friendly fighters. Seated at front left is Pilot Officer Hulton-Harrop, who was killed. Standing, back right, is Pilot Officer Rose who was unhurt. He was killed in action over France in May 1940.

BATTLE OF BARKING CREEK

On 6 September 1939, RAF Fighter Command suffered its first air battle fatality. However, the tragedy was that it was a 'friendly fire' incident, with Spitfires attacking the Hurricanes.

With Britain's defences at high readiness, and hordes of German bombers expected any time, the RAF's response to perceived threats was on a hair trigger.

With aircraft reported over Essex by anti-aircraft batteries at 06.15, RAF North Weald were notified and duly 'scrambled' eighteen Hurricanes of 56 and 151 Squadrons. Meanwhile, air raid sirens wailed across Essex and Kent and Spitfires of 54, 65 and 74 Squadron were 'scrambled' from Hornchurch.

Exactly what happened next is confused, but suffice to say that both groups of fighters were expecting to meet enemy aircraft. Ultimately, the Spitfires of 74 Squadron attacked the Hurricanes of 56 Squadron before the mistake was realised. Two of the Hurricanes were shot down.

Pilot Officer Montagu Hulton-Harrop was killed while Pilot officer Frank Rose made a safe force-landing in his damaged fighter. Meanwhile, anti-aircraft guns opened fire on the Spitfires of 65 and 74 Squadron, damaging one of the 65 Squadron aircraft.

It was a debacle with tragic consequences which became known as 'The Battle of Barking Creek'. Although Pilot Officer Rose survived the incident, he was one of the many fighter casualties in France, being shot down and killed on 18 May 1940.

Above The Hurricanes of 56 Squadron were accidentally attacked by Spitfires over Essex on 6 September 1939. Two of them were shot down.

BACKGROUND TO BATTLE

Top The RAF's light and medium bomber force, which had been deployed to France, took very substantial casualties. Being serviced in primitive outdoor conditions at Plivot, France, this is Bristol Blenheim Mark IV, N6227, XD-M, of 139 Squadron.
Above One of the 1,067 RAF aircraft of all types lost during the Battle of France was this 605 Squadron Hurricane which has landed on a French beach and became the object of curiosity for a group of German soldiers.
Right 'Cometh the hour, cometh the man'. Winston Churchill became Prime Minister on 10 May 1940, just as the German Blitzkrieg in the west was unleashed. He led Britain with his indomitable bulldog spirit throughout the Battle of Britain and for the remainder of the war.

THE BATTLE OF BRITAIN IN COLOUR

BATTLE JOINED

Although the Battle of Britain was officially declared to have begun on 10 July 1940, engagements between RAF Fighter Command and enemy aircraft had been going on since the Luftwaffe commenced air operations against the British Isles in October 1939. Between that time and the middle of July 1940, several Luftwaffe bombers were brought down over Britain and in its coastal waters. These included a Heinkel 111 H‑4 of Stab II/KG4, shot down in the early hours of 19 June 1940, at Cley-next-the-Sea, and which 'ditched' just offshore with its crew all captured. Photographs of the battered tail section of the aircraft were widely published in newspapers of the period. Another aircraft destroyed by RAF fighters before the official start of the Battle of Britain was a Dornier 17-Z of 8/KG77, downed at Horsmonden, Kent, on 3 July. Two crew members were killed, the other two were captured but injured. Again, the wreck of the aircraft was widely photographed for newspaper publication, the British public not yet used to regularly seeing pictures of downed enemy aircraft. That would change over the coming few months!

The unit emblem was salvaged from the Dornier and can be found today in the Army Air Corps Museum at Middle Wallop.

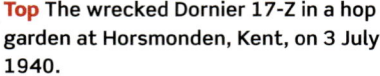

Top The wrecked Dornier 17-Z in a hop garden at Horsmonden, Kent, on 3 July 1940.
Above Sightseeing in Paris. Hitler with his entourage visited a conquered Paris on 23 June 1940, just before the Battle of Britain properly got underway.
Left The unit emblem cut from the Dornier is now preserved and on display in a UK museum.
Below left Desperate measures for desperate time. As the RAF shouldered responsibility of the air defence of the British Isles during the summer of 1940, so the Home Guard helped to bolster the ground defences in what were frequently do-or-die measures. This was an improvised armoured car in use in Berkshire, known as the 'Malcolm Campbell' car. When Sir Malcolm Campbell was the provost company commander of the 56th London Division, Home Guard, he designed and built the prototype of the Dodge armoured car. Seventy of them were constructed by Briggs Motor Bodies of Dagenham.

BACKGROUND TO BATTLE

Above The Boulton Paul Defiant became heavily involved in the air actions covering the Dunkirk evacuations. Although the aircraft suffered losses, the Defiant crews also claimed considerable success – albeit that such success was later shown to be on the rather optimistic side. The aircraft went on to serve during the Battle of Britain where it fared rather badly.

be able to achieve this meant attaining control of that narrow waterway. The Royal Navy had ruled the waves for more than 100 years, and the Kriegsmarine could pose no serious or long-term threat to Britain's command of the oceans. The Channel, though, was not the high seas.

With the Germans now in control of airfields in France and Belgium, their aircraft could range easily over the Channel. For all its might, the Royal Navy could not risk its capital ships to the dangers of aerial attack, or indeed that of enemy submarines, in the confines of the Channel. So, whilst the Royal Navy in terms of Coastal Forces would play its part in the defence of Great Britain, it would be the RAF that would carry the greatest burden.

The Luftwaffe was immensely powerful and had benefitted from considerable investment by the German government in the years running up to the war. That investment translated itself into the Luftwaffe being the most potent continental air force, equipped with the most modern aircraft.

The estimated number of aircraft available for the proposed attack on the British Isles were:
Bombers: Heinkel 111, Dornier 17,
Junkers 88 1,200
Dive-bombers: Junkers 87 280
Single-engine fighters:
Messerschmitt 109 760
Twin-engine fighters:
Messerschmitt 110 220
Long-range reconnaissance aircraft:
Dornier 17, Heinkel 111, Junkers 88
and Messerschmitt 110 50

This gave a total of around 2,500 front-line aircraft, though the actual number of serviceable aircraft available at any one time was far less than this, and possibly as little as half. This was still significantly greater than what were around 600 fighters available to Fighter Command.

Preparation For Assault

When Hitler decided on attacking Britain, he faced not just an efficient air force, but a whole nation. Why then did the German dictator attempt such an operation against a people he openly admired, a nation backed by its industrial might and the resources of the world's largest and most loyal Empire? The reality is that it was a battle that Hitler did not want, and one that neither he nor his generals and admirals had either carefully planned for or seriously envisaged. However, Hitler ultimately decided to launch an invasion of the British Isles in an operation called Seelöwe, or Operation Sealion. For such an operation to have even a chance of success, then air superiority was necessary. Thus, the Luftwaffe were charged with the destruction or neutralisation of the RAF.

After the evacuation from France in May and early June 1940, there was a respite of a few weeks before the Luftwaffe air assault got properly underway. This short time frame allowed a breathing space for RAF Fighter Command to ready itself for what was to come. However, the fact of the matter was that German air attacks against the British Isles had been going on since October 1940, and these were air attacks which were already being countered by RAF Fighter Command. But what was to come was clearly to be a far more devastating blow as Luftwaffe bomber and fighter forces moved into France and Belgium, right up to the English Channel coast, in preparation for the assault.

The air attacks against the British mainland, and against shipping in coastal waters, gradually gathered in momentum and intensity in early July 1940.

The Battle of Britain was about to begin. ■

THE BATTLE OF BRITAIN IN COLOUR

Leader of the 'Few'

Air Chief Marshal Hugh Dowding is rightly given credit for not only preparing Britain's air defence system which ultimately brought success in the Battle of Britain, but also in his brilliant leadership of RAF Fighter Command during that battle.

Air Chief Marshal Hugh Caswall Tremenheere Dowding was born in Moffat on 24 April 1882, and educated at St Ninian's School and Winchester College. He trained at the Royal Military Academy before being commissioned in the Royal Garrison Artillery in 1900.

Promoted to lieutenant on 8 May 1902, he served with the RGA before becoming interested in aviation. Gaining his Aviator's Certificate in 1913, he attended the Central Flying School, where he was awarded his wings. Although added to the Reserve List of the Royal Flying Corps, Dowding resumed his RGA duties.

In August 1914, he joined the RFC as a pilot on 7 Squadron and was promoted to Major in 1915. In 1916, having been promoted to temporary lieutenant colonel in 1916, he was given command of 7 Wing at Farnborough, transferring to command 9 Wing in France in June. Returning to England, he was promoted to temporary colonel on 1 January 1917, as commander of Southern Group Command, and became temporary brigadier-general in June 1917, before commanding Southern Training Brigade in August. Sent to York as chief staff officer in April 1918, he was made Companion of the Order of St Michael and St George in January 1919.

Dowding was given a permanent commission in the RAF in August 1919, with the rank of group captain, commanding 16 Group from October 1919 and 1 Group from February 1920. Promoted to air commodore on 1 January 1922, he was appointed Chief Staff Officer for RAF Iraq Command in August 1924.

In May 1926, Dowding was director of training at the Air Ministry and made a Companion of the Order of the Bath on 2 January 1928, being promoted to air vice marshal on 1 January 1929.

He became Air Officer Commanding Fighting Area, Air Defence of Great Britain, in December 1929, joining the Air Council as Air Member for Supply and Research in September 1930. He was promoted to air marshal on 1 January 1933, and advanced to Knight Commander of the Order of the Bath on 3 June 1933.

The 'Dowding System'

In July 1936, Dowding was the first commander of the new RAF Fighter Command, conceiving the 'Dowding System' of integrated air defence. He also introduced modern aircraft into service during the pre-war period, including the Spitfire and Hurricane. He was promoted to air chief marshal on 1 January 1937, and became Knight Grand Cross of the Royal Victorian Order in January 1937. Due to retire in June 1939, Dowding was asked to stay on until March 1940 because of the international situation, and was again permitted to continue through the Battle of Britain until November 1940.

In 1940, Dowding, nicknamed "Stuffy", was unwilling to sacrifice aircraft and pilots in the Battle of France, resisting requests to weaken home defence by sending precious squadrons to France.

Beyond the system of integrated air defence, his major contribution was to marshal resources (including replacement aircraft and aircrew) and maintain significant reserves while leaving subordinate commanders' hands free to run the battle in detail.

Dowding was known for humility and

Above Removed from command in November 1940, Dowding maintained an interest in his 'dear fighter boys'. Here, in bowler hat, he is flanked by participants in the Battle of Britain outside the Air Ministry on the 1942 anniversary of the battle.

great sincerity, and was characterised as caring for his men, with their best interests at heart. He referred to his fighter pilots as his "chicks": indeed, his son Derek was one of the 'Few', a Spitfire pilot with 74 Squadron.

Because of his brilliant preparation of air defences, and prudent management of resources, Dowding is given large credit for victory in the Battle of Britain.

Dowding was made Knight Grand Cross of the Order of the Bath in October 1940. He unwillingly relinquished command on 24 November 1940, but was elevated to the peerage in June 1943.

Post war, he developed interests in spiritualism and was a leading anti-vivisectionist. In 1969, in the film *Battle of Britain*, he was played by Laurence Olivier.

He died in Tunbridge Wells on 15 February 1970. His cremated remains were buried beneath the Battle of Britain window in Westminster Abbey, recognising the unique place he held in ensuring Britain's survival during the Second World War. ■

THE COMMANDERS

Air Chief Marshal Hugh Caswall Tremenheere Dowding, C-in-C, RAF Fighter Command, 1940.

THE BATTLE OF BRITAIN IN COLOUR

Hermann Göring

The commander-in-chief of the Luftwaffe during the Battle of Britain was Hermann Göring, an ineffectual and boastful leader throughout the war. He was instrumental in the German failure of being unable to wrest air superiority from the RAF in 1940.

On 26 February 1935, Adolf Hitler signed a secret decree authorising the establishment of the Luftwaffe as Germany's third military service. This was independent of the Heer (Army) and Kriegsmarine (Navy), the decree also appointing Hermann Göring as commander-in-chief of the newly formed service.

Hermann Göring was born to a Bavarian foreign service officer and his peasant wife in 1893, later attending the Berlin Lichterfelde Military Academy before joining the Prince Wilhelm Regiment (112th Infantry) in 1912. After a severe bout of rheumatism, which supposedly resulted from exposure to dampness during trench warfare, he arranged in 1916 for his own transfer, through connections fostered with nobility, to Feldflieger Abteilung 25 (Field Flying Unit 25), initially as an observer. Drawn to the glory of becoming a fighter pilot, he completed his flying training and was eventually posted to Jagdstaffel 26 (Fighter Squadron 26) in February 1917.

Through the next year, he became a successful fighter pilot and was made commander of Jasta 27, amassing 18 accredited victories. Afraid that the war would end before he reached 20 victories, the number required to be considered for the coveted *Pour le Merite* (the famous 'Blue Max'), he persuaded an influential friend to lobby for him and was awarded the prestigious decoration on 2 June 1918, ahead of the requisite 20 'kills', although he did eventually claim 22.

He was adroit at leveraging connections, and when Manfred von Richthofen's replacement was killed in July 1918, while test flying an aircraft, Oberleutnant Göring had himself appointed as the next – and last – commander of Jagdgeschwader 1, the famous 'Richthofen Flying Circus'.

Critical Errors

In 1922, he married into money and Swedish nobility, going on to do a little 'barnstorming' flying before moving to Munich to study political science. Here, he met and became enthralled with Adolf Hitler and joined the NSDAP. Göring came into his own as a Nazi politician, being elected to the Reichstag in 1928, and arranging to have himself appointed Prussia's Minister of the Interior, which gave him control of the state police.

When Hitler came to power, he initially appointed Göring to his Cabinet as minister without portfolio. Once made commander-in-chief of the Luftwaffe, he oversaw its development and expansion, mostly as a basis for promoting his own power and influence. Prior to the start of the Second World War, Göring only exerted command authority over personnel moves and aircraft production. He was not an airpower expert, had not flown an aircraft since 1922, had no knowledge or experience in air campaigning and initially left doctrine, technological development and combat operations to the professionals.

In the summer of 1940, however, Hitler ordered preparations for an invasion of Britain, but for any chance of success, the Germans needed to secure air superiority.

Göring ultimately assumed overall control and direction of the air campaign,

Above Hermann Göring's prisoner photographs after he was captured by the Allies in May 1945.

arguing a sustained air assault against Britain would achieve the decisive victory needed to make invasion a possibility. But he made critical errors during the battle, including a failure to fully understand the importance of radar in Britain's defence and his ultimate decision to shift Luftwaffe's attacks away from RAF targets and onto London in September 1940.

His influence declined after the Luftwaffe's failure in the Battle of Britain and against Soviet forces on the Eastern Front, as well as its inability to respond effectively to Allied strategic bombing.

In the last weeks of the war, with Hitler trapped in an encircled Berlin, Göring sought authorisation to assume power but was denounced as a traitor. Following the surrender in May 1945, he was arrested and became the highest-ranking Nazi tried at the Nuremberg war crimes tribunal. Convicted of crimes against peace, war crimes and crimes against humanity, he was sentenced to death.

Göring committed suicide on 15 October 1946 – the night before his scheduled execution. ■

THE COMMANDERS

THE BATTLE OF BRITAIN IN COLOUR

A Day in the Life

Life for a fighter pilot during the Battle of Britain was gruelling. Whether engaging the enemy, or awaiting the call to battle, physical and mental exhaustion was also the enemy.

The RAF fighter pilot during the Battle of Britain was, typically, just 21 years old. His life on a front-line fighter squadron was demanding and exhausting, although levels of activity varied considerably, the days began early and usually ended just before dusk. During that time, a pilot or aircrew member could be called upon to make operational flights two or three times or more in a single day. Waiting for action was nerve jangling, and the wait for a call to action was particularly stressful. When it came, action could be brief and frantic. Or it could involve prolonged and exhausting dogfighting, where the mental effort could be debilitating.

Although pilots and squadrons were often 'rested' and moved to quieter Groups or Sectors, it sometimes became impossible for them to be released from duty on rest days as Dowding intended. For example, 501 Squadron served the entirety of the battle on the front line without ever being rested. On the other hand, some squadrons saw comparatively little action. And some pilots never once saw the enemy.

Overall, it was a tough and dangerous life with a high probability of death or serious injury. Despite public perception that the fighter pilot's life was a rather glamorous one, it was far from being so. And it was often short.

The Waiting Game
A day in the life of a fighter pilot generally began around 4am, with officer pilots roused by their batmen with a cup of tea. On the other hand, sergeant pilots got themselves up to make their own tea before a truck collected all flying personnel to drive them out to squadron dispersal points at around dawn. Far too early to have made use of the station's mess facilities for breakfast. In any event, nervous tension did not generally enhance appetite for food. If the fliers wanted to eat, ground personnel at Dispersal cooked bacon and eggs. Tea and cocoa were in plentiful supply, but eating or drinking was the last thing

THE RAF FIGHTER PILOT

Facing page Squadron Leader Rupert Leigh, the CO of 66 Squadron, prepares for another sortie during the Battle of Britain as his fitter, equipped with tin helmet and gas cape, helps him strap in. The emblem under the cockpit is the rank marking for a squadron leader. Rupert Leigh survived the war.

Above Sergeant Pilot Douglas Corfe of 610 Squadron waits at readiness in the cockpit of his Spitfire during the summer of 1940. On 22 August, he was shot down in flames near Folkestone, and on 18 September he was shot down again, baling out near Canterbury. Douglas Corfe survived the Battle of Britain but was killed in action over Malta on 25 April 1942.

THE BATTLE OF BRITAIN IN COLOUR

THE JARGON

A range of code-words and official terminology was in use during the Battle of Britain by aircrew and controllers. It was known as 'The Fighter Code'.

The code words were not slang terms. Instead, they were words for specific actions etc. They are set out below in the order in which instructions might typically be issued:

- Take off and set
  course immediately: ....SCRAMBLE
- Climb to: ....ANGELS
- Alter Course to:......................VECTOR
- Increase speed to
  normal full speed:.................BUSTER
- Increase speed to
  maximum full speed:..................GATE
- Reduce speed to
  normal cruising speed:..............LINER
- Circle and search: ....ORBIT
- Enemy:.....................................BANDIT
- Unidentified aircraft:..................BOGY
- Enemy sighted:....................TALLY-HO
- Return to Base: ....PANCAKE

on the mind of a Battle of Britain pilot during operational periods.

At dispersal, the squadron commander (or flight commander) made sure his pilots had been allocated their aircraft, updating them with specific orders, and information and instructions for the day. Meanwhile, fitters, riggers and armourers got 'their' aircraft ready for the day, checking fuel, oil, oxygen and ammunition and carrying out routine Daily Inspections. With everything signed-off and ready for flight and fight, the accumulator starter trolley was plugged in and the aircraft started up by the fitter. With the engine run up and warmed, the aircraft stood ready for instant action as the pilot checked final cockpit details: gun-sight working and illuminated, seat and rudder pedals adjusted for his height, parachute and flying helmet stowed and ready. Now, the CO (or flight commander) rang through to the Sector Operations Room to declare his squadron ready for business. His men were now declared 'AVAILABLE'. Now, the waiting game began.

If they were lucky, pilots might be released from dispersal, one section at a time, for breakfast, lunch or dinner. Otherwise, it was a case of impromptu meals at Dispersal. Here, waiting was taken up with reading - or maybe playing chess, cards or darts. Anything to ease nervous tension and boredom as they lounged on the grass or in deck chairs. If chilly, the pilots assembled in the Dispersal Hut where a pot-bellied stove provided some comfort during the cold mornings and evenings of the latter stages of the battle. At Dispersal, there was no rigid segregation between officer and NCO pilots which was found elsewhere on the station, or in normal service life.

'Scramble!'

Sometimes, waiting at Dispersal would become interminably nerve-jangling. But when it was shattered it was inevitably by telephone. The tight nervous knot in the stomach of every waiting pilot was something that never went away. Even the most seasoned fighter pilots privately admitted they were often afraid. They would say of those who claimed they

THE RAF FIGHTER PILOT

were not afraid that they were either liars or foolish. However, a strident jangling of the telephone could mean several things. Sometimes, to intense relief, it could send a message to 'Stand Down'. Other times, it called pilots to readiness, and then to the heart-pounding order: 'SCRAMBLE!'

Years afterwards, veterans of the Battle of Britain told how they hated the sound of a ringing telephone.

On the order to scramble, there was a mad rush by pilots to their allotted aircraft where the fitter and rigger were ready and waiting: the rigger on the wing ready to help in his pilot, and the fitter standing by with the starter plugged in on the starboard side of the engine. Heaving himself into the cockpit, the pilot went through a number of tasks: helmet pulled on, oxygen plugged in, radio jack-plug in its socket, magneto switches 'on', Ki-Gas cylinder priming pump given a couple of brief strokes and thumb ready on the starter. Meanwhile, leaning into the cockpit, the Fitter helped the pilot with his parachute harness straps, then his Sutton seat harness.

By this time, the starter button was pushed after a thumbs-up from the fitter, who unplugged the starter trolley, ensuring it was clear of the aircraft. Unable to communicate over the roar of the Merlin engine, the pilot and rigger exchanged thumbs up signals, the rigger slapping his pilot on the shoulder to convey reassurance and good-luck as he leapt from the wing. As he jumped, the aircraft was already rolling, and the rigger dodged out of the way of the tail-plane, buffeted by the slipstream which was kicking up dust and grass. Getting out of the way, he was hit by a blast of hot exhaust gasses. Now, the aircraft gathered speed ahead, into wind, bouncing and rocking across the grass airfield. Others careered along around it, in the organised chaos that was a squadron scramble.

Getting airborne, the pilots concentrated on keeping station as they selected 'Gear Up', closing the cockpit canopy while listening out for instructions from the CO or flight commander who was talking to the Sector Operations Room and garnering instructions as to heading, altitude and

Facing page Pilots of 19 Squadron are delivered to their dispersal point at RAF Duxford ready for operations early one morning during the summer of 1940.
Above Their relaxed look perhaps concealing the tension, these Hurricane pilots of 501 Squadron pose for the camera during the summer of 1940. All of them saw action. Several of them shot down enemy aircraft and some of them were killed.

what it was they were intercepting. It may have been an instruction along the lines of: "MITOR Squadron, ANGELS 18, Vector Two-three-zero. Fifty Plus. BUSTER." Listening in, the other pilots could interpret these coded instructions: "41 Squadron to climb to 18,000 ft on a heading of 230 degrees. Fifty plus enemy aircraft. Maximum cruising speed."

Mentally and Physically Draining

Settling into the climb, the pilots automatically slid into section order and the preferred squadron formation. Meanwhile, the CO or flight commander concentrated on setting course as the

THE BATTLE OF BRITAIN IN COLOUR

THE RAF FIGHTER PILOT

other pilots concentrated on what was going on in their cockpits: oil temperatures and pressures, fuel state, oxygen contents checked and selected to 'On', microphone not on 'Transmit' (this could effectively block all other transmissions), straps tight, gun-sight 'On' and illuminated, straps tight and canopy firmly shut. A surprising number would carry out a little good luck routine like feeling for a lucky charm, or even crossing themselves.

Now, the workload was high, and still they needed to concentrate on formation keeping while permanently keeping a wary eye open for the enemy and quartering the sky in a relentless search. A moment of relapse could literally spell death. The squadron 'Weaver', winding from side to side, kept a rather more wary eye open than the rest, as the squadron got closer by the second to their quarry. Brief instructions might crackle through the headphones: 'Close up Red 2' or, on receipt of further instructions from the Fighter Controller: 'Turning to Port. Go!'

Meanwhile, pilots fiddled with the radio tuner, struggling to tune and re-tune their wireless sets in a constant battle to receive and properly understand the messages. Sometimes, a squawk of static drowned out everything, sometimes resulting in one section haring off suddenly, upwards or downwards, the rest of the squadron watching in bemusement and puzzled because they received no transmission, or else just couldn't understand what had been said. Meanwhile, constant juggling of the throttle setting with the left hand, and judicious adjustment of position through the control column and rudder pedal inputs, were all necessary just to keep station. It was incredibly hard work, and mentally and physically draining.

By now, the squadron was 'on oxygen', masks clamped securely to pilot's faces as cold began to permeate the cockpits. Now, with all the hard work of take-off, formation flying and getting to altitude, came further nervous tension with realisation that the enemy were near. Then, a tight knot of fear returned as the gunsight was checked and the SAFE and FIRE ring on the gun button turned, ready, to the FIRE position. Goggles pulled down. And then the shout:

'BANDITS! Ten o'clock, above. Coming down now! Break, break, break....'

Chatter Of Gunfire

Suddenly, to avoid the 'bounce' of fighters coming out of the sun, the squadron had dispersed in a pre-ordered plan. Now, the enemy fighters were among them. This time, there was no

Facing page Although posed for a news cameraman, the squadron telephone orderly shouts instructions for a 'scramble' as pilots lounge in the dispersal hut. The smartly dressed officer is Duty Pilot – the pilot rostered for ground admin tasks such as recording take-off and landing times etc.

Above It was not unusual for aircraft to return damaged after an engagement and with pilots wounded. This brand-new Spitfire had just been delivered to 602 Squadron at RAF Westhampnett when it was hit by cannon shells from a Messerschmitt 109 in a combat on 18 August 1940. The aircraft was written off and Flight Lieutenant Dunlop Urie wounded in his feet.

chance of a well-ordered textbook: 'Number One Attack'. Instead, it was every man for himself, but with 'wing men' desperately trying to maintain station and protect their section leader.

Now, the pilots were climbing and hanging on their props, the sun glaring and blinding as they turned, all the while listening out and looking out. Now, there were shouts: "Behind you Blue 3!", permeated by chattering gunfire. A cacophony of shouts and static made communication unintelligible. One pilot may be drawing a bead on a

THE BATTLE OF BRITAIN IN COLOUR

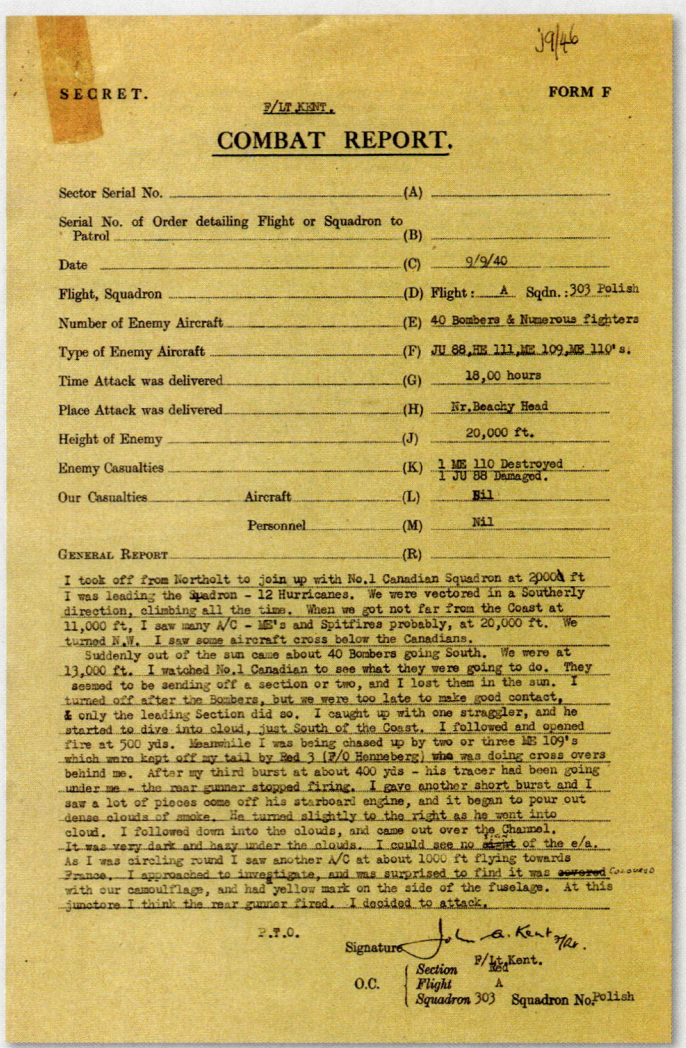

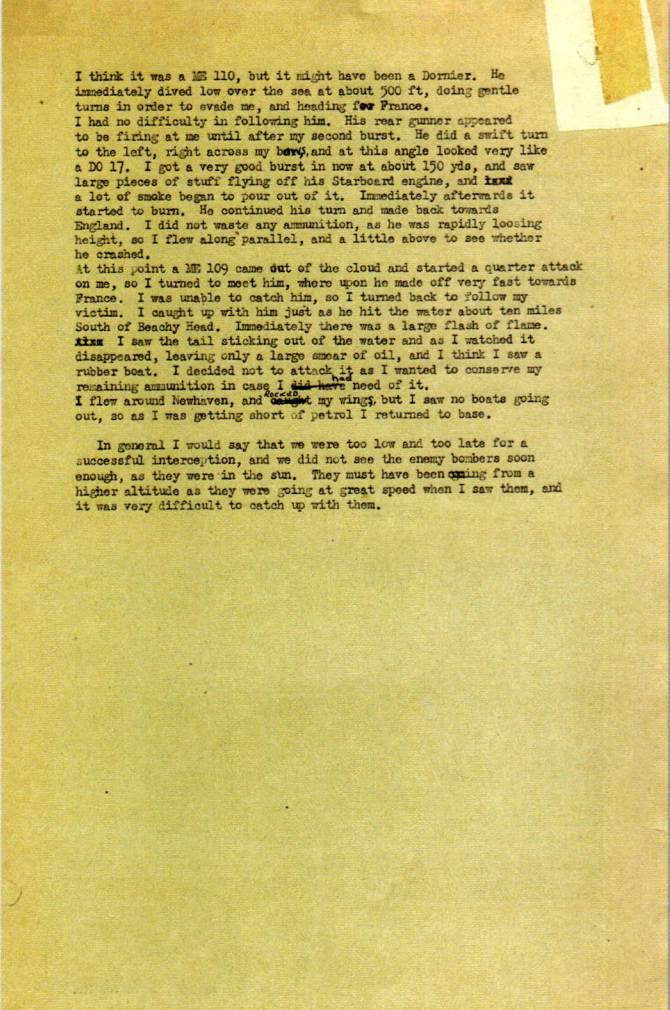

REPORTING THE 'KILLS'

On returning from operations, each pilot had to submit a combat report if an engagement with the enemy had taken place. The official criteria for allocating a claim of destroyed, probably destroyed or damaged is set out below:

'DESTROYED – to cover all cases in which the enemy aircraft is positively reported to have been seen to hit the ground or sea, to break up in the air, or to descend in flames whether or not confirmation by second source is available. This term to cover cases in which the enemy aircraft is forced to descend and is captured.

PROBABLY DESTROYED – to be applied to those cases in which the enemy aircraft is seen to break off combat in circumstances that lead to the conclusion that it must be a loss.

DAMAGED – to be applied to those cases in which the enemy aircraft was obviously considered damaged when under attack, such as: undercarriage dropped or engine stopped, or aircraft part shot away.'

Using these criteria, the Squadron Intelligence Officer determined the allocation of victories. However, they were very often confirmed rather arbitrarily, based solely on what the pilot said he witnessed. In many cases, and in the heat and stress of battle, aircraft claimed as 'Destroyed', and granted as such, were not always definite 'kills'. Sometimes, multiple pilots claimed the same aircraft, over-claiming becoming commonplace in the confusion of battle.

RAF fighter pilots during the Battle of Britain sometimes claimed Messerschmitt 109s as destroyed, probably destroyed or damaged when they were seen to dive away emitting black smoke. This was often when the enemy pilot put his aircraft into a full-power dive, resulting in black smoke from the exhausts, which led some pilots to incorrectly believe they had scored a victory.

Above Canadian "Johnny" Kent, pictured here as a Squadron Leader when commanding the Spitfire-equipped 92 Squadron at RAF Biggin Hill. His Canadian heritage is signified by a maple leaf, with a Polish badge superimposed, painted under the cockpit. The Polish emblem being a 'nod' to his previous service with 303(Polish) Squadron.

THE RAF FIGHTER PILOT

Facing page An example of a pilot's Combat Report from 1940. This report was made by Flight Lieutenant 'Johnny' Kent, who led one of the flights of 303(Polish) Squadron.

Left On returning from an air battle, fighter pilots were required to complete a Combat Report. Here, Sergeant Pilot Alan Feary, a Spitfire pilot with 19 Squadron, dictates details of his combat to the squadron's Intelligence Officer. Feary destroyed a number of aircraft during the Battle of Britain, but was shot down on 7 October 1940, over Weymouth, although died when he baled-out too low and his parachute failed to open.

Below "I saw the Messerschmitt land in a field near Maidstone. The pilot got out and waved at me." Pilots who saw their victims crash would carefully note and record the details, such as in relation to this Luftwaffe casualty when Leutnant Wilhelm Frönhofer of 9/JG26 crash-landed in a field at Ulcombe, Kent, on 31 August 1940. His aircraft has been covered with straw to camouflage it and prevent attack by passing German aircraft. The German pilot was taken Prisoner of War.

THE BATTLE OF BRITAIN IN COLOUR

"Scamble!" Although this scene has been recreated by re-enactors, it is a photograph which demonstrates not only what a typical scramble might have looked like but also the variety of flying clothing and equipment in use.

THE RAF FIGHTER PILOT

THE BATTLE OF BRITAIN IN COLOUR

Above Dressed for Battle. The full headgear of a Battle of Britain pilot, ready for action.
Right What the typical RAF fighter pilot wore into combat during the Battle of Britain: flying jacket, helmet, goggles, oxygen mask, gauntlets, flying boots and Mae West lifejacket.
Facing page, top "Refuel! Re-arm!" So goes the shout as a Spitfire of 19 Squadron returns to RAF Duxford after an operational sortie. Armourers swarm to replenish the wing guns as the fitter and rigger work on re-fuelling. The tattered red fabric on the gun ports, and smoke streaks under the wing, show this aircraft has just been in action.
Facing page, bottom left The post-mortem. Spitfire pilots of 610 Squadron gather after a sortie to discuss the action and to mull over claims and losses and figure out who has not come back.
Facing page, bottom right Down, but not out. A Spitfire pilot shot down over Kent leaps across the fence from the field where he has just landed. He could be back in action tomorrow – or even later that day.

Messerschmitt 109 who had overshot, his three second burst missing by a mile – merely hosing the air well ahead of his quarry who was now diving away.

A distinct cry of panic from an unidentified pilot might be followed by the briefest glimpse of a Spitfire falling away, vertically, trailing orange-red streaks of flame and a ghastly banner of oily black smoke. But no time to watch, however awfully mesmerising the sight and however strong the desire to know who it was. Just the nagging worry: did he get out safely?

BATTLE KIT

A universal clothing and equipment rig for pilots and aircrew of RAF Fighter Command during 1940 did not exist. Much was simply down to individual choice, although certain items were a standard requirement. Even then, there were variations on a theme. There were, however, common 'styles' – although what was worn, and how, depended on personal preferences. However, taking a typical pilot we would expect to find: flying helmet, flying goggles, oxygen mask, lifejacket, flying gauntlets and parachute harness and pack. These could not be variable.

Pilots and aircrew sometimes wore just uniform tunic, trousers and shoes into action – with nothing else apart from the headgear, lifejacket etc. However, one piece flying suits or overalls were often worn. Sometimes, knitted woollen sweaters were worn under the pilot's jacket.

Mostly, aircrew wore flying boots with thick knitted socks. Operating at high altitude, in sub-zero temperatures, keeping warm was paramount.

Less common was the Irvin sheepskin leather flying jacket. Bulky and cumbersome, they were too restrictive inside the confines of a cockpit, especially when worn with lifejacket and parachute harness. Warm and stylish they may have been. But they were hardly practical for fighter cockpits. Typically, it was regarded as de rigeur for fighter pilots to wear the top button of their uniform tunics undone. Never officially condoned, a blind eye was generally turned to this 'mark' of the fighter pilot.

The life jacket in use during 1940 was issued in drab khaki. As pilots noted, this was the same colour as the English Channel on an average day, and many pilots painted theirs yellow for greater visibility if brought down in the sea. (Examples of lifejackets painted yellow, and in their issued colour, can be seen throughout this publication.)

The leather flying helmet with headphones, and its attached oxygen mask with wireless microphone, was not an optional piece of kit. Without it, the pilot could neither communicate nor breathe at altitude. Headphones were incorporated into zipped ear cups of the helmet. The oxygen mask, in green fabric and chamois lined, clipped to the helmet. An oxygen tube led from the mask to a socket in the cockpit and leads to the microphone and headphones fed into a cable which plugged into a cockpit socket. The goggles worn with the helmet, however, varied in pattern. Some were issued, and some purchased privately by the pilot himself.

Flying gauntlets were essential, not only as protection against cold but also against burns.

Most important was the parachute. This was often stowed in the bucket seat pan of fighter aircraft, with straps left adjusted to fit and ready to be fastened. Some pilots preferred to keep theirs on the tail-plane, and to be helped into it by the fitter.

Flying clothing and equipment, then, was often a case of mix-and-match. It was worn with comfort, practicality and often superstition influencing individual choice.

– 26 –

THE RAF FIGHTER PILOT

THE BATTLE OF BRITAIN IN COLOUR

NOT TOO YOUNG TO DIE...
Summing it all up, Battle of Britain pilot Wing Commander 'Paddy' Barthropp* said:
- "In 1940 he had total control of a 350mph fighter and eight machine guns – with no radar, no auto-pilot and no electronics.
- At the touch of a button, he could unleash thirteen pounds of shot in three seconds. He had a total of fourteen seconds of ammunition. He needed to be less than 250 yards away from the enemy to be effective.
- He and his foe could manoeuvre in three dimensions at varying speeds and with an infinite number of angles relative to each other. His job was to solve the sighting equation without becoming a target himself.
- His aircraft carried 90 gallons of fuel between his chest and his engine.
- He often flew at over 20,000 ft with no cockpit heating or pressurisation. He endured up to six times the force of gravity, but with no 'G' Suit.
- He had no crash helmet or protective clothing other than ineffective flying boots and gloves.
- He had about three seconds in which to identify his foe and slightly longer to abandon his aircraft if hit. He had no ejector seat.
- Often, as in my case, he was only nineteen years old. He was considered too young and irresponsible to vote, but not too young to die.
- His pay was the modern equivalent of around sixty pence per day in 1940.
- Should he have been stupid enough to be shot down and taken prisoner, a third

of that sum was deducted at source by a grateful country and never returned.
- However, every hour of every day was an unforgettable and marvellous experience spent in the company of the finest characters who ever lived."

*Wing Commander Patrick 'Paddy' Barthropp DFC AFC, served with 602 Squadron on Spitfires during the Battle of Britain as a Pilot Officer. He was shot down over France and taken POW on 17 May 1942. He died on 16 April 2008.

In a matter of minutes, the pilot had pulled excessive 'G', almost greyed out, been shot at, briefly shot at something himself, rolled, dived, bunted and looped in desperate efforts to avoid hostile fire or to get on the tail of an enemy. The artificial horizon and compass would spin wildly, nausea overcoming the sweating, aching and frightened young pilot. Sometimes, he was sick. A combination of airsickness and fear.

Typically, he was now alone. Not an aircraft was in sight. He could no longer hear anything in his headphones - his wireless now completely off-tune, anyway. In a short span of time he had lost 10,000 feet of altitude. His fuel state and low ammunition meant he could not hang around. It was a case of setting course, alone, back to his home airfield – checking all the while on his aircraft for damage. Was everything still OK? Pressures and temperatures? Fuel state? Meanwhile, he was a sitting duck and alone. Constant head-swivelling was essential to make sure no unseen Messerschmitt should sneak up, or dive at him out of the sun.

Bullet Holes
On finals to his home airfield, and on a wide curving approach, his canopy was pulled back, and locked. Airspeed, checked. Gear down - indicated by green lights on the instrument panel. Flaps, set. Over the hedge. One bounce. Two. Then down. A careful taxy to Dispersal, fish-tailing the aircraft for visibility ahead, and already checking to see who was back. A quick blip of the throttle and the aircraft was swung around, already pointing back into wind and ready for next sortie. Then, switch off. The propeller staggered to a stop, with the sound of metal contracting, tinking and pinging, as the engine cooled.

Exhausted, sweating and shaking the pilot pulled off his helmet and mask. The rigger, on the wing, asking an enthusiastic: 'Any luck, Sir?' He perhaps hadn't noticed the vomit-stained Mae West and his pilot's grey pallor. Exhausted, the pilot hauled himself from the cockpit to face a barrage of questions. Crowding round, the armourer, rigger and fitter need to know any snags as they ready the aircraft for immediate action once more. 'No. All fine' might be all he could mumble. And then the Intelligence Officer was badgering for details of the engagement, insisting on the pilot completing his Combat Report.

The halting account might well be interrupted by a shout from his rigger: 'Sir! Take a look here!' Neat bullet holes in the fuselage are pointed out. 'Nothing important hit, sir!'

The information cheerily shrugged aside, the pilot hid his feelings. Those holes were eighteen inches from where he sat. He wasn't even aware. But death had come perilously close.

Reinforcing things, word came through

– 28 –

THE RAF FIGHTER PILOT

that the new Sergeant Pilot in Blue Section, 'Blue Three', was the man down in flames. 'Blue Two' had watched as he baled-out, but then he fell, faster and faster, like a flaming comet, his burning parachute trailing uselessly behind him.

Bullet holes in his own aircraft. One man down and dead. And dead in the most horrible of circumstances. Now, he must be ready to go again. Perhaps in twenty minutes. Perhaps twice more that day. And again tomorrow. If he lived.

Now, there was a nervous wait to see who else wasn't coming back. Then, a stand-down for a break. But nobody felt like eating or drinking. Then, back to the wait by the aircraft. And maybe some nervous fiddling with the aircraft. Checking and re-checking things like the gunsight bulbs. Then, more waiting. Just waiting, waiting, waiting…

Exhaustion took over, and perhaps he fell fast asleep - if nerves and nagging fear hadn't beaten his fatigue. The yearned for sleep didn't always come easily. It wasn't even mid-afternoon. Still a good six hours before the squadron would be stood down for the day.

Those with enough energy might make it to the local pub. Most would not have the energy. In a few short hours, it will start all over again. ■

Top left Wing Commander "Paddy" Barthropp, DFC, AFC.
Above "Patrol Hastings, Angels 20!" The Spitfires of 610 Squadron, high above southern England during 1940, on a squadron patrol.
  Based at RAF Biggin Hill for a greater part of the Battle of Britain, the squadron took heavy casualties and was eventually 'rested' in the north at RAF Acklington, and away from the main area of action, from 13 September 1940. However, despite its losses, the squadron also claimed a significant tally of enemy aircraft destroyed, with at least 63 victories confirmed during July and August.

THE BATTLE OF BRITAIN IN COLOUR

Attackers & Defenders

Two modern air forces were ranged against each other across the English Channel and North Sea during the Battle of Britain. Essentially, these were the fighter aircraft of both sides and the Luftwaffe's fleet of medium bombers.

In the pre-war and expansion years of the RAF, across the 1920s and 1930s, Britain had modernised and re-armed. By 1939, it possessed a force in RAF Fighter Command of cutting-edge and high-performance fighters.

Mostly, this force comprised eight-gun fighters in the form of Spitfires and Hurricanes, but included a few squadrons of four-gun turret fighters, the Boulton Paul Defiant. Additionally, a handful of Gloster Gladiator biplanes, armed with four machine guns, were also thrown into the fray. A few Bristol Blenheims and Beafighters also made up the numbers, each type theoretically allocated the tasks to which the aircraft was best suited.

Mostly, the aircraft were equipped with the .303 Browning machine gun, the Blenheim utilising a .303 Vickers 'K' gun. For the Spitfire and Hurricane backbone of Fighter Command, the Rolls Royce Merlin III was the reliable power plant. The same engine also powered the Defiant.

By the early summer of 1940, all these aircraft types were thrown into the life-and-death struggle in Britain's skies.

The Opposition
For the Luftwaffe, the main types used over Britain were the Dornier 17-Z, Heinkel III, Junkers 88 and Junkers 87 'Stuka' which comprised the bomber force. The German fighters were exclusively the Messerschmitt 109 and 110, although both had limitations when it came to operations over Britain.

With the Messerschmitt 109, the problem was range and duration over Britain – and this was even when operating from bases right on the Channel coast. In fact, it was often the case that Messerschmitt 109s flying over Britain to escort the bombers had to turn for home early when they ran low on fuel. Any number of Messerschmitt 109s were forced down in England, or the Channel, as they ran out of fuel.

With the Messerschmitt 110, the type was not ideally suited to close dogfighting combat with Spitfires and Hurricanes, although in the hands of skilled and competent pilots it could still be a fearsome foe and it packed a deadly punch from the nose battery of machine guns and cannon.

The bomber types, though, could range far and wide and the length of Britain – albeit with limited or no fighter protection anywhere north of London. They were, though, only medium bombers with relatively limited payloads, the Germans never bringing into production heavy long-range bombers which were later employed by the Allies. ■

Above With the modernisation of the RAF in the pre-war years, one of the most iconic and innovative new designs coming into service was the sleek Supermarine Spitfire. Shown here are the Spitfire I aircraft of 65 Squadron. The squadron first took delivery of the type in March 1939.

THE HARDWARE: THE DEFENDERS

Boulton Paul Defiant Mk I

The Defiant was of relatively conventional construction, but its all-important turret singled it out as unusual for a single-engine fighter. It had been conceived very much as a bomber formation destroyer at a time when the concept of fighter-escorted bombers attacking Britain had not been foreseen.

Whilst conventional wisdom might have us believe that this was a hopelessly outmoded design concept for modern air fighting, it was certainly not as ill-conceived as has subsequently been suggested. Such suggestions inevitably arise from its poor performance during the daylight fighting of the Battle of Britain where it proved to be no match against enemy fighters and the tactics then being employed by both sides.

Certainly, the Defiant lacked forward-firing guns and had to be manoeuvred into a fighting position by its pilot for the gunner to be able to get a bead on his quarry. However, it was never designed for fighter-on-fighter combat. Consequently, its daylight participation in the Battle of Britain had to be curtailed in light of its poor performance against single-seat fighters. However, there is no truth in the story that German fighter pilots, having first mistaken the Defiants they encountered for Hurricanes, learned how to deal with the turreted fighters as a consequence.

After the Battle of Britain, it saw rather more useful service in the night fighter role.

Technical data:
- Dimensions:
  Span – 39ft 4in, Length – 35ft 4 in.
- Power Plant: Rolls Royce Merlin III, delivering 1,030hp at 16,250ft.
- Maximum Speed: 304mph
- Service Ceiling: 30,020ft
- Armament: Four x .303 Browning machine guns in a power-operated turret.

Above Defiants of 264 Squadron during the Battle of Britain.
Right The power-operated four-gun turret of the Defiant.
Below The Defiant, when withdrawn from the day fighting role, was re-deployed by RAF Fighter Command as a night-fighter.

THE BATTLE OF BRITAIN IN COLOUR

Bristol Blenheim Mk IF

Between 1934 and the spring of 1935, the Bristol Aeroplane Company Ltd built a civilian transport aircraft which had a high speed and was of advanced design. This was to the order of Lord Rothermere, a private customer. When this proved faster than most contemporary military aircraft, Lord Rothermere presented the aircraft to the nation.

From Rothermere's aircraft, the manufacturer developed the Blenheim Mk I bomber, of which the prototype first flew in June 1936. At the request of the Air Ministry, the Bristol Aeroplane Company also developed a fighter version, the Blenheim Mk IF.

During the Battle of Britain, the Blenheim Mk IF was used as both a day and night fighter. As a day fighter it had limited value unless used against unescorted bombers, although by 1940 it was unable to catch even the German bombers then in use if engaged in a tail-chase. The Blenheim could not be pitched against escorted raids of the nature being experienced, for example, in the 11 Group area at the height of the battle and was clearly no match for either the Messerschmitt 109 or Messerschmitt 110.

It also had broad similarities to the Junkers 88, and there were unfortunate incidents when Blenheims were mistakenly shot down by other RAF fighters in 'friendly fire' episodes.

Technical data:
- Dimensions: Span 56 ft 4 in, Length 39 ft 9 in
- Power Plant: Two x Bristol Mercury VIII engines, each delivering 840 hp
- Maximum Speed: 260 mph
- Initial Rate of Climb: 1,540 ft per minute
- Service Ceiling: 27,280 ft
- Armament: Four x .303 Browning machine guns in ventral pack plus one in port wing.

Top Blenheims of 25 Squadron are prepared for operations at RAF Martlesham Heath in July 1940. As day fighters during the Battle of Britain, these were hopelessly outclassed in all but interceptions against unescorted bombers.
Left The mid-upper gun turret with its single Vickers 'K' gun can be clearly seen in this rare air-to-air photograph of a Blenheim Mk IF of 25 Squadron.
Below left The Blenheim IF, however, proved a useful stopgap night-fighter during the Battle of Britain. Here, the crew of a 29 Squadron aircraft climb aboard ready for night operations.

THE HARDWARE: THE DEFENDERS

Bristol Beaufighter I F

Like the Blenheim, the Beaufighter had started out as a private-venture design for a twin-engine and cannon armed fighter. However, by July 1938, the Air Ministry had decided to adopt the type and it immediately went into production.

By the end of 1940, only 110 Beafighters had been built, but the aircraft entered service in August 1940. Although originally intended as a day fighter, it quickly became apparent that it was better suited to the night-fighter role, largely because of ample space in which to fit the new Airborne Interception (AI) radar.

Like other cannon-equipped RAF aircraft that were put into service around this time, the weapon proved troublesome with feed mechanism issues and vibration in the mountings causing inaccurate firing. Once these problems were ironed out, the Beaufighter became an impressive night-fighter.

The Beaufighter was only just coming into service with a few Fighter Command squadrons and units as the Battle of Britain drew towards its zenith, with the first (day) sortie being carried out by 29 Squadron on 18 September. No successful engagements had taken place by the end of September, though, and by this time it was being employed exclusively in the night-fighting role.

Technical Data
- Dimensions: Span 57 ft 10 in, Length 41 ft 8 in
- Power Plants: Two x Bristol Hercules III radial engines
- Maximum Speed: 320 mph
- Initial Rate of Climb: 1,600 ft per minute
- Armament: Four x 20 mm Hispano cannon

Left When it became evident that the Beaufighter was not best suited to the day-fighter role during the Battle of Britain, it was diverted to night-fighting. In this capacity, it was a successful weapon. This was especially due to the fact that the capacious fuselage allowed for the easy installation of the new Airborne Interception (AI) Radar.

Centre Although only 110 Beaufighters had been built by the end of 1940, a total of 5,562 had been constructed by September 1945 – the aircraft turning out to be a versatile and successful one, most notably in the shipping strike and ground attack roles.

Below The Beaufighter IF was only just coming into service during the late summer of 1940, this aircraft being a machine of 25 Squadron which was the first unit operationally equipped with the Beaufighter.

THE BATTLE OF BRITAIN IN COLOUR

Gloster Gladiator Mk II

The Gladiator biplane single-seat fighter was developed by the Gloster Aircraft Co Ltd as a private venture but found to conform to an Air Ministry Specification of 1930 which was a requirement for a new RAF fighter. The prototype first flew in September 1934. Production models were built to an amended specification drawn up in 1935, the type then entering service as a front-line fighter with the RAF.

During the Battle of Britain, the Gladiator, although obsolescent, continued to be used by one flight of 247 Sqn operating from a rudimentary airstrip at Roborough, near Plymouth, which was unsuitable for Spitfires or Hurricanes. From here, fighter protection could be provided for the Royal Navy Dockyard at Plymouth. On 28 October 1940, for example, Flying Officer R A Winter intercepted a Heinkel 111 over the city.

The Gladiator was not suited, generally, for modern air combat against fighters such as the Messerschmitt 109, but it had already given a good account of itself in the Norwegian campaign against Heinkel 111s, Junkers 88s and Messerschmitt 110s. Over Greece, in 1941, Squadron Leader 'Pat' Pattle, DFC & Bar, shot down 15 of his 50 plus tally of enemy aircraft claimed as destroyed when flying the Gladiator.

The aircraft was the last of the RAF's biplane fighters.

Technical Data
- Dimensions: Span 32 ft 3 in, length 27 ft 5 in
- Power Plant: Bristol Mercury IX delivering 840 hp
- Maximum Speed: 253 mph
- Initial Rate of Climb: 2,300 ft per minute
- Service Ceiling: 33,000 ft
- Armament: Four x .303 Browning machine guns

Top During the 'Phoney War', Gladiators were still part of Britain's front-line air defence. These aircraft and pilots of 615 (County of Surrey) Squadron await the call to action at Vitry, France, in 1939. The squadron were later re-equipped with Hurricanes.
Above One of the Roborough based Gladiators of 247 Squadron pictured during 1940. The airfield was unsuitable for Spitfires and Hurricanes, but it was an essential base at which to locate air protection assets to cover the Royal Navy Dockyard at Plymouth, and the Gladiator was able to operate from the small and often muddy grass airfield.
Left The cockpit of the Gloster Gladiator.

THE HARDWARE: THE DEFENDERS

Hawker Hurricane I

The Hurricane low-wing monoplane single seat fighter was designed by Sydney Camm and developed by Hawker Aircraft Ltd as a private venture. At one time, Hawkers proposed modifying the aircraft in order to conform to a specification for a new fighter for the RAF. Eventually, though, the Air Ministry drew up an amended specification which preserved the salient features of the original Hawker design.

The prototype first flew on 6 November 1935, the Hurricane coming in to front-line service with the RAF in January 1938. It became the most numerous fighter aircraft in RAF service during the Battle of Britain.

The airframe was extremely rugged and could take considerable punishment, due in part to its fabric, wood and tubular steel rear fuselage construction and a sturdy airframe centre-section. Its wide undercarriage was also a useful attribute when landing.

The aircraft also afforded an excellent gun platform for its battery of eight .303 machine guns. Although the wings were initially fabric covered, these were later replaced with all-metal wings in time for the Battle of Britain.

It was generally intended, where possible, that Hurricanes dealt with bomber formations and Spitfires dealt with the fighters. That was not always possible, but the Hurricane had no trouble engaging with fighters. Indeed, many Hurricane pilots scored high 'kill' rates when engaging Messerschmitt 109s.

Technical Data
- Dimensions: Span 40 ft, length 31 ft 5in
- Power Plant: Rolls-Royce Merlin III delivering 1,030 at 16,250 ft
- Maximum Speed: 325 mph
- Initial Rate of Climb: 2,420 ft per minute
- Service Ceiling: 34,000 ft
- Armament: Eight x .303 machine guns

Top When the Hurricane first came into service, they were fitted with two-bladed fixed-pitch wooden propellers and fabric covered wings. These were later replaced with three-bladed variable pitch propellers and metal wings. This 1 Squadron aircraft at Tangmere in 1938 is fitted with the early propeller and wings. The squadron went on to see operations in the Battle of France and the Battle of Britain.

Above At various times across 1939 and 1940, the RAF decreed that the undersides of its fighters be finished in black and white, or black, silver and white. This scheme – intended to aid recognition of friendly aircraft from the ground - is seen to good advantage on this Hurricane.

Left The Hawker Hurricane production line at Langley, near Slough, during the early part of the war.

THE BATTLE OF BRITAIN IN COLOUR

Supermarine Spitfire I

The Spitfire, a low-wing monoplane single-seat fighter, manufactured by the Supermarine division of Vickers-Armstrong Ltd, was developed from the record-breaking seaplanes built by Supermarine Ltd for the international Schneider Trophy contest. The designer was R J Mitchell, with his first design for a high-performance retractable-undercarriage fighter with enclosed cockpit meeting the Air Ministry's specification for a new fighter, the aircraft being designed around a Rolls Royce Merlin engine.

The prototype first flew on 5 March 1936, and after the Spitfire went into production it first entered service with the RAF in 1938. Together with the Hurricane, the Spitfire formed the backbone of RAF Fighter Command's defensive force during the Battle of Britain.

Many variants of the Spitfire were built, using several wing configurations as well as uprated armament and engines - including the Rolls-Royce Griffon in later marks. The Spitfire was produced in greater numbers than any other British aircraft and was also the only British fighter produced continuously throughout the war.

Technical Data
- Dimensions: Span 36 ft 10 in, length 29 ft 11 in
- Power Plant: Rolls-Royce Merlin III delivering 1.030 hp at 16,250 ft
- Maximum Speed: 355 mph
- Initial Rate of Climb: 2,530 ft per minute
- Armament: Eight x .303 Browning machine guns (The Spitfire IB was equipped with two x 20mm cannon, but only very few of these were in operational use during 1940)

Above left Spitfires of 41 Squadron take off over a parked Spitfire of 610 Squadron during the Battle of Britain.
Top The Supermarine Spitfire, along with the Hawker Hurricane, formed the backbone of RAF Fighter Command during 1940, with the Spitfire remaining in service as a front-line fighter throughout the war. These aircraft, parked at 'Dispersal', are machines of 65 Squadron.
Above Perhaps rather more than the Hurricane, it was the perceived 'glamour' of the Spitfire, and the men who flew them, which captured the imagination of the British public. Widespread fondness for the aircraft has not diminished across some 80 years.

HARDWARE: THE ATTACKERS

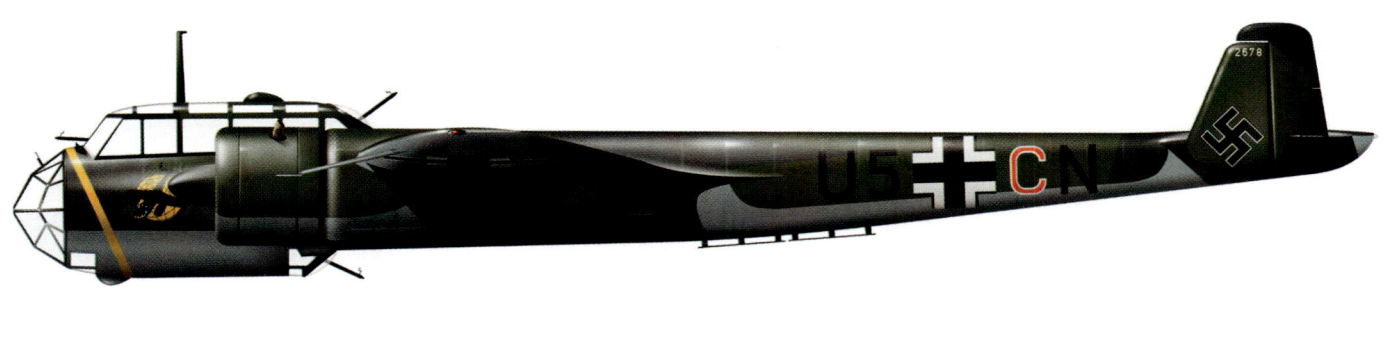

Above The other version of the type is use during the Battle of Britain was the Dornier 17-P which was employed the reconnaissance role. From this photograph of the Dornier 17-P, it is clear why the aircraft became known as the 'Flying Pencil'.
Bottom right The Dornier 17-Z was one of the primary bomber types in use by the Luftwaffe during the Battle of Britain, taking part in most of the major assaults and later during the night Blitz.
Below right Some examples of the Dornier 17-Z were equipped with a single 20mm cannon firing through the nose glazing, the weapon being utilised in the ground attack role.

Dornier 17

The Dornier 17 high-wing monoplane was intended by the Dornier-Werke G.m.b.H as a commercial aircraft, but a demonstration of the prototype in the autumn of 1934 brought no orders from the German airline, Lufthansa.

A bomber version first flew in 1935 and was developed for the Luftwaffe. It went on achieve some success in the Spanish Civil War. In total, eight variants of the Dornier 17, in addition to two variants of a type known as the Dornier 215, were used in 1940 as bombers or reconnaissance aircraft. The bomber versions of the Dornier 17 were all types in the 'Z' series, with the reconnaissance version being the 'P'.

The slim fuselage of the Dornier 17 earned it the nickname 'Flying Pencil'. As a bomber, the aircraft served on through the Blitz and into the early part of 1941, but it was otherwise pretty much phased-out later in the war - especially with the development of the improved Dornier 217.

The Dornier 17-Z carried a crew of four and had a relatively modest bomb capacity. The type was also used in ground attack operations against RAF airfields etc. In this role, a few units used the Dornier 17-Z fitted with a 20mm cannon in the nose.

Technical Data (Dornier 17-Z 2)
- Dimensions: Span 59 ft, length 53 ft 5.5 in
- Power Plants: Two x Bramo-Fafnir 323 P radial engines, each delivering 1,000 hp
- Maximum Speed: 265 mph with normal load
- Service Ceiling: 26,740 ft
- Range: Normal, 745 miles (with overload tank 1,860 miles)
- Bomb Load: Normal: 1,100kg (With maximum fuel: 500kg)

THE BATTLE OF BRITAIN IN COLOUR

Heinkel 111

The Heinkel 111 was a low-wing, twin engine monoplane long-range bomber with a crew of four, although sometimes five crew members were carried. It was developed by Ernst Heinkel Flugzeugwerke G.m.b.H and first flew in 1935, before entering service with the expanding Luftwaffe in 1937. Early models of the type took part in the Spanish Civil War, and it became one of the mainstay bombers across all Luftwaffe air fleets during 1940.

The Heinkel 111 was the first aircraft type to be shot down over the British Isles during the Second World War, with aircraft of KG26 operating at long range over the North Sea against Scotland and the north east of England. In different versions, the aircraft remained in service with the Luftwaffe throughout the war.

Nine different variants were used during 1940, including a version that operated with the Daimler-Benz DB 601 engine. The aircraft proved too slow and too lightly armed to escape heavy losses during daylight action, although it became a successful night bomber. For simplicity, the technical data (below) selects just one of the models commonly in use: the Heinkel 111 H-3.

Technical Data
- Dimensions: Span 74 ft 3 in, length 54 ft 6 in
- Power Plants: Two x Junkers Jumo 211 D-1 engines, each delivering 1,200 hp
- Maximum Speed: 255 mph with normal load
- Service Ceiling: 25,500 ft
- Range: Normal – 1,540 miles; with additional fuel, 2,640 miles
- Bomb Load: Maximum 2,000kg (with increased fuel load 1,000kg)

Top A Heinkel 111 delivers its mixed payload of 250kg and 50kg bombs.
Above The nose gondola of the Heinkel 111 was the position occupied by the observer who also had the role of bomb aimer. A defensive MG15 was also fitted in the revolving front blister.
Left The Heinkel 111 bomber was one of the main Luftwaffe bomber types during the Battle of Britain, and had been used in air operations against the British Isles since the outbreak of war in 1939. The first enemy aircraft brought down in the air war against Britain was this Heinkel 111 of Stab/KG26, shot down at Humbie, Scotland, on 28 October 1939.

HARDWARE: THE ATTACKERS

Junkers 87 'Stuka'

The crank-winged and angular Junkers 87 'Stuka' dive-bomber was one of the most recognisable Luftwaffe types in use during the Battle of Britain.

The aircraft was deployed mostly in attacks against Channel shipping and in raids on RAF airfields and radar stations along Britain's south coast. It first flew in 1935, and was introduced into operational service in 1937.

In Poland, France and the Low Countries it was used to devastating effect, although its successes in the Battle of Britain were limited and offset by significant losses. It was little used against British targets after 18 August 1940, although carried out a series of anti-shipping strikes in the English Channel in late 1940 and early 1941. By mid-August 1940, though, the Junkers 87 units were all concentrated in the Pas-de-Calais region where they were held in readiness to provide potential support for the planned invasion of the British Isles.

As a pin-point weapon, it was extremely accurate and effective – albeit that its participation in the Battle of Britain was relatively limited. Despite its disappointing performance in that battle, the aircraft remained in production and service up until the end of the war and proved a useful weapon on the Eastern Front, Mediterranean and in North Africa.

It carried a crew of two. Three variants of the type were used during 1940: B-1, B-2 and the R versions.

Technical data:
- Dimensions: Span 45 ft 4 in, Length 36 ft 5 in
- Power Plant: One x Junkers Jumo 211-D, delivering 1,150 hp
- Maximum Speed: 232 mph
- Service Ceiling: 24,500 ft
- Range: Junkers 87 B-1 and B-2, 370 miles with normal bomb load; Junkers 87 R, 875 miles with reduced bomb load and additional fuel in supplementary tanks
- Bomb Load: Normally, one 250kg bomb beneath the fuselage and four 50kg bombs under the wings, or one 500kg beneath the fuselage.
- Armament: One x rearward firing flexible 7.92 mm MG 15 machine gun, two x fixed forward firing 7.92 mm MG 17 machine guns

Top Crew members of a Junkers 87-R unit are briefed before another sortie during 1940. The 'R' version of the Stuka had a longer range and was fitted with underwing auxiliary fuel tanks which can be seen in this photograph. The tanks were fitted where the wing bomb racks were installed on the 'B' versions.

Above Massed 'Stuka' formations were a chilling sight to behold, but after 18 August 1940, they were rarely seen in Britain's skies.

THE BATTLE OF BRITAIN IN COLOUR

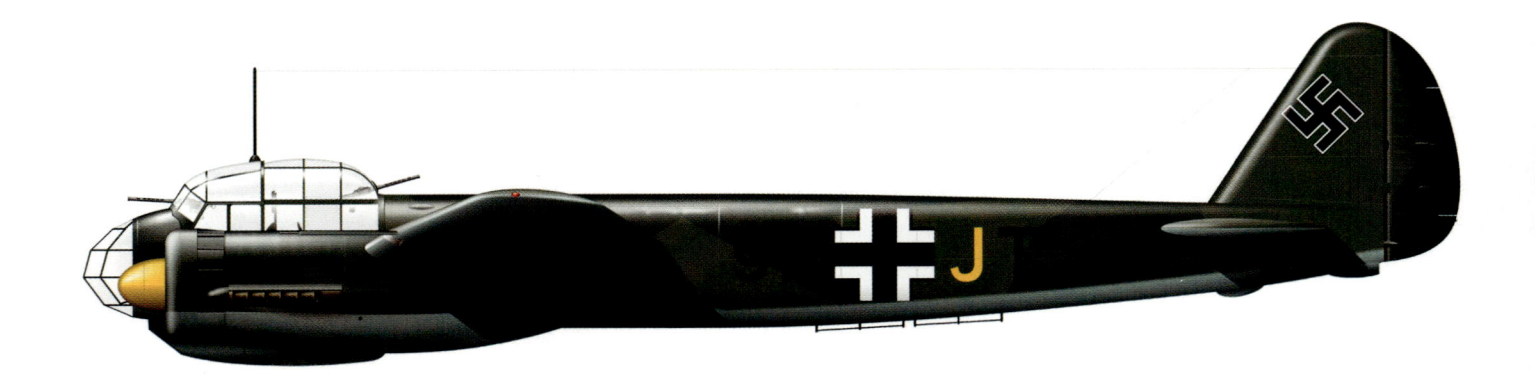

Junkers 88

The Junkers 88 low-wing monoplane first flew in December 1936, with the manufacturers, Junkers Flugzeug und Moterenwerke A.G, intending the aircraft to be a high-performance bomber with a turn of speed that would enable it to dispense with any fighter escort. Hopes of outdistancing any pursuing fighters were dashed, however, with the advent of the Spitfire and Hurricane. However, it remained a fast and agile aircraft and was considered the hardest of the German bombers to catch and shoot down.

The aircraft was one of the Luftwaffe's more successful medium bombers of the Battle of Britain, the Blitz, Eastern Front and Mediterranean. It was also developed as a night-fighter version and in this capacity carried out intruder sorties over Britain, looking for RAF bombers that were taking-off or landing at their home airfields.

It proved to be a popular aircraft with its pilots and aircrew, although losses of the type over Britain were not insignificant and broadly in line with the other bomber aircraft in use.

The Junkers 88, or developments and versions of the aircraft, remained in production and use right up until the end of the war.

Two variants, the A-1 and A-5, were used in 1940. They both carried a crew of four.

Technical Data (Junkers 88 A-1)
- Dimensions: Span, 59 ft 10.75 in (increased in the A-5 to 65 ft 10.5 in) length, 47 ft 1 in
- Power Plants: Two x Junkers Jumo 211 B-1 engines, each delivering 1,200 hp
- Maximum Speed: 286 mph
- Service Ceiling: 26,500 ft
- Range: Normal, 1,553 miles
- Bomb Load: Normal, 1,800 kg; Maximum 2,300 kg

Top The Junkers 88 was a fast and versatile aircraft and proved to be an important and valuable part of the Luftwaffe's bomber fleet during the Battle of Britain.

Above Bombs away! A Junkers 88 is captured from an unusual angle at the point of bomb release. In this photograph, two x 500 kg bombs fall away from the aircraft's inner wing racks. The ventral gondola, with its single MG15 machine gun protruding, can also be seen.

Left The crew members of a Junkers 88 don their flying clothing in preparation for another sortie over Britain during the summer of 1940.

HARDWARE: THE ATTACKERS

Messerschmitt 109 E

This was the principal Luftwaffe fighter of the Battle of Britain and was first flown in 1935. It entered service in 1937, seeing action in the Spanish Civil War in the B and C types. Several variants of the E model were used in 1940, including the E-1, E-3 and E-4.

One asset of the type was its fuel injection system which gave an advantage by allowing the aircraft to go into a steep dive without loss of power. The aircraft was less robust and more difficult to handle than the Spitfire or Hurricane and prone to landing mishaps.

As an escort fighter, the Messerschmitt 109 had a theoretical radius of around 200 miles at a cruising speed of 298 mph, but this was greatly reduced by the distance covered in rendezvousing with the bombers and evasive action etc. Its fighting time over Britain was thus limited, and a considerable number of Messerschmitt 109s were lost in the Channel or just managed to make France due to fuel shortages.

Contrary to popular belief, the Messerschmitt 109 E did not have a cannon firing through the propeller boss, although the E-4 did have wing mounted 20mm cannon. The aircraft was also modified for use as a fighter-bomber later in 1940 with a centrally mounted single 250 kg bomb.

Note: As early as 25 October 1940, the Messerschmitt 109-F with a DB 601 E engine was coming into limited operational use.

Technical Data (all for Me 109 E-3)
- Dimemsions: Span 32 ft 4 in, Length 26 ft 8 in
- Power plant: Daimler-Benz DB 601 A engine delivering 1,150 hp (direct fuel injection)
- Maximum Speed: 354 mph
- Initial rate of Climb: 3,100 ft per minute
- Service Ceiling: 36,000 ft
- Armament: Two x 7.92mm MG 17 machine guns above the engine and one in each wing, or two x 7.92mm MG 17 machine guns above the engine and one 20mm MG FF cannon in each wing on the E-4.

Top The Messerschmitt 109 was a nimble and effective fighter, and more-or-less on a par with its Spitfire counterpart during the Battle of Britain. In upgraded versions, it remained in service throughout the war and became one of the mainstays of the German fighter arm.

Centre Limited range was a handicap for the Messerschmitt 109 during the Battle of Britain, especially when escorting bombers over the Channel, possibly getting involved in engagements with the enemy and then having to make the return crossing whilst low on fuel.

Left Ground handling in the Messerschmitt 109 was always a challenge for pilots. Many were lost or damaged in take-off or landing accidents. This aircraft has suffered a collapse of its port undercarriage leg during landing.

THE BATTLE OF BRITAIN IN COLOUR

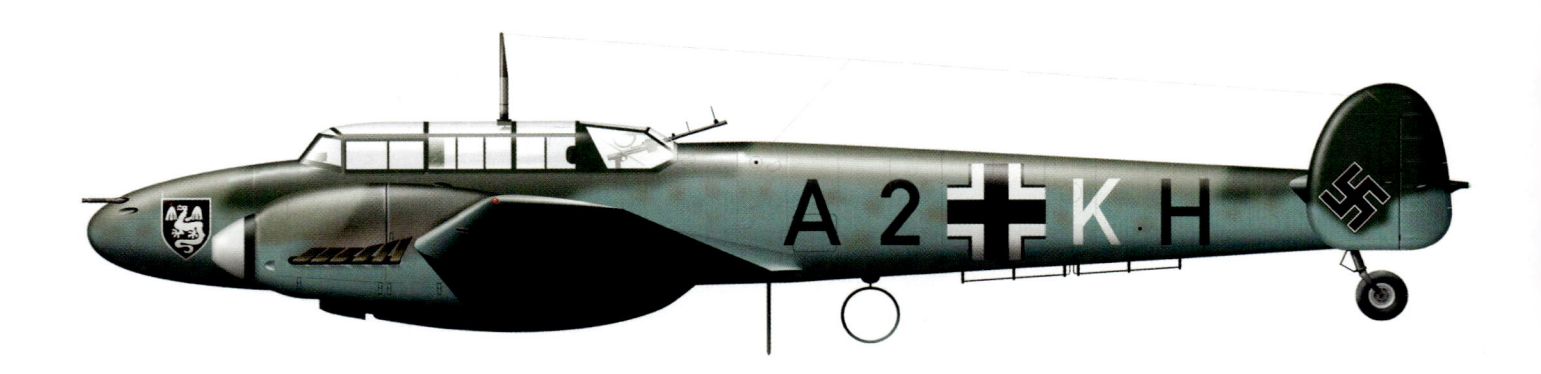

Messerschmitt 110

The Messerschmitt 110 was a low wing two-seat monoplane, intended for use as a long-range escort fighter and was built by Messerschmitt A.G. The prototype first flew in May 1936, the type eventually going into production in 1937. The aircraft became known as the Zerstörer (Destroyer) and in different variants it went on to serve on all fronts throughout the war.

During the Battle of Britain, it was outmanoeuvred with ease by the RAF's Spitfire and Hurricane and its value as an escort fighter was thus limited. However, it had a powerful punch in the nose with two closely spaced 20mm cannon and four 7.92mm machine guns.

Two types, the 'C' and 'D', were used during the Battle of Britain, with the 'D' variant being deployed as a fast fighter-bomber where it achieved a degree of success. It was also used in the photo reconnaissance role. The Messerschmitt 110 carried one rearward firing 7.92mm machine gun operated by a wireless operator/air gunner.

The aircraft was later used very successfully in the night-fighter role in the defence of the Reich.

Technical Data (Based on the 'C' model)
- Dimensions: Span 53 ft 5 in, Length 40 ft 4 in
- Power Plants: Two x Daimler Benz DB 601-A (or 601-N) engines, each delivering around 1,100 hp
- Maximum Speed: 340 mph
- Initial Rate of Climb: 2,120 ft per minute
- Service Ceiling: 32,000 ft
- Armament: Four x 7.92mm MG 17 machine guns and two x 20mm MG FF cannon firing forward and one 7.92mm MG 15 flexibly mounted machine gun in dorsal position

Above With its crew of two, the Messerschmitt 110 had some limited rearward facing defence in the form of a single 7.92mm MG15 machine gun.

Left The Messerschmitt 110, intended as a long-range heavy escort fighter, played a major part in Luftwaffe fighter operations over Britain in 1940. However, it was not a success when pitched against the agile Spitfires and Hurricanes of the RAF. This aircraft wears the distinctive red and white shark's mouth insignia of ZG26.

HARDWARE: THE ATTACKERS

The 'Heinkel 113' Fighter

An aircraft which appears frequently in the narrative of the Battle of Britain is a fighter which didn't even exist: the Heinkel He 113. But if it didn't exist, why are there numerous photographs of the type? And why did RAF pilots claim to have shot so many of them down?

A mistake frequently made by RAF fighter pilots and aircrew in 1940 was to sometimes identify Messerschmitt 109s as Heinkel 113s. In reality, that aircraft was actually the Heinkel He 100 D-1. The type was built in very small numbers, mostly pre-production models, and the aircraft never went into full-scale production or front-line Luftwaffe service.

Although it was comparable in many respects to the Messerschmitt 109, the He 100 had rather 'missed the boat' since Messerschmitt 109 production was already fully underway. As a result, no more than 20 of the He 100 fighters were built. Nevertheless, this handful of aircraft would serve the German Ministry of Propaganda well, and the existing He 100s were given the pseudonym 'He 113'.

In the event, German propaganda imagery in 1940 showed the few aircraft that had been built, grouped together, and with spurious unit markings in different settings and billed as the He 113. The intention was that the RAF would believe a new type was both in service. The ruse worked perfectly.

The German Propaganda Ministry boastfully described the type's success in the Norwegian campaign and its use across Europe. This claim, coupled with photographs seemingly showing the aircraft 'on the front line', resulted in RAF Intelligence being convinced that the Luftwaffe had the type in service in France during 1940. Often, RAF Combat Reports of the period have accounts of engagements with 'He 113 fighters'. Some of the first engagements were by Hurricanes of 56 Squadron off Dover on 13 July 1940.

In truth, none of these aircraft ever made it to operational service. For the most part, the RAF airmen involved in these combats had engaged Messerschmitt 109s. Unfortunately, there is also evidence that Hurricanes were sometimes shot down by other RAF pilots who claimed their victim was a 'He 113'. Thus, an unintended consequence of the German deception.

Only when the battle was over, and it was apparent that not a single He 113 had been found on the ground, did the RAF realise they had been duped. However,

Above Three 'Heinkel 113' fighters are posed in a photograph by the German Propaganda Kompanie (PK) to appear as though they are in front-line service and operating from a makeshift airfield in Northern France during the Battle of Britain. The aircraft have been painted in camouflage colours and with completely fictitious unit emblems. An air raid shelter slit trench has also been constructed to further complete the illusion.

this was not before Air Chief Marshal Sir Hugh Dowding, the C-in-C of Fighter Command in 1940, wrote of the type in his 1946 despatch to the *London Gazette* on the Battle of Britain.

In it, he said:

"The Heinkel 113 fighter made its appearance in limited numbers during the Battle. It was a single seater, generally resembling the Me 109. Its main attributes were high performance and ceiling, so that it was generally used in the highest of the several layers in which attacking formations were made up."

The deception had gone right to the very top of the RAF's Fighter Command. It had been the perfect ruse. ■

THE BATTLE OF BRITAIN IN COLOUR

Browning .303 Machine Gun

The Browning .303 entered service during the crucial re-armament phase of the mid-1930s. It was fitted to both the new eight-gun fighters of the RAF, the Hurricane and Spitfire, and was also employed as defensive armament on bombers and other aircraft types. It remained in service throughout the war

No individual British or Allied weapon can be singled out as responsible for winning the war. However, the overall contribution of individual types of weaponry can at least be measured to some degree. To that end, the contribution made by the Browning machine-gun should certainly be recognised as significant. And as the principal weapon in use during the Battle of Britain, it would not be unreasonable to state that it was certainly the gun that 'won' the battle.

However, by 1940 it was already recognised that rifle calibre ammunition was outmoded in terms of air fighting, and air forces began to look to heavy calibre weapons such as the .50 calibre and 20 mm cannon. The damage inflicted by such guns could be overwhelming and catastrophic, whereas aircraft could often endure multiple hits from .303 rounds.

As the standard wing-mounted gun in the Spitfire and Hurricane during the Battle of Britain, the Browning .303 was carried in batteries of four x guns in each wing. In the case of the Defiant, a battery of four guns was carried in a power-operated turret.

A Spitfire carried ammunition for 15 seconds of firing (slightly more in a Hurricane), typically fired in bursts of two to eight seconds.

The gun was gas-operated, air-cooled and could fire 1,100 rounds per minute.

Fig. 1 A Spitfire fires its battery of .303 Browning machine guns at the firing butts. Spent cases and belt links cascade out from ejector chutes under the wing.
Fig. 2 Good shooting! Although the .303 rifle calibre bullet against German aircraft could often be ineffectual, this Heinkel 111 looks like a colander after a sustained attack. This aircraft was shot down near Whitby before the Battle of Britain, on 3 February 1940.
Fig. 3 Good shooting! This Messerschmitt 109, photographed going down over Kent in September 1940, seems to have taken such punishment from .303 bullets that the rear fuselage and its tail section is crumpling. Despite the relatively small calibre, the .303 Browning was still an effective weapon.  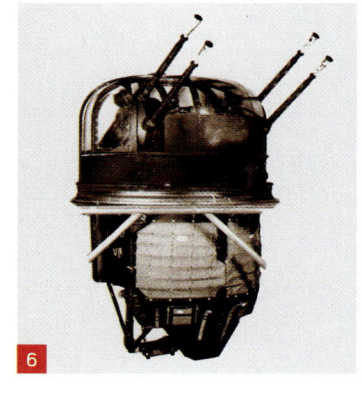 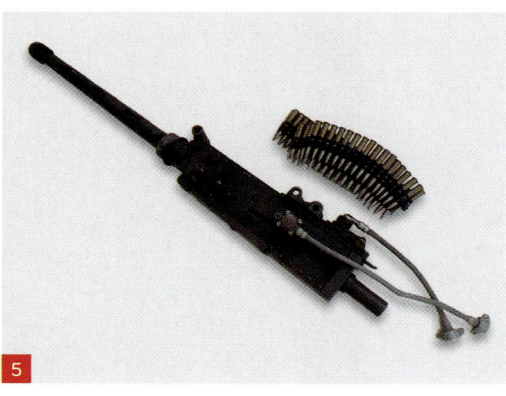
Fig. 4 A view of a Spitfire I starboard wing, showing the .303 gun bays.
Fig. 5 The wing mounted .303 Browning machine gun, as fitted to the Spitfire, Hurricane, Defiant, Blenheim and Gladiator aircraft during the Battle of Britain.
Fig. 6 The power-operated turret for the Defiant which contained a battery of four .303 Brownings.

THE HARDWARE: WEAPONRY

Vickers Gas-Operated Mk I No 1 or Vickers 'K' Gun

The Vickers Gas Operated .303 machine gun was adopted in service with the RAF in 1937 as the Vickers G.O. Gun No.1 Mark 1. During its service, the gun was also known by as the 'Class K'; 'Vickers K' and as the 'VGO'.

Fed by a 100-round drum, the gun performed well, and although it was later replaced by the Browning .303 machine gun as the standard RAF turret gun, it equipped the turret of the Bristol Blenheim IF during the Battle of Britain.

The Vickers G.O was eventually replaced in RAF service by the Browning but apart from use as a turret gun on the Blenheim during the Battle of Britain, it was also used defensively in several other types during 1940, such as the Short Sunderland, Westland Lysander and the Avro Anson.

It could fire between 950 and 1,100 rounds per minute across 1,000 yards.

Fig. 1 The turret on the Bristol Blenheim FI was equipped with a single Vickers 'K' gun, although the aircraft carried a belly pack of four .303 Browning machine guns firing forward. This turret is fitted with a Vickers 'K' camera gun – a 'gun' specially devised for training.

Fig. 2 This 'experimental' Hurricane with 151 Squadron during the Battle of Britain had one 20 mm cannon under each wing. It was not successful, although the cannon was developed and, internally mounted in the wing, became the standard armament for RAF Spitfires and Hurricanes later in the war.

OPERATIONAL FLYING WITH 20MM CANNON, RAF FIGHTER COMMAND, 1940

"Early in July 1940 I noticed a Hurricane in the hangar with tubes sticking out of each wing and I asked what they were. '20mm cannon', I was told. At this time, they were dead secret. Normally, they would have been at the Experimental Establishments at Martlesham Heath or Boscombe Down, but this aircraft was L1750 and marked up with the squadron code letters, DZ – Z. It had two cannon which were cocked and fired by a very tricky procedure, and as I'd always been keen on guns, I asked why it wasn't being flown. I was told the other pilots considered it was less safe than the rest of the Hurricanes because it was much slower, less manoeuvrable and had guns which were unreliable and prone to stoppages. We were short of aircraft, and the idea of flying it appealed to me. I was also now leading 'B' Flight, and often the squadron, and having the leader with a slower aircraft helped the rest of the pilots keep up. I flew DZ-Z routinely, and although the cannons were unreliable, they improved by virtue of flying and firing them. The cannons were mounted upright, as opposed to the Spitfires of 19 Squadron which were mounted on their sides and had to be withdrawn. However, by the time I left 151 Squadron, I'd flown 133 sorties in a cannon Hurricane."

Flight Lieutenant Roderick 'Black' Smith, 151 Squadron, 1940.

20mm Hispano Cannon Mk I

The Hispano 20mm cannon was one of the most important guns used by the RAF and was first introduced during the Battle of Britain when Duxford-based 19 Squadron unsuccessfully equipped with a few cannon-armed Spitfires. Additionally, a few Hurricanes of 151 Sqn were experimentally fitted. Once teething problems were ironed out, the gun became the standard RAF fighter armament.

The 20 mm Hispano in armament terms is a cannon and fired at a rate of 650 rounds per minute, the Mark.1 gun being fitted with a 60-round magazine drum.

By 1941, the weapon was coming into widespread use, but during the Battle of Britain, apart from its limited deployment in a few Spitfires and Hurricanes, it was the main frontal armament in the Bristol Beaufighter.

— 45 —

THE BATTLE OF BRITAIN IN COLOUR

GUNSIGHTS AND SHOOTING

RAF Fighter Command's early warning and control system's chain ended at the gun sight, gun button and machine-gun barrel of its frontline fighters.

The Spitfire and Hurricane were both fitted with Barr & Stroud Reflector gun sights, featuring a lens through which a circular graticule was projected onto a glass screen in front of the pilot. This was bisected by a cross, the horizontal bar broken in the centre and the range setting being determined by adjusting two knurled rings around the base of the sight. The internal mechanism then set the gap in the graticule crossbar according to the required range. A central dot was added as a further aiming point.

The radius of the ring gave the deflection shooting allowance for hitting a target crossing at 100mph. It was illuminated by a 12-volt light bulb held and a clip of spare bulbs was stowed on the side of the cockpit. A 'Sorbo' rubber pad was fitted across the front of the sight to protect the pilot from injury in the event of crash-landing.

In sighting the guns on an enemy – and depending on the angle and attitude at which the aircraft was engaged – it was necessary for the pilot to adopt 'sighting off'. In other words, aiming ahead of the enemy by carefully calculated margins. That way, the enemy aircraft would theoretically fly through the stream of bullets. Conversely, if the point of aim was directly at the aircraft itself, then the target would usually have moved forward by the time the bullets reached that spot.

As to the wing mounted guns, these would be harmonised so that all the bullets converged at a fixed-point ahead and at the optimum point to hit the enemy aircraft.

Writing of the sight and sighting in his 'Notes on Air Gunnery and Fighting', Battle of Britain pilot Wing Commander E M 'Teddy' Donaldson, DSO, AFC, set out his thoughts:

"I do recommend that a range be set on the sight and that range should be for a 60 ft target on 300 yds, this being the size of the average bomber target. I say 300 yds, because one is inclined to watch the enemy until it fills the range gap and then open fire so that one is always very much closer when the trigger is pressed than the range one has set on the sight. This means that one opens fire at the best possible range of 250 yards."

He then went on to discuss the harmonisation point which should be set for the guns:

"I have found it most effective to harmonise the two inboard guns to 200 yds, the next pair at 225 yds, the next pair at 250, and so on. If one draws a plan of the path of the bullets from each gun, then with a five-foot target you practically cover it with a maximum density of bullets at all ranges from 175 yds onwards."

To fire the guns, the pilot operated a single gun button with his right thumb. The button was situated at the eleven-o-clock position on the control column top and was surrounded by a knurled ring marked SAFE and FIRE. Before going into action, the pilot turned the ring to FIRE, and was now set to engage the enemy. Depressing the button opened a valve and allowed compressed air to flow through the system from an air reservoir and fired all the guns simultaneously.

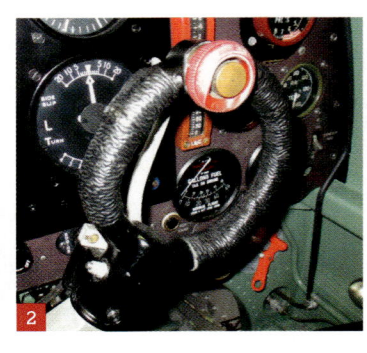

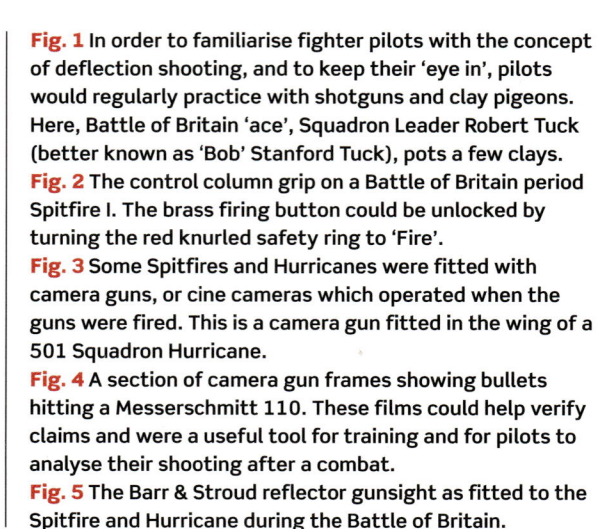

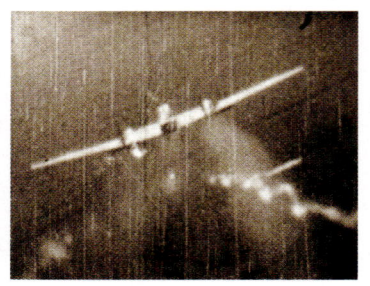

Fig. 1 In order to familiarise fighter pilots with the concept of deflection shooting, and to keep their 'eye in', pilots would regularly practice with shotguns and clay pigeons. Here, Battle of Britain 'ace', Squadron Leader Robert Tuck (better known as 'Bob' Stanford Tuck), pots a few clays.
Fig. 2 The control column grip on a Battle of Britain period Spitfire I. The brass firing button could be unlocked by turning the red knurled safety ring to 'Fire'.
Fig. 3 Some Spitfires and Hurricanes were fitted with camera guns, or cine cameras which operated when the guns were fired. This is a camera gun fitted in the wing of a 501 Squadron Hurricane.
Fig. 4 A section of camera gun frames showing bullets hitting a Messerschmitt 110. These films could help verify claims and were a useful tool for training and for pilots to analyse their shooting after a combat.
Fig. 5 The Barr & Stroud reflector gunsight as fitted to the Spitfire and Hurricane during the Battle of Britain.

-46-

THE HARDWARE: WEAPONRY

Fig. 1 This Heinkel 111 gunner has fitted a double MG15 mount in his aircraft. Usually, they were employed singly.

Fig. 2 Two Luftwaffe fighter pilots practice deflection shooting techniques on a model Spitfire using a 'Revi' gunsight.

Fig. 3 Armourers load belted 7.92 rounds into the ammunition tanks of a Messerschmitt 110, summer 1940.

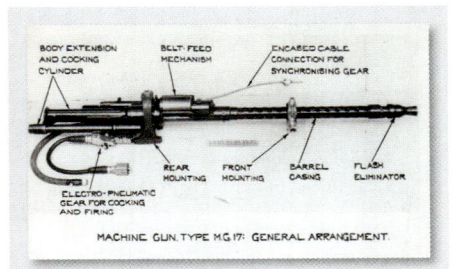

The MG17 Machine Gun

Like the MG15, the MG17 was 7.92 mm calibre but was belt fed and fitted in the Messerschmitt 109 and 110. Its calibre was roughly comparable to the RAF's .303 machine guns.

Based on the older MG30 light machine gun, it became the standard forward firing offensive Luftwaffe gun during the early part of the war. Produced by Rheinmetall-Borsig, the weapon also saw limited use as a fixed rearward defensive gun in the tail of the Heinkel 111.

The gun fired 1,200 rounds per minute, with 500 rounds in each belt. In fighters, it was sighted via a 'Revi' reflector gunsight.

The MG15 Machine Gun

During the Battle of Britain, the MG15 was the Luftwaffe bomber's flexibly mounted standard defensive weapon. It was a 7.92mm gun which operated smoothly, firing from an open bolt which stayed cocked when the gun was ready to fire. This made it unnecessary to re-cock after changing magazines. By pulling the trigger, the bolt released and stripped a round from the magazine, which was pushed into the chamber, a trip lever releasing the firing pin and firing the gun. The recoil would push the barrel back to eject the fired cartridge case which was flung it out. This cycle continued while the trigger was held down, the gun firing 1,000 rounds per minute.

The saddle-drum magazines held 75 rounds, distributed in both sides. One magazine gave a burst of about 4.5 seconds, each gun having around 10 spare magazines. It was sighted through a ring-and-bead sight mounted on the barrel.

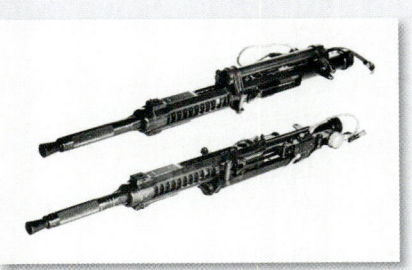

The 20 mm MG FF Cannon

During the Battle of Britain, the MG FF gun was fitted in pairs in the nose of the Messerschmitt 110. In the Messerschmitt 109 E-4, one was fitted in each wing. It was developed in 1936, by Ikaria Werke, Berlin. Some were fitted in the nose of Dornier 17-Zs for ground attack operations.

The weapon was drum fed, with each drum holding 60 high explosive rounds.

It had a low rate of fire at 520 rounds per minute, but hits from a single round could be devastating.

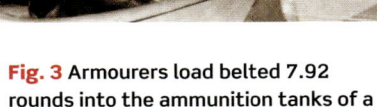

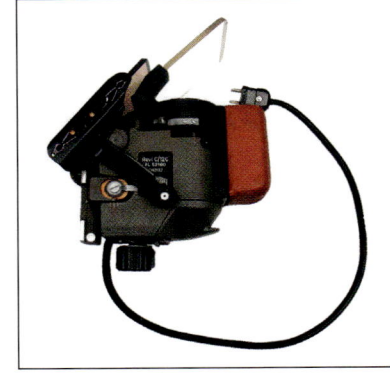

The 'Revi' Gunsight

The 'Revi' gunsight was similar in operation to the RAF's Barr & Stroud reflector gunsight where a graticule ring of light was projected onto a glass screen. It was used in the Messerschmitt 109 and 110. The pilot sighted his guns through the screen, using the ring of light for aiming. Degrees of deflection were needed so that the bullets fired slightly ahead of the enemy who, in theory, would fly into that fire. The 'Revi' sight, along with the RAF's gunsight, was very much the cutting-edge technology of its day, both being forerunner of the head-up displays found in modern jet fighters.

THE BATTLE OF BRITAIN IN COLOUR

The Spitfire Fund

During the dark days of the Battle of Britain, inspired by the deeds of the 'Few', the British public subscribed to a fund-raising scheme to buy Spitfire fighters for the RAF. It was the 1940 version of crowd funding.

Perhaps driven more by a patriotic desire to help the war effort than to have any realistic effect on the pace or quantity of Spitfire production, the Spitfire Fund of 1940 became something of a public outpouring of appreciation for the fighter pilots of the day. However, the real shortages for RAF Fighter Command during the Battle of Britain rested with pilots and aircrew, rather than with the production and supply of fighters. Nevertheless, the Spitfire caught the imagination of the British public as well as Commonwealth and ex-patriate communities overseas. And it was the Spitfire, rather more than the equally worthy Hurricane, which captured the spirit of the nation and encapsulated public perception of the glamour tied to that aircraft and its pilots, and to the ultimate promise of victory. Thus, the Government encouraged and endorsed the implementation of community based 'Spitfire Funds'.

These funds comprised locally organised collections, based on cities, towns and villages etc, as well as other fund-raising schemes set up by companies and organisations and to which their employees or members could contribute. A multitude of fund-raising efforts became common, and the Ministry of Aircraft Production decided that the nominal cost of a Spitfire in 1940 should be set at £5,000. And the nation, collectively, very soon rose to the challenge of buying Spitfires.

Once the requisite sum had been handed over to the Ministry of Aircraft Production, the donor became entitled to name the aircraft. In many instances, that was simply the name of the donor town or village. In other cases, rather more flamboyant titles and even town or family coats of arms might be added. Many businesses and companies, too, got in on the act. For example, the Hoover Company named theirs 'Sky Sweeper' and Marks & Spencer decided on 'Marksman', while a certain battery manufacturer claimed their Spitfire was 'Ever Ready'. For the most part, though, such Spitfires were funded by employees rather than entirely by the corporate body.

Other companies were keen to promote their brand and product, too. Even during wartime. The potato crisp company, Smiths, went simply for 'Crisp', with Lloyd's Bank selecting, almost

– 48 –

THE HARDWARE

Above left The British public were encouraged to support various local Spitfire Funds through an advertising campaign. In truth, and once the campaign took hold, very little encouragement was required.

Above right This Messerschmitt 109 of JG27, flown by Oberleutnant Gunther Bode, was forced down at Mayfield, East Sussex, on 9 September 1940. Later, it was used in fund-raising exhibitions around the country to help collect money for the Spitfire fund. It is seen here on display at Stanhay's Garage in Ashford, Kent.

Facing page The beauty of the Spitfire, its undeniable allure and perceived 'glamour' went a long way towards encouraging the British public to subscribe to the Spitfire Funds of 1940. This rebuilt Spitfire I, serial number P9374, was estimated to have cost £5,000 to build in 1940. In recent years it sold for £3 million – thus proving that the magic of the Spitfire endures.

Above One of the organisations gifting a Spitfire was the Observer Corps. Their Spitfire, duly named, went to 41 Squadron at RAF Hornchurch. It is seen here, wearing its name and the emblem of the Corps. Below the cockpit, two swastikas signify victories over German aircraft.

Right The London Borough of Hendon organised collecting cards to encourage members of the public to make regular contributions to the borough's 'Four Fighter Fund', their donations marked by savings stamps. On filling the card, the holder earned a 'Stamp of Honour'.

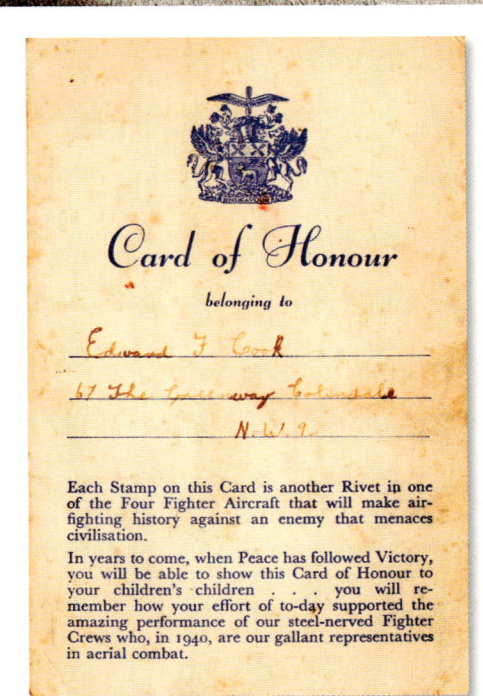

THE BATTLE OF BRITAIN IN COLOUR

inevitably, 'Black Horse'. But it was the Kennel Club, however, who chose the singularly appropriate 'Dog Fighter'.

Spoils Of War
Whilst there were a few generous individual donors, the majority of what became known as Presentation Spitfires came from counties, towns and cities (and sometimes villages) around Britain. One small village, Fairwarp in East Sussex, was notable for donating an astonishing five Spitfires to the RAF. This was largely due to the single contribution of a parish resident, Baronet Sir Bernard Eckstein. As a result, five Spitfires bearing the name of the village flew with the RAF.

Not quite five Spitfires, but in another example of this remarkable community effort were the four Spitfires given by the people of Hendon following on from the Municipal Borough of Hendon's 'Four Fighter Fund'. One method of donating for Hendon's campaign was by collecting saving stamps on cards issued to residents of the borough, with the donor being rewarded with a colourful 'Stamp of Honour' if they filled each of the 24 stamp spaces on their collecting cards. Single contributions could range from a modest one penny up to a pound.

Hendon, though, was like every other donating community, and aside from the initial morale-boosting publicity photographs of 'their' Spitfire, the public got to know nothing of the service history of 'their' aircraft or the pilots who flew them. Perhaps that was just as well. In many cases, the operational life of the donated Spitfires was depressingly short. In the case of one of the Hendon Spitfires, for example, the aircraft (named 'Hendon Pegasus') was lost through a mid-air collision in September 1941, not long after delivery from the factory. And the good folk of Eastbourne, for example, would have been dismayed to learn that their gifted Spitfire had been lost over France in 1941. This was just a couple of months after it was built, with its pilot POW.

By and large, however, the finished and delivered Presentation Spitfires tended to be coming on-stream with the RAF very much towards the end of 1940 and into 1941, notwithstanding the fact that the funds were actually being set up and collected during the period of the Battle of Britain. Indeed, many of the fund-raising efforts revolved around the public display of shot down Messerschmitt 109s

'It was the Spitfire, rather more than the equally worthy Hurricane, which captured the spirit of the nation and encapsulated public perception of the glamour tied to that aircraft and its pilots, and to the ultimate promise of victory.'

THE HARDWARE

Figs. 1-4 All manner of fund-raising efforts were utilised to collect money for Spitfire funds. These included the various enterprises depicted here: a book, a Spitfire song sheet, a dance and sales of a postcard depicting a displayed Messerschmitt 109 for the Croydon fund, with its caption 'Made in Germany, Finished in England'.
Above A Spitfire Fund lapel pin.
Top right Donors of Spitfire aircraft were presented with commemorative plaques. This one recognises the gift of a Spitfire by the brewers, Charrington and Co.Ltd, which was appropriately named 'Toby'.

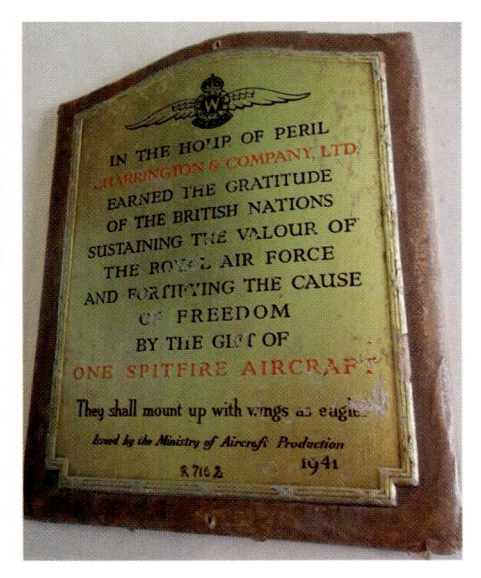

COST OF A SPITFIRE

In 1940, the Ministry of Aircraft Production issue a breakdown of the cost of a Spitfire aircraft:
'Here is an early costing of a Spitfire, which amounts to a sum considerably in excess of £5,000:

Engine:	£2,000 – 0 – 0
Fuselage:	£2,500 – 0 – 0
Wings:	£1,800 – 0 – 0
Undercarriage:	£800 – 0 – 0
Guns:	£800 – 0 – 0
Airscrew:	£350 – 0 – 0
Tail:	£500 – 0 – 0
Petrol Tank (top):	£40 – 0 – 0
Petrol Tank (bottom):	£25 – 0 – 0
Oil Tank:	£25 – 0 – 0
Compass:	£5 – 0 – 0
Clock:	£2 – 10 – 0
Thermometer:	£1 – 1 – 0
Sparking Plug:	£0 – 8 – 0
Rivet:	£0 – 0 – 6d

It has been agreed that the sum of £5,000 should be the share of the voluntary contributor and enable him to name the machine.'

that were taken around the country for exhibition. Those coming to view these spoils of war were either required to pay to see them, or else collecting tins were vigorously rattled. In some cases, it was even possible to sit in the cockpit of these captured fighters. The going rate for such a 'Messerschmitt experience' was usually 6d, although it would have needed a total of 200,000 sixpences to get to the required £5,000. But, every little helped, with community fund-raising efforts being as widespread as they were varied: bring-and-buy sales, dances, raffles, whist drives and tea dances all featured in collective efforts to buy Spitfires.

In today's money, the requisite £5,000 would equate to roughly £280,000. However, in 2020, fully restored or rebuilt Spitfires in flying condition can sell for as much as £3 million.

However, the patriotic outpouring in donations to buy Spitfires led at least 1,500 being presented. An astonishing achievement in what might be described as the 1940s form of crowdfunding! ■

THE BATTLE OF BRITAIN IN COLOUR

A Weapon for Victory

Key to success during the Battle of Britain was the Command and Control system of RAF Fighter Command and its central reliance on radar. The Luftwaffe, however, failed to understand how it all worked and how the 'Few' were controlled from the ground.

The Air Defence of Great Britain during the Battle of Britain was based around the 'Dowding System' which provided an organised plan of defence with a centralised command-and-control structure. This had largely been developed since Fighter Command was formed in the inter-war years, with Air Chief Marshal Hugh Dowding in command. Its success was the ability to integrate the command of fighter squadrons, balloon defences and anti-aircraft guns by drawing on a radar-based advanced early-warning system.

Incredibly, it was only in 1935 that work began by Robert Watson-Watt on the development of a system to detect distant aircraft through radio signals. Development was conducted at such a pace that by 1937 the new system was adopted by the RAF, and the construction of radar stations commenced immediately, integrated as a vital part of the command and control system. With the Battle of Britain just three years away, its introduction was very timely.

Integrated Command & Control

In the overall picture of the Battle of Britain, RAF Fighter Command was the sharp end of defence. Essentially, the RAF's early warning system was reliant on radar and the Observer Corps, with information provided from these two sources, disseminated enabling fighters to be directed onto hostile aircraft.

It was, however, a far cry from Allied defeat in Europe during the spring of 1940, where air supremacy was a contributing factor to German success. Although RAF and French Air Force fighters performed well, they were hampered by the absence of command and control. Fighters could only patrol up and down hoping to engage the enemy by chance and there was no mechanism to properly guide fighters towards hostile aircraft It was often a game of hit-and-miss. Otherwise, fighter squadrons would be sent off following reports that enemy aircraft were attacking particular locations. Usually, the enemy were long gone before the fighters arrived.

COMMAND AND CONTROL

Left The RAF Sector Station Operations Room at Duxford. These Operations Rooms controlled squadrons operating in their local sector, and relied on information cascaded down from Group Operations Rooms and fed back up the system to them from Observer Corps posts.

Right The workings of RAF Fighter Command's command and control system, as explained to the public in an HMSO information booklet on the Battle of Britain published in 1940. For security reasons, one crucial element was missing from this schematic: radar. The diagram would seem to infer that the source of all information coming into RAF Fighter Command was from the Observer Corps.

However, as the RAF withdrew from France, Fighter Command hunkered down behind the bulwarks of Britain's defence to await the onslaught. But now they could now rely on their 'secret weapon': radar.

Serious Disadvantage

Britain's system of early warning, interception and control was the first of its kind in the world, comprising a network stretching from northern Scotland down to the south of England, the workings of the system remaining a closely guarded secret. However, a surprising public glimpse was given in 1941, in an illustrated booklet: 'The Battle of Britain: August – October 1940', published with an outline of how it all worked. However, the booklet was economical with detail. Importantly, and for security reasons, it left one element out of the explanation: radar.

Although the Germans were aware of radar and had their own, failure to understand its place in RAF fighter defences placed them at a disadvantage. However, they were aware of the stations which had sprung up around Britain, with their huge aerials and concrete bunkers. Although they appreciated the sites were significant, they didn't understand to what extent and attacks on them were piecemeal. However, the relatively few attacks had some results with stations knocked off the air, albeit temporarily. Had sustained efforts been made to attack them, the RAF could have been 'blinded' and the eventual outcome different. As it was, the Luftwaffe could not 'see' their efforts; the towers were impossible to topple, and the hardened structures difficult to hit or make much impression on. This overlooked the fact that infrastructures were hit and stations disabled as a result - even if there was no visible sign of damage or destruction.

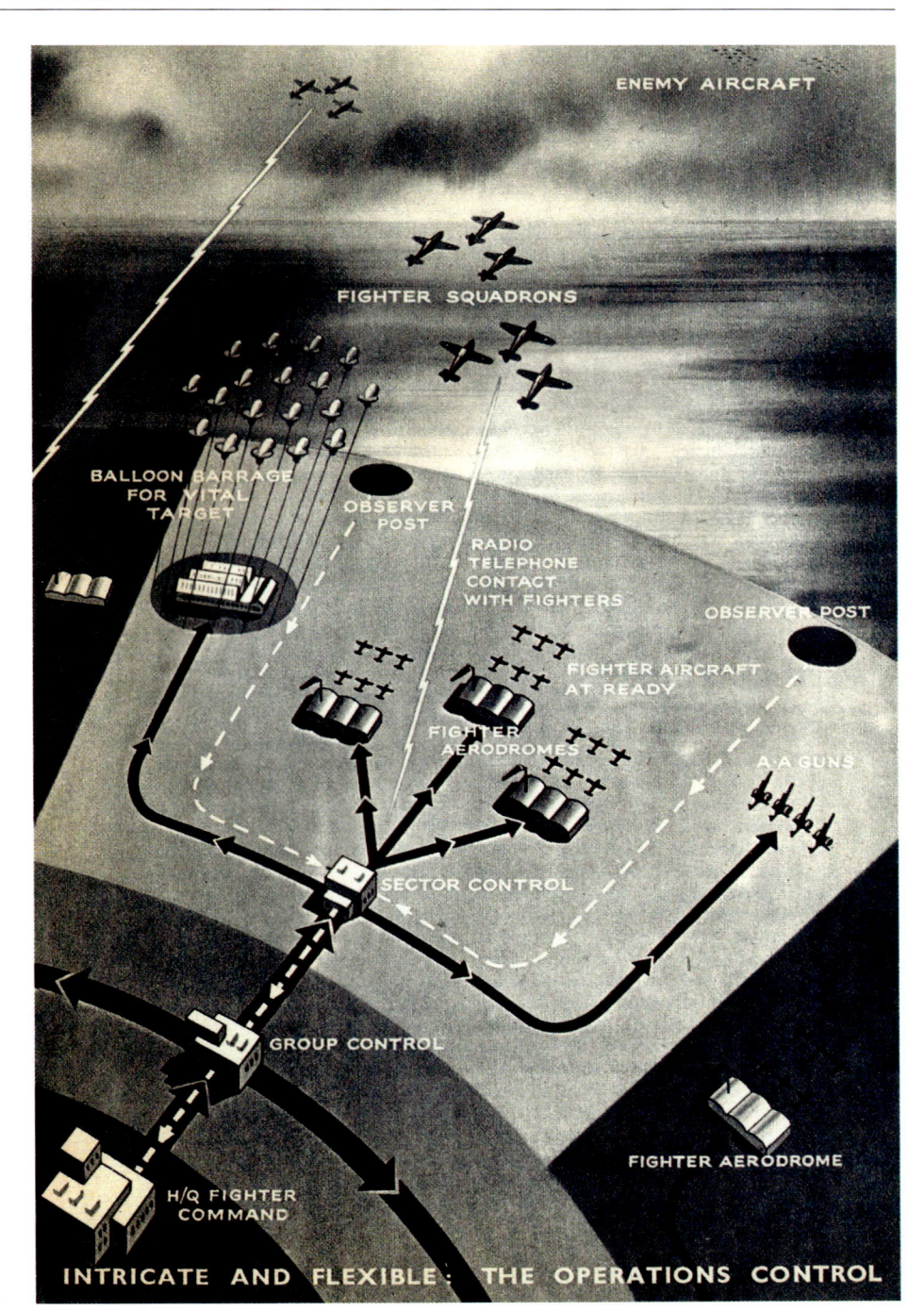

Unbroken Chain

In summary, RAF Fighter Command's Early Warning, Interception and Control System was not exclusively a radar set-up but was reliant on many components: Observer Corps, Filter Room, Command Operations Room, Group Operations Room and Sector Operations Room. The keystone, however, was the network of R.D.F (radar) stations.

In the summer of 1940, the radar chain comprised 22 x "chain home" (C.H) stations, supplemented by 30 x "chain home low" (C.H.L) stations – the latter for detecting low-flying aircraft. These stations were positioned to ensure that every aircraft approaching from the east, the south, or south-west would be detected by at least two stations.

The existence of these stations, with impossible-to-hide 350-foot masts, was known before the war to the Germans, who sent the airship *Graf Zeppelin* to reconnoitre them in the 1930s. Göring's advisers, however, believed the men who worked them would be unable, at times of stress, to distinguish between large and small formations, and the system would fail if large numbers of aircraft approached the country simultaneously.

The C.H. stations were capable, in theory, of detecting aircraft at ranges at up to 200 miles, but performance was limited by atmospheric conditions,

-53-

THE BATTLE OF BRITAIN IN COLOUR

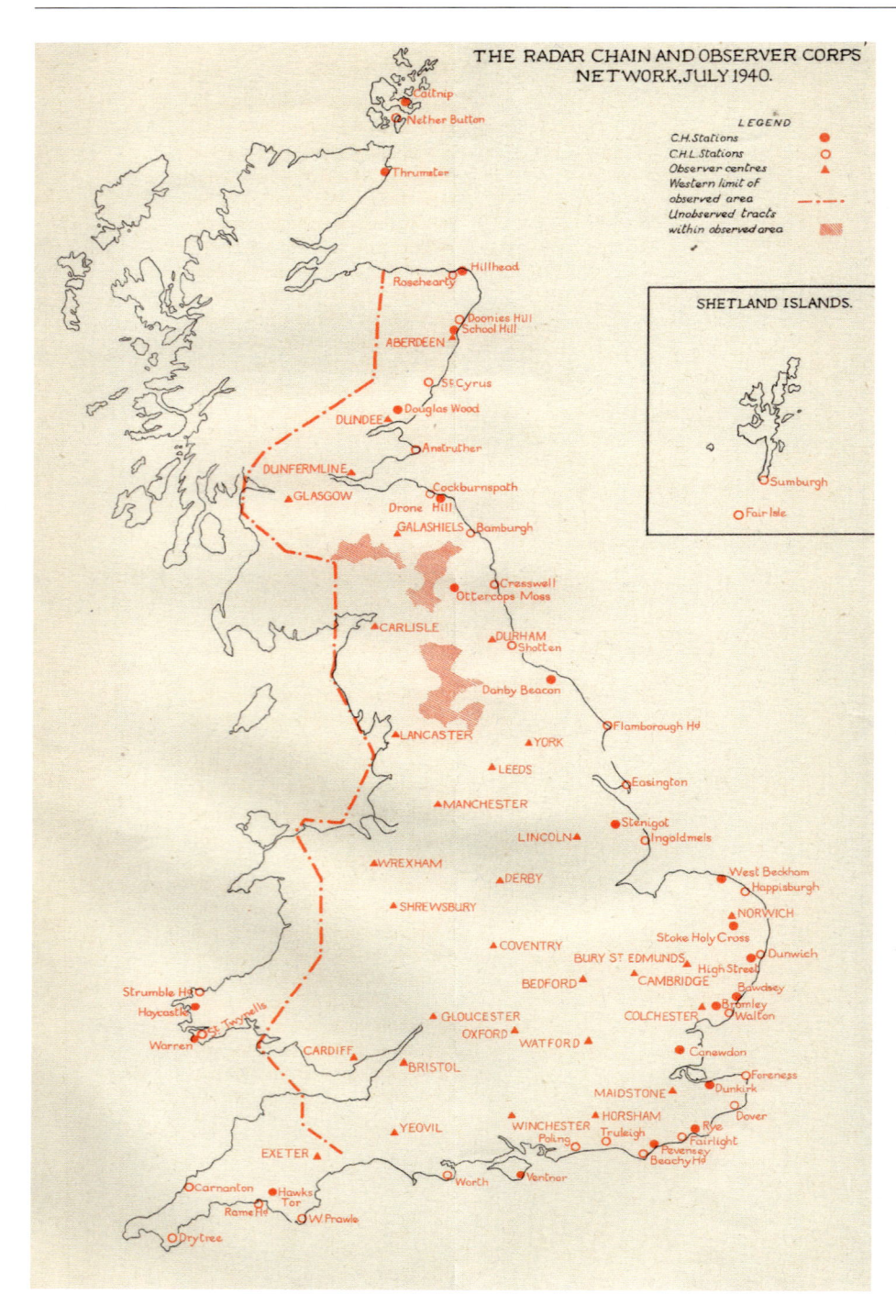

Left The radar chain and Observer Corps Centres at the start of the Battle of Britain, July 1940.
Below This wartime image of a CH radar station shows the four transmitter masts and the smaller wooden receiver masts.
Bottom The lattice steel transmitter masts at RAF Chain Home radar stations were 360 ft high, with each station having four such masts. The receiver masts were shorter wooden constructions. Today, just a few of the masts survive - this example being at Stenigot, Lincolnshire.

operator skill, the height of the enemy and echoes from friendly aircraft or natural features. Accurate location on approaching raids at 60 to 80 miles or more from the coast was not uncommon, and estimates of strength, although often vague, became more reliable as the range shortened.

'Death Ray' Stations

All radar stations, except those in the west of the country, passed information by landline to an underground Filter Room at RAF Bentley Priory, HQ, RAF Fighter Command. Here, the information was sorted and displayed on a gridded map and passed to the Command Operations Room and operations rooms of appropriate regional Groups within RAF Fighter Command. Usually, about four minutes elapsed from the first observation by radar to the appearance of map plots in operations rooms.

Officially, RDF (or Radar) sites around Britain's coast were known as Air Ministry Experimental Stations, this euphemistic name further obscuring their true purpose. Considerable speculation surrounded the building of these stations, the most popular rumour being that the tall aerials emitted a 'death ray' to stop the engines of enemy aircraft. Had they known the truth, the public would have been equally amazed to learn that the masts could detect, at very long range, approaching aircraft.

Operationally, radar stations had failings and weaknesses - including the interpretation of results. But they had one major failing; a fixed line of sight. In other words, they could only 'see' in the direction the radar was pointed, and this was away from the coast and towards the anticipated approach of any threat. In other words, once the threat had passed over the radar sites and was inland, then the plots became invisible. From this moment on, approaching threats were

COMMAND AND CONTROL

monitored visually (or audibly if at night or poor visibility) by a network of ground-based observers: the Observer Corps.

Vital Link
Once radar picked up an enemy sighting, and the information passed on to Fighter Command HQ, the Observer Corps Command Centre was notified. They, in turn, alerted the relevant Observer Posts where the detected enemy formation would likely be sighted. As soon as the call was received, the post, normally manned by three to five men, scanned the skies with binoculars and kept a keen ear for the sound of aero engines.

In inclement weather or low cloud, visual sighting was often impossible with detection only being made by sound.

Once a sighting was made, observers had to detect the types of aircraft, how many, the heading they were taking and their height. All these factors were vital, because it would be this picture which gave a view of the true situation. Unlike radar stations which gave Fighter Command HQ their sighting and contact first, the Observer Corps gave details of their first sighting to the local RAF Sector Fighter Station (further down the command structure) in their area, and so that fighters could be 'Scrambled' once

> **Above** A vital part of the RAF's early warning and command and control system relied on volunteer personnel of the Observer Corps, who manned stations dotted right across the country, 365 days a year, 24 hours a day. They were the eyes and ears of Fighter Command. In 1940, they were the Observer Corps, but in 1941 became the Royal Observer Corps.

the enemy was crossing the coast. The observers truly a vital link, and would give the type of aircraft detected and were trained to observe formations and accurately estimate its strength, reporting it as '50 +' or '100 +' etc.

—55—

THE BATTLE OF BRITAIN IN COLOUR

Right The Group Operations Room at HQ, No. 11 Group, RAF Fighter Command, Uxbridge, with its General Situation Map, clocks and wall information 'Tote' boards all set at 11.30 am on Sunday, 15 September 1940, exactly as it would have been seen by Prime Minister Winston Churchill when he visited the bunker. The site is now a museum location, open to the public.
Facing page Today, the Duxford Sector Operations Room has been preserved exactly as it was in 1940 and is part of the Imperial War Museums Duxford site. The attention to detail in exactly recreating the 1940 scene is noteworthy.
Fig. 1 When plots arrived on Operations Room tables, they were marked with arrows to indicate the track and with wooden blocks carrying numbered and lettered plaques to show the composition of the plot. In this instance: H = Hostile, comprising 50 + aircraft.
Fig. 2 This marker indicates intercepting squadrons (in this instance, Spitfire squadrons - no 72 and 92) together with the number of aircraft and their altitude.

Channelled For Assessment

Essentially, there were three levels of Operations Rooms in RAF Fighter Command during 1940: Command, Group and Sector. Each had clearly defined functions and this hierarchical system allowed information and orders to cascade down but was reliant on information also being relayed back up the system via its eyes and ears in the field (the Observer Corps) to allow it to properly function.

Without information, orders could not be disseminated, and the point of entry for raw information from radar and the Observer Corps at HQ Fighter Command was the Filter Room.

The Filter Room at HQ Fighter Command, Bentley Priory, was the most important link in the whole air defence command and control chain. In simplistic terms, all incoming information from radar stations was channelled for assessment and action. It was then passed, simultaneously, to the Command Operations Room for dissemination to the relevant Group Operations Rooms. Upon judgements made in the Filter Room rested the decisions made for the deployment of defensive forces. As the Air Ministry noted:

'The accuracy of filtering is of vital importance. At only one point in the whole vast network of the radar system does the information collected and forwarded by the radar chain assume a tangible form on which fighter action may be taken.'

Monitoring The Battle

Whilst the Fighter Command Operations Room at the Bentley Priory HQ was the very nerve centre of the Battle of Britain, it was really the Group and Sector Operations Rooms which more actively controlled the battle. That said, the Command Operations Room gave the C-in-C (or a nominated senior officer) an immediate overview of the situation across the entire country. From his gallery position, the C-in-C could monitor the overall progress of battle at any given moment by looking down on the General Situation Map with its constantly changing display of counters and markers being moved around by RAF and WAAF personnel. However, there were two important functions carried out by Command Operations.

The first of these, from an overview of the situation, was to allocate specific incoming raids to the appropriate Group. Depending upon which ground the raid was encroaching, then it designated the particular raid to that Group. Once handed on to the relevant Group, then that Group's Operations Room would, in turn, delegate down to the appropriate Sector or Sectors and that Sector's own Operations Rooms.

The second function was to disseminate air raid warnings to the appropriate civil defence regions in the country, and this was based on the information coming in from radar stations.

Once a raid had been allocated to a specific Group within Fighter Command, the Group Controller would cascade down his instructions to the Sector Operations Rooms within his area of command. In turn, the Sector Operations Rooms had, under their command, small numbers of fighter squadrons, and it was the Sector Operations Room that issued instructions for specific squadrons (or even sub-sections of squadrons) to 'scramble' and intercept threats.

In sending squadrons off, the Sector

'The radar stations were positioned to ensure that every aircraft approaching from the east, the south, or south-west would be detected by at least two stations situated in an unbroken chain along Britain's coasts, from the Shetland Isles to Pembrokeshire.'

COMMAND AND CONTROL

Controller had information which had been passed up the chain from the radar stations, and then trickled back down to his level of command in a matter of two or three minutes. In effect, he became the 'hands-on' controller who controlled the battle itself, and also had the benefit of real time information being fed directly up to him from Observer Corps posts in his operating area.

Weapon For Victory

Radar was thus the essential 'front end' of the system on which Britain's air defence was reliant. Without radar, the rest of the system couldn't have worked. Reporting on the system overall, and of its success, Air Chief Marshal Dowding said:

'The system, as a whole, had been built up by successive steps over a period of about four years, and I was not dissatisfied with the way in which it stood the test of war.'

It was, perhaps, a rather modestly understated assessment of the system which he had designed around the radar chain. It could be said that radar had been a weapon for victory, and that Dowding's system won the day and held the line.

For his part, Prime Minister Winston Churchill was rather more effusive:

'All the ascendancy of the Hurricanes and Spitfires would have been fruitless but for this system which had been devised and built before the war. It had been shaped and refined in constant action, and all was now fused together into a most elaborate instrument of war, the like of which existed nowhere in the world.'

On the German side, there continued to be a failure to recognise the importance of the system. In the preliminary stages of the battle, the Germans realised, through interception of radio messages, that British fighters were directed towards them with great accuracy. And although they knew of the British radar system before the war, they had no idea about the highly developed system linked to fighter control. Their assessment of that system on 7 August 1940, showed a very serious misconception:

'Since British fighters are controlled from the ground by W/T they are tied to their respective ground stations and thus restricted in mobility. Consequently, the assembly of strong fighter forces at determined points and at short notice is not to be expected. A massed German attack on a target area can therefore count on the same conditions of light fighter opposition as in attacks on widely scattered targets. It can, indeed, be assumed that considerable confusion in the defensive networks will be unavoidable during mass attacks, and that the effectiveness of the defences may thereby be reduced.'

The conclusion the Luftwaffe had arrived at was the opposite of the truth. Radar, and the linked-in command and control system, saved the day. ■

The Operations Room Clock

A distinctive and colourful feature of RAF Operations Rooms, the clock was a vitally important feature of the 'Dowding System' which used information about incoming enemy raids from radar stations and the Observer Corps.

The clock was marked with coloured triangular markers in a circle below the numbers 1 to 12, the triangles pointing upwards between each of the numbers in five-minute intervals and coloured alternately: red, yellow and blue. Information received from radar stations was 'filtered' in the Filter Room at RAF Bentley Priory and then passed to the Operations Room once confirmed as an enemy raid. The Operations Room clock was essential in ensuring that information on incoming aircraft raids remained current.

The direction of raids was plotted onto the situation map using coloured arrows, and the colour of the arrow corresponded to the time of arrival of the information. This was tied to the coloured segment the minute hand had fallen on when the information came in.

Once the minute hand moved into a new colour, all the old arrows in that colour were removed in order to repeat the process and ensure that all information on the situation map was never more than 15 minutes old.

THE BATTLE OF BRITAIN IN COLOUR

Fierce Days of Fighting

Not every day during the Battle of Britain was filled with action and dogfights, but some were far more heavily fought than others. Those days have greater significance in the overall picture of the battle and its eventual outcome.

From the British perspective, the Battle of Britain was fought between 10 July and 31 October 1940. From the German standpoint, there was no 'Battle of Britain' *per se* – it was simply a period of escalating intensity in the air war against the British Isles which had been waged since October 1939, in pursuance of German war aims.

In the early summer of 1940, however, and with the fall of France, Winston Churchill stated:

"What General Weygand called the Battle of France is over, I expect that the Battle of Britain is about to begin."

The term 'Battle of Britain' was thus born.

By 1941, the Air Ministry had published an information booklet called *"The Battle of Britain"*. This explained the battle had begun on 8 August and ended on 31 October 1940. In truth, these were artificial dates.

In 1946, Air Chief Marshal Sir Hugh Dowding (Commander-in-Chief of RAF Fighter Command during 1940), wrote a dispatch for the *London Gazette* in which he re-appraised things, saying that although there was merit in choosing 8 August as the start date, he had subsequently concluded that it began on 10 July. He acknowledged, though, that even this date was "somewhat arbitrary". Neither was it a date which bore any real significance in terms of Luftwaffe air operations. It was simply the day, retrospectively chosen by the British, as that upon which the battle was deemed to have commenced. In truth, it was just another date in an air campaign which had been underway for some while.

In fact, the pilots of RAF Fighter Command thought they had been

FIERCE DAYS OF FIGHTING

Far Left An iconic image of the Battle of Britain as vapour trails tangle above the London skyline during the summer of 1940.
Above A London newsvendor keeps a wary eye on the battle as he chalks up the 'score' on a blackboard – albeit with what are probably rather exaggerated tallies.

fighting the Battle of Britain for some time already, the Operations Record Book of Spitfire equipped 54 Squadron remarked on 10 July – the very day when the battle supposedly commenced – that:

"As a result of the first phase of the Battle of Britain, the squadron could only muster eight aircraft and thirteen pilots."

Equally contentious is the day marked in Britain and its Commonwealth as Battle of Britain Day. That date is 15 September, with national commemorative services and events held on the nearest Sunday. However, subsequent research shows that 15 September 1940, was *not* the hardest fought day of the battle at all. It was, though, a date selected on the basis that 185 German aircraft had been *claimed* as shot down. That claim, with the benefit of post-war research, is discredited. Simply a case of over-claiming the number of enemy aircraft destroyed. In fact, the hardest fought day was Sunday, 18 August 1940.

There were, of course, other heavily contested days. Among them, for instance, the 12th, 13th, 15th, 16th, 26th and 30th August. Into September, and the 9th, 11th, 27th and 30th are all notable – as was 7th October.

Here, we look at a small selection of some notable days during the Battle of Britain: fierce days of fighting, but just three days out of the 114 across which the battle had raged.

In truth, not each of those 114 days were filled with fierce fighting. On some days, weather conditions were such that air operations were impossible – for either side. On other days, the Luftwaffe simply carried out very few air operations over Britain.

In fact, no date was definitively a 'turning point' in the battle. And no outright victory could be claimed to have occurred by 31 October. Instead, each day of air fighting merged almost insensibly into the next. And neither did the air fighting simply stop on 31 October. In fact, it carried on – to greater or lesser degrees – into November and December. By then, however, the night Blitz had largely replaced the daylight fighting, continuing almost unabated through to the spring of 1941. ■

THE BATTLE OF BRITAIN IN COLOUR

Convoy 'Peewit'

During the early stages of the Battle of Britain, the Luftwaffe concentrated attacks on shipping in the English Channel. One of those heaviest fought actions took place on 8 August 1940 - initially, the date identified as the beginning of the battle.

The background to the actions fought on 8 August 1940, lay with the sailing of a convoy of over 20 merchant ships from Southend during the morning of 7 August. The convoy was CW9 'Peewit'. With a Royal Navy escort, and covering RAF fighters, the mass of shipping sailed round North Foreland and out into the Dover Strait. Sailing with them were four Royal Navy vessels towing barrage balloons to guard against air attack, including one towed by what was a converted Belgian pilot ship, HMS *Borealis*.

As the convoy passed down the Channel, and hugging the shore, the convoy was spotted from the French coast as it sailed westward in fading daylight. The bobbing barrage balloons gave the game away, having been seen against the sunset. The trap was sprung.

At Boulogne, several German torpedo boats (E-Boats) left port in the early hours to take up position off Beachy Head, watching and waiting for the convoy. With horrendous suddenness, the E-Boats were among the ships like wolves in a flock of sheep. Three of the merchant ships were sunk, the German boats scattering the convoy. Mayhem ensued until the E-Boats called off the attack in the gathering light of dawn. The rest would be left to the Luftwaffe.

Timeline: 06.20

The scattered remnants of CW9 'Peewit' eventually formed some sort of order south west of Selsey Bill when they were spotted by a reconnaissance Dornier 17-P, which had just been missed by six Hurricanes of 601 Squadron from RAF Tangmere which landed back there at 06.25 hrs. Unhindered in its work, the Dornier landed with vital information on the course, speed and composition of the convoy. The information was flashed to Luftwaffe planners who mobilised a formidable force of Stuka dive bombers. Briefed for the raid, one crew member noted:

"At the briefing we were told that our target was a British convoy trying to force the Channel route. We were given a codename for our attack: 'Puma'. We had no proper location as such, so had to fly our mission most accurately by compass."

The scene was set for the 'Puma' to pounce on the 'Peewit'.

Timeline: 08.00

Fifty-seven Ju 87 Stukas, laden with a total of 285 high-explosive bombs, departed the Cherbourg Peninsula escorted by a huge force of Messerschmitt 109s. South of the Isle of Wight, the Ju 87s found a group of six merchant vessels sailing to meet CW9 'Peewit' and attacked these instead. The SS *Coquetdale* and SS *Ajax* were sunk.

DAYS OF BATTLE

Facing page Messerschmitt 109 pilot, Oberleutnant Julius Neumann of 6/JG27, took part in fighter escort operations over the Channel on 8 August. He was shot down on the Isle of Wight and captured ten days later, on 18 August 1940.

Right The converted Belgian pilot vessel, HMS Borealis, was one of the craft employed towing barrage balloons to protect Convoy CW9 'Peewit' from air attack on 8 August 1940. In the event, her balloon was spotted from France against the setting sun as the convoy proceeded down the English Channel. The trap was thus sprung, and the Germans were able to launch their attacks. Ultimately, HMS Borealis would not see the next sunset.

Far right Overnight, Kriegsmarine E-Boats launched a surprise attack on the convoy off Beachy Head. They sank three of the ships and scattered the rest of the convoy - the exploits of these fast Channel raiders being covered in this propaganda title, part of the 'War Books for German Youth' series.

Below Aircrew of Stukageschwader 1 getting a last-minute briefing prior to a sortie are pictured in this original colour photograph by the Propaganda Kompanie. The Junkers 87 Stukas of this unit participated in the various actions on 8 August 1940 over Convoy CW9 'Peewit'.

Writing of his experiences that day, one merchant seaman wrote:

"The whole side of our ship was blown out. When I glanced into the water as I made my way to our bullet-holed lifeboat I could see a body with great streaks of blood around it on the white foam of a wave crest. He was bobbing face down, surrounded by bits of smashed wood, clothes, bits of paper and charts, personal belongings, kapok lifejackets, sodden loaves of bread and uncoiling pieces of rope. I was shaking uncontrollably. One lad of about sixteen or seventeen was crying like a baby. Mercifully, I couldn't hear his pathetic wails as I was deaf from a bomb blast. He had also wet and soiled himself in this living hell where the Germans were still gunning and bombing us."

Meanwhile, the barrage balloons – including the one above HMS *Borealis* – were simply shot from the sky in flames, impotent to the guns of German fighters.

Overhead, as other RAF fighters were being rushed to the scene, it was only the Hurricanes of 145 Squadron who engaged the raiders. Flight Lieutenant Adrian Boyd DFC had a remarkable escape when engaging the Messerschmitt 109 escort: "Suddenly, and for no reason at all, one of them did a half roll and went straight into the sea. I hadn't fired at him and it looked as if he had committed suicide. I was so astonished I couldn't believe my eyes. While I was looking, there was a crash behind my head. A bullet came through

THE BATTLE OF BRITAIN IN COLOUR

my hood, passed through the back of my helmet, tore through the back of my goggles and before I knew where I was the hood had flown back and my goggles disappeared."

Escapes didn't come any closer.

Timeline: 11.45
Another forty-nine Stukas, carrying 245 bombs between them, set out for CW9 'Peewit' and attacked the convoy, sinking the Commodore's ship, SS *Empire Crusader*. Before the dive-bombing attack, fighters shot down in flames all the convoy's protective barrage balloons. Four other ships were hit and damaged. This time, Hurricanes and Spitfires of 145, 213, 238, 257, 601 and 609 Squadrons were scrambled to intercept the Stukas and their escort of Messerschmitt 109s and Messerschmitt 110s. One RAF pilot, Squadron Leader Harold Fenton, was shot down into the sea after going out to search for some pilots who had been lost in that engagement. He was rescued by HMS *Basset*, along with a Stuka pilot, Oberleutnant Martin Müller. It was recorded that:

"HMS Basset also picked up a German officer whose total luggage comprised a Verey pistol with cartridges and a large packet of twelve contraceptives which gave the crew an amusing interlude. Whilst Squadron Leader Fenton and the Bosche were drying out, they enjoyed tea and buttered toast together but were much interrupted by German bombs which were falling with insistent regularity."

During this mid-day battle, as with the earlier engagement, several RAF and Luftwaffe aircraft had been shot down.

Timeline: 15.45
Yet again, another force of Stukas was despatched in the final assault against CW9 'Peewit'. This time, 82 dive bombers set out with 30 Messerschmitt 109s and 20 Messerschmitt 110s providing cover. In total, 132 aircraft.

Sent to meet them were 48 Hurricanes and nine Spitfires of 43, 145, 152 and 238 Squadrons. In the biggest aerial engagement to date, massive dogfights ensued in a small space of sky, with a number of raiders and defenders shot down. Once again, the attackers failed to find the convoy but chanced upon a motley selection of shipping that had been sent out to aid vessels crippled earlier.

In the bombing, HMS *Borealis*, damaged in an earlier attack, was sunk - although the defenders exacted a heavy toll. Nevertheless, one of the fighter pilots, Sergeant Frank Carey of 43 Squadron, said:

"It was a raid so terrible and inexorable that it was like trying to stop a steam roller."

Meanwhile, his CO, Squadron Leader 'Tubby' Badger, astonished by the awesome spectacle of the approaching bombers, said of the aircraft stepped up in serried tiers:

"It was like looking up a crowded escalator on the Piccadilly Underground."

In the maelstrom, however, Pilot Officer Peter Parrot of 145 Squadron hit one of the Stukas before it dropped its bombs, sending it down to crash at St Lawrence, above Orchard Bay on the Isle of Wight. Parrot hit the bomber at less than 100ft over the sea, killing the rear gunner and severing the main fuel line to the engine.

As it wobbled back over the coast, a young local boy, Alan Twigg, grabbed his 'Daisy' .22 air rifle and took a pot shot at the Stuka as it passed overhead, only to be admonished by a rather excitable adult:

"What if you'd have hit one of the bombs, you stupid, stupid boy? You'd have blown us all to kingdom-come!"

It had been a heavily fought day, with the wreckages of ships and aircraft strewn along the Channel from Beachy Head to the Isle of Wight.

— 62 —

DAYS OF BATTLE

Left Originally earmarked for test flying by the RAF, the Junkers 87 shot down on the Isle of Wight ended up in the aircraft scrap re-processing yard at Cowley, Oxfordshire.
Below The grim reality of war. This was the gunner's position in the Stuka shot down at St Lawrence, its Perspex splattered with the unfortunate crew man's blood.

Above One of the Junkers 87 raiders on 8 August was this aircraft of 4./StG77, shot down at St Lawrence on the Isle of Wight by a Hurricane of 145 Squadron, flown by Pilot Officer Peter Parrot. The pilot of the Stuka was captured, his gunner killed.
Above Left The Messerschmitt 109s of Jagdgeschwader 27 participated in escort operations covering the Junkers 87s during attacks against the convoy.
Left Blazing ships were left in the wake of the convoy on 8 August 1940 - from Beachy Head in the east to the Isle of Wight in the west.

SCRAPYARD FODDER

When the Junkers 87 Stuka hit by Pilot Officer Parrot came to earth in a bumpy crash-landing at St Lawrence on the Isle of Wight on 8 August 1940, it had suffered relatively little damage with just eight .303 bullet strikes.

The Stuka was in such good condition that it was earmarked by RAF technical intelligence officers to be carefully taken apart and moved to the Royal Aircraft Establishment at Farnborough for repair and test flying, being the first relatively intact Stuka to be captured.

By the time the airframe had been brought back to the mainland, yet another example of the aircraft type had fallen into RAF hands. This had been brought down virtually intact on 18 August and was earmarked for evaluation and testing in place of the Isle of Wight example. The latter was duly consigned to the scrapyard.

Unfortunately, it transpired that the better example was extensively vandalised before the RAF could remove it, and it was damaged by souvenir hunters to such an extent that a return to flight was no longer viable.

The Junkers 87 brought down at St Lawrence on 8 August 1940, was a machine of 4/StG77, piloted by Unteroffizier Pittroff, who was taken POW. His gunner, Unteroffizier Rudolf Schubert, was killed by one of the few bullets which struck the aircraft.

THE DAY SUMMARISED

It had been the German's biggest air effort to date, and its biggest failure.

In total, 23 Luftwaffe aircrew were killed or missing in operations on 8 August. Another 12 were wounded and three taken POW. Additionally, 24 Luftwaffe aircraft had been lost and many damaged, some badly. The RAF had coincidentally lost the same number of men killed or missing and lost 22 aircraft. Man-for-man, aircraft-for-aircraft, it was almost a score draw.

The reality, however, was that the Luftwaffe couldn't afford such wastage against little merchant ships plying the Channel. They were insignificant targets in either securing air superiority or paving the way for invasion.

The tactics and direction of German air attacks needed to change if they were to succeed.

THE BATTLE OF BRITAIN IN COLOUR

A Hurricane of 32 Squadron at 'Readiness' during the summer of 1940. The groundcrew have chalked 'Petrol OK' and a time on the engine cowling. Meanwhile, the pilot sits in the cockpit attended by his Fitter and Rigger, with the aircraft plugged into a trolley accumulator ready for a rapid start. This squadron were heavily engaged during the fighting on 18 August 1940.

DAYS OF BATTLE

The Hardest Day

Post-war research has identified the most fiercely fought day of the Battle of Britain, in terms of the numbers of aircraft brought down, was Sunday, 18 August 1940. It subsequently became known as 'The Hardest Day'.

THE BATTLE OF BRITAIN IN COLOUR

As with many of the big days of fighting during the Battle of Britain, 18 August 1940 started quietly enough – a quietness which belied what was to come. Initially, German air activity was restricted to a few reconnaissance sorties across the South of England. Significantly, the track of these flights took the aircraft over many of the RAF's airfields. It was a portent of what was to come later that day, although one of the aircraft, a Messerschmitt 110, was chased and shot down into the sea by two Spitfires of 54 Squadron off the French coast and its two crew members killed. Its loss, though, neither hampered nor postponed the Luftwaffe's plans for the day's attacks. Initially, though, those plans were hampered by a summer haze. Once it lifted, however, the German assault got into its stride with a ferocious intensity.

Timeline: 13.04

Shortly after 12.30 a large force of enemy aircraft was picked up by radar as it formed-up and crossed the Channel. The formation comprised some 60 Messerschmitt 109s of JG3 and JG26 which performed a *Frei jagd* (Free Hunt) ahead of the formation of 12 Junkers 88s, 27 Dornier 17s and 60 Heinkel 111s which crossed the coast between Dover and Dungeness. Already airborne were the Hurricanes of 56 and 501 Squadrons and the Spitfires of 54 Squadron, although the Hurricanes of 501 Squadron were taken disastrously by surprise over Whitstable by the Me 109s of JG26.

Here, Oberleutnant Gerhard Schoepfel crept up, unseen, on the squadron's Hurricanes who were flying an outmoded and dangerous pre-war tight combat formation which allowed no flexibility and gave little chance of spotting an enemy about to pounce. Taking advantage of the situation, Schoepfel shot down no less than four Hurricanes, one after the other in quick succession, killing one pilot and wounding the three others without the rest of the squadron even noticing. The last aircraft, though, splattered oil and debris across Schoepfel's windscreen and he had to break away from his killing spree.

Schoepfel, temporarily commanding III/JG26, later wrote of his experiences that day:

"Our Me 109s, and others from JG3, were on a roaming free-hunt ahead of a raiding force of Dornier 17s and Heinkel 111s bound for British airfields. In total, our force comprised about 40 fighters. Soon after we crossed the Kent coast, I caught sight of the enemy. As usual, they were waiting for us. But this day they were not very watchful. It was also my lucky day!

"The enemy, a force of Hurricanes, were climbing in a wide spiral in close

Above Hurricanes of 501 pictured during a 'Scramble' take-off on 15 August 1940. On 18 August, both these aircraft were shot down on 18 August 1940. The pilot of the nearest aircraft (P3049), Pilot Officer Kenneth Lee, baled out injured over Whitstable. The pilot of the other aircraft (P3208), Pilot Officer John Bland, was killed when his aircraft crashed at Sturry, near Canterbury. Both aircraft were brought down by Oberleutnant Gerhard Schoepfel.

formation and in vics of three. The pilots must have all been concentrating on keeping good formation, and not colliding with their fellows. Anyway, they were too busy to be looking out for their enemy. I signalled to my pilots to remain above and give cover, as I dived down behind them. As a single aircraft, I could achieve surprise, but if the whole formation had dived on them, then we probably would have been seen. It worked, as I could tell they had not seen me as they continued as if nothing was the matter.

"I stalked up like a cat stalking a bird and got into position behind the two Hurricanes weaving above and behind the formation. In seconds, I'd got bursts into both and they went down. With them out of the way, I closed on the formation – surprised that they hadn't noticed anything. Then, "Brrrrr...."another short burst into the rear Hurricane. It caught fire at once, and down he went.

– 66 –

Surely, they must see me, now? No! On they went. So, I moved up to the next Hurricane, but I got in too close and after my burst of fire I was hit by debris and oil and I couldn't see properly.

"I had to break away, but if I'd carried on, then I think I could have continued knocking them out of the sky so long as I still had ammunition."

Meanwhile, the bomber formations behind the fighters advanced on their targets: RAF Biggin Hill and RAF Kenley. Unseen to the radar, though, had been another nine Dornier 17s of 9/KG76 who, further west, were at that moment sliding past Beachy Head just above the wave tops. Spotted by the Observer Corps on the cliff top, the raiders swung in through Cuckmere Haven, still at ultra-low-level. As they snaked past Seaford, Margaret Birch watched from her home on top of the hills:

"We stood and looked down on the pencil-like 'planes, creeping along with the South Downs as a backdrop and hopping over trees and hedges. We couldn't see their markings, but there was something sinister about their appearance and behaviour."

At Kenley, as the raider's approach was plotted, so the squadrons were scrambled to get into the air. Squadron Leader A R D 'Donald' Mac Donnell, of 64 Squadron, described what it was like:

"When the order came, the airman on the telephone would shout 'SCRAMBLE!' at the top of his voice and each pilot would dash for his aircraft. By the time one got there a mechanic would already have started up the engine; the other would be holding the parachute up to help me strap it on. Once that was done, I would clamber into the cockpit. He would then pass my seat straps over my shoulders and help me fasten them. When I gave the 'thumbs-up' signal, he would slam shut the side door and I would pull tight the various straps. Next, I'd pull on my helmet, plug in the wireless lead and check that the engine was running properly. If all was well, I'd wave to the ground crew to pull away the wheel chocks. Then, I'd open the throttle and move forward out of the blast pen and across the grass to the take-off position. Once there, I would line up and open the throttle and begin the take-off run with the rest of my pilots following as fast as they could. Once airborne, I'd take instructions from the Sector Controller who would give me a course and altitude and give me the position of the raid. From the scramble order to the last aircraft leaving the ground, took about a minute and a half. At most."

Timeline: 13.20

The nine Dornier 17s seen by Margaret Birch certainly had 'sinister' intent, however, and streaked across Sussex, low level all the way, towards RAF Kenley. Tracked by the Observer Corps, the information was fed directly to the Sector Controller at Kenley and he had little doubt that the attackers were coming for his airfield. With minutes to spare, and without waiting for orders from Group Control, he scrambled all fighters still on the ground at Kenley in a 'survival scramble.' Almost immediately, the nine bombers roared over the airfield perimeter and scattered bombs across hangars, buildings and runways and machine gunning as they went. The attack was over in just seconds, but in the mayhem one of the Dorniers was hit by anti-aircraft defences and crashed in flames, exploding just beyond the airfield boundary. Others were hit, too. One pilot was shot and killed with a crew member incredibly wresting control, heaving the dead pilot of his seat and flying the aircraft back home.

Now, the fighters pounced and of the nine raiders, four were shot down and the other five all returned damaged and some with dead, dying or badly injured crew members on board. On the ground at Kenley, nine soldiers and airmen were killed, and others wounded, whilst four Hurricanes and a Blenheim had been destroyed, two Hurricanes and a Spitfire damaged and a further four non-operational aircraft destroyed, along with hangars and buildings. The funeral pyre from the burning buildings could be seen on the coast at Brighton, 35 miles away.

Wilhelm Raab was one of the Dornier pilots struggling to get home:

"We were shot to pieces. Over the sea, the left motor packed up and a long line of black smoke trailed behind us. Our speed was dropping, but I had no idea what it was because my air speed indicator had a bullet hole right through it. Suddenly, a shudder went through the aircraft as though it was about to break up. This was it. There was nothing but to set down on the sea and we did the best job we could, but the waves smashed straight through the Perspex front leaving us gasping for breath in the water. We scrambled out, but the flight engineer couldn't inflate his life jacket and was drowned. I think he was dragged under by our bomber. His life jacket had most likely been punctured by bullets. Later, they called this 'The Hardest Day.' It certainly was for us."

Timeline: 13.20

The other bomber formations advancing across Kent had now reached their objectives at Biggin Hill and the already battered Kenley. With 501 Squadron engaged by the Messerschmitts, and the other RAF fighters too far away to the north, the bombers had slipped through unmolested and Biggin Hill was bombed along with more bombs being dropped on Kenley and at RAF Croydon. The squadrons at Biggin Hill, 32 Sqn (Hurricanes) and 610 Sqn (Spitfires), were both scrambled to avoid losses on the ground. After the attack, WAAF Sergeant Elizabeth Mortimer coolly helped defuse unexploded German bombs, a deed which won her the Military Medal.

"I was just doing my job and was only the Flight Sergeant Bomb Disposal specialist's assistant. We simply dug down to the bombs and then put a special tool on the fuse to short-out the electrical condenser fitted to them, then we could lift them out. Some were probably delayed action that hadn't gone off yet, others were just duds. But even the duds could suddenly turn nasty. But it was nothing, really."

Timeline: 13.59

The radar station at Poling, West Sussex, picked up echoes from a force assembling north of Cherbourg and, within minutes, had calculated a force of 150 plus heading for the south coast. To start with, the heading of the force towards the Selsey area made it appear that a repeat of an attack made on RAF Tangmere two days earlier was incoming. In fact, before the formation reached the coast it split up into different elements but not before some 68 RAF fighters, Spitfires and Hurricanes, were scrambled and despatched to deal with the threat. The German formation had comprised

> "Now, I looked round at my wireless operator and he was hanging forward in his straps, his machine gun pointing aimlessly into the sky. I didn't realise that either he or the aircraft had been hit."
> Hauptmann Otto Schmid, I/StG77

THE BATTLE OF BRITAIN IN COLOUR

some 55 Me 109s and 109 Junkers 87 Stuka dive bombers. Off the Isle of Wight, at about 14.30, two groups swung north-west and two more headed east. Moments later, dive bombing attacks began at Gosport (a naval air station), RAF Thorney Island (a RAF Coastal Command airfield) and Ford (another naval air station) and the radar site which had detected them, RAF Poling.

Considerable damage was done at each location, although the only site of any real significance which was dive-bombed was Poling radar station which was knocked off the air. A number of Stukas were downed around the West Sussex area and in the English Channel, but the RAF fared badly, too. The other airfields, although damaged severely, were not any of Fighter Command's vital aerodromes. Once again, the Luftwaffe had expended needles effort and taken unnecessary losses going after targets that really were not important in the greater picture of the air defence of Great Britain. At Ford, though, the devastation was significant.

Buildings were wrecked and set on fire, many aircraft destroyed and 25 people were killed – Royal Navy and Army personnel and civilians, including a young Irish girl who had arrived at the main gate to meet her boyfriend at just the wrong time. Local Bobby, PC Jack Hamblin, was horrified at the scene which met him on arrival:

"Lying in the bottom of a bath in the shower block was a naval rating of about 20. His body was lying in its own blood, almost severed in the middle. The walls, such as were still standing, were splattered in blood. At the main gate I found the body of Lt Cdr Michael de Courcy who had been firing his .45 revolver in frustration at a diving Stuka and was caught in a bomb blast. His dismembered body was found outside the Wardroom, his right hand still firmly gripping his service revolver."

One of the raiding Junkers 87 Stuka pilots attacking RAF Thorney Island was Hauptmann Otto Schmid of I/StG77. He later recalled taking part in one of the significant actions of the Battle of Britain:

"Take off was at 13.30 hrs, but we were not unduly excited by it. Since the start of the war, I'd flown 65 sorties, including against Dunkirk and Channel targets, and always returned unscathed.

"We remained in close formation, led by the commander who gave hand signals as our three groups gained height to about 12,000 ft and at a speed of about 200 mph. It was a beautiful summer day,

Top Left Oberleutnant Gerhard Schoepfel sits in the cockpit of his Messerschmitt 109 as he prepares for another sortie during 1940.
Top Right Aircraft of Schoepfel's unit sit waiting for action on their improvised airfield, a farmer's cornfield, in the Pas de Calais, France.
Bottom Left The rudder of Oberleutnant Gerhard Schoepfel's Messerschmitt 109, marked with 'kill' tallies, including those recording his four victories on 18 August 1940.
Bottom Right Viewed through a gunsight, the aircraft of 9/KG76 approach the point where they crossed the coast at Seven Sisters, east of Seaford.

– 68 –

DAYS OF BATTLE

Above The Dornier 17s of 9/KG76 race in at low-level, past Beachy Head and its famous lighthouse, heading for the attack on RAF Kenley on 18 August 1940.
Left Viewed from the cockpit of one of the attacking Dorniers, this is RAF Kenley under attack on 18 August 1940. Smoke from bullets and cannon shells wreathe the dispersal points and taxiway and a solitary 64 Squadron Spitfire sits in its protective E-Pen.

Right Squadron Leader Aeneas Ranald Donald 'Don' MacDonell, the CO of 64 Squadron at RAF Kenley, August 1940.
Above One of the Stuka pilots of the attacking force on 18 August was Oberleutnant Johannes Wilhelm of 2/StG77. Shot down over Fishbourne, West Sussex, he was sprayed with oil as he abandoned his aircraft. Under escort at Chichester Railway station, curious commuters gape at the German as one of the escorting soldiers kindly slips his enemy a packet of fags! In this image, the oil-stained collar of Wilhem's shirt is clearly visible.

-69-

THE BATTLE OF BRITAIN IN COLOUR

Above A Junkers 87 Stuka stirs up the dust as it starts-up, preparatory to yet another sortie over Britain during the summer of 1940. On 18 August 1940, the last mass attack by Stukas was carried out against Britain.

Right Aftermath. One of the attacking Dorniers crashed into the garden of a residential property, just on the northern boundary of RAF Kenley. Airfield defences that day had included parachute and cable devices. These fired steel cables skywards, which then descended slowly on parachutes in the path of attacking aircraft.

Below right The Messerschmitt 109 of Oberleutnant Helmut Tiedmann at Abbey Farm, Leeds, Kent, on 18 August 1940. It has been covered in straw to camouflage it against attack and destruction by passing Luftwaffe aircraft.

and although our fighter escort hadn't shown up, we were sure they were in the vicinity. It was calm and peaceful. As the coast popped up in front of us, we could make out Thorney Island and intended to go down one after the other on the target. The leading Stukas looked like a string of pearls as they started to go in. Then, I saw the first British fighters screaming towards us. Initial evasive action brought my own flight to safety, but the last flight in our formation took the brunt.

"One Ju 87 went into the sea like a flaming torch. There were no sounds or words on the radio. There was no time to think about what was happening. The main thing was to remember the correct moment to start the attack. And now it was my turn! First, I made the wing-waggle (indicating I was about to dive) then I was going down with my nose pointed on the target. Now, my vision was only downwards but couldn't help sparing a thought for my radio operator. All he could do was gaze upwards, not knowing when the bombs left the aircraft or if his pilot was efficient. Or even still alive! As for myself, I was completely concentrating on the target.

"The hangar complex grew in my sight, and I dropped lower and lower. At last, there was just one hangar in my cross wire. I pressed my bomb release, and my job was done. All I had to do now was

ON THE RUN...

When the radiator of twenty-two-year-old Oberleutnant Helmut Tiedmann's Messerschmitt 109 was hit during combat over southern England in the early afternoon action on 18 August 1940, he was forced to make a wheels-up belly landing at Abbey Farm, Leeds, in Kent. Tiedmann, the Staffelkapitän of 2/JG3, managed to get clear of his aircraft long before the military or Police arrived on the scene. He is said to have been at large and on the run in the Kent countryside for some twelve hours.

Home on leave in nearby Hollingbourne, RAF airman Dennis Rolph raced to the spot to view the crashed Messerschmitt. Cannily, he had quickly changed into his RAF uniform before setting off on his bicycle with a group of friends. All of them wanted to view the German aircraft.

On arrival at the scene, the group discovered the aircraft was already heavily guarded, and any close access to it was forbidden.

However, Dennis' quick change into his uniform had paid dividends. Seeing his RAF blue, the guards lifted the rope barrier and allowed him to pass. Rather smugly, he got a close-up look and noted that the pilot had recorded a victory over an RAF aircraft on 15 August 1940, the tally marked on the Messerschmitt's fin.

Later, the aircraft was covered in straw to make it less visible from the air and to hopefully prevent its destruction by any passing Luftwaffe aircraft. Eventually, curious civilians were allowed to come closer to view the aircraft.

— 70 —

DAYS OF BATTLE

make for home. Making a wide turn, I went to re-join the formation. Normally, we re-formed into flights without much trouble. Then, behind me, looming ever larger, was a Spitfire trying to get into a firing position. I had to act fast to get out of his way. Turning wouldn't save me. So, I side-slipped, and he was foiled. Now, I looked round at my wireless operator. He was hanging forward in his straps, his machine gun pointing aimlessly into the sky. I didn't realise that he or the aircraft had been hit. In the meantime, the Spitfire turned and was coming in for another attack. It was obvious that he had selected me as his personal target. He must have seen my helpless gunner, and made for my tail. But I side slipped him and he went screaming past.

"Then, one of comrade in low-level flight, suddenly plunged into the sea and disappeared. And another Ju 87 was shot down, bouncing on the surface of the water and vanishing. The situation became frightening as another Spitfire joined in the attack on me, but followed my side-slip, touched the water with its wingtip, and met its end. Then, I felt a blow and lost so much height that I touched the sea with my undercarriage.

"For the first time, I noticed blood on my arm and realised I'd been hit. Then, I was back over Caen. With relief, I got my Ju 87 on the ground. And that was my next surprise! My landing was rough and fast, and only then I realised my undercarriage had been torn away.

"The ground crew took my radio operator out of the cockpit and found more than 80 hits in the aircraft. From my own Staffel, only one other aircraft escaped; an inexperienced pilot was so unnerved by what happened that he was grounded and never flew again. My poor radio operator died a few weeks later."

It was the last attack in any force by the Stuka during the Battle of Britain. ■

Top Left WAAF Sergeant Elizabeth Mortimer, awarded the MM for bravery on 18 August.
Top Middle Two Polish pilots of 501 Squadron: Sergeant Anton Glowacki (left) and Pilot Officer Stefan Witorzenc - both in action on 18 August.
Top Right Hauptmann Horst Tietzen (left) and Leutnant Hans Lessing of 5/JG51, were both shot down and killed by Pilot Officer Witorzenc and another Polish pilot off Kent on 18 August.
Above One of the losses on 18 August 1940 was Flight Lieutenant R A 'Dickie' Lee of 85 Squadron. He was last seen chasing Messerschmitt 109s out to sea off Southend at around 6pm when flying this Hurricane.

THE DAY SUMMARISED

During all three main air operations against Britain that day, the scale of the fighting had been unprecedented and subsequent analysis allows an objective assessment which rates this, by far, as the hardest fought day of the entire battle. At the end of the day, 68 British (although only 31 of these were in the air) and 69 German aircraft had been totally destroyed. The Luftwaffe had lost 94 aircrew killed, 40 POW and had many more injured, plus 27 aircraft had returned home damaged, some seriously. The RAF, meanwhile, had lost 11 pilots killed and nineteen had been wounded, some so seriously that they would not return to the battle. Others, RAF ground personnel, had been killed on the ground and serious damage had been caused to airfields and installations.

Despite all of this, however, it would be 15 September that was subsequently chosen as 'Battle of Britain Day', purely on the very unsound basis that it was the day when British fighter claims, as opposed to actual Luftwaffe losses, was the apparently the highest.

But that is not to say, either, that 18 August proved to be a turning point in the battle, because it didn't.

Instead, it was simply the hardest fought day.

THE BATTLE OF BRITAIN IN COLOUR

Battle of Britain Day

Notable for fierce air fighting over London and the south east of England, Sunday 15 September 1940 is still marked as the day on which the Battle of Britain is remembered nationally.

Celebrated ever since 1940 as 'Battle of Britain Day', there is little basis for such recognition in terms of the scale of air fighting or number of losses on either side. As we have seen, the fighting on 18 August might be better suited as the day to be thus celebrated. That said, the air fighting on 15 September did cause German High Command to finally realise that the Luftwaffe would not achieve air superiority over the RAF before the weather broke in the autumn. However, the RAF had no way of knowing this to be the case until long after the event. In fact, it only became gradually clearer to the defenders, as September drew to a close, that large-scale escorted daylight bomber operations would eventually be abandoned.

There would yet be one or two more such raids after 15 September, however, but it is largely for the fighting over central London, and the RAF's initial claim of 185 German aircraft destroyed, for which the day is remembered.

Timeline: 11.00

By 11.00 hours, it was obvious from the forces massing near Calais that a big attack was imminent, and a large force of British fighters were sent into the air over the next 25 minutes to counter the threat. For once, the controller at 11 Group not only had time to assemble his squadrons into 'wings', but he was able to bring in reinforcements from adjacent groups before the first German formations crossed the coast. In total, seventeen full squadrons were in position and waiting to meet the Luftwaffe formations now advancing on the Capital and southern England.

The sight of so many fighters must have been a shock to those Luftwaffe aircrews who might have believed Göring's assurances that the RAF was down to its last few fighters. As the

DAYS OF BATTLE

Top Left Pilot Officer Roy Marchand of 73 Squadron in his Hurricane, chats with his airman fitter during the summer of 1940. On 15 September 1940, Pilot Officer Marchand was shot down and killed over Sittingbourne, Kent.
Top Right A Dornier 17-Z bombersof 2/KG76 with its striking nose-art which conveys a powerful message about the Luftwaffe's assault on Britain. Aircraft of this unit participated in the attacks on 15 September 1940.
Right A crew member stands by a Dornier 17-Z of 7/KG3 which is being readied for its cargo of 50 kg bombs. Aircraft of this unit participated in the attacks on 15 September 1940.

massed formations approached London, and then flew over the city itself, large air battles and dogfights ranged widely across Kent, Sussex and the Capital.

One Luftwaffe fighter pilot already disabused of Goring's claim was Leutnant Hans Bertel of Stab.I/JG52. That day, and solely due to rising combat losses, his unit could only put up 13 fighters instead of the usual 26. Over Kent, it would be his turn to be shot down. Baling-out, he recalled:

"I must have been going down very fast when I was finally thrown clear of my out-of-control Messerschmitt, because once I was outside it sounded like a thunderstorm. I opened my parachute very high up and blacked out due to lack of oxygen. Coming-to, a squadron of Hurricanes came past and I thought they were going to shoot me on my parachute - but they circled me, gave a friendly wave, and flew off. I landed in a hedge and was captured by two Home Guardsmen in civilian clothes carrying shotguns. They took me to a village where there was a funny old man with a long knife who wanted to kill me. Later, I could laugh about it - but even when a car was sent to pick me up, he tried to attack me through the open window of the car!"

Timeline: 12.00

Most of the bombs which fell on London fell in the ten minutes after noon, but the official account of the RAF's Air Historical Branch later recorded that: 'In short, it achieved very little. An electricity station at Beckenham was hit, houses in Lewisham, Battersea, Camberwell and Lambeth were hit along with two bridges between Clapham Junction and Victoria being struck and an unexploded bomb falling on the lawns of Buckingham Palace.' In fact, the Palace was hit on no less than sixteen occasions during the Battle of Britain and the Blitz, and one of the most famous incidents of the entire battle involved a Dornier 17 being hit and destroyed almost over the Palace itself

THE BATTLE OF BRITAIN IN COLOUR

and falling onto the forecourt of Victoria Station. It has often been suggested that this raider was specifically targeting Buckingham Palace and that it was deliberately rammed from the sky by a defending fighter. Neither assertion is accurate.

The bomber in question was one of a formation from I/KG76 that was tasked with bombing central London but was hit and attacked by at least nine different fighters. In frenzied air fighting, the bomber was eventually struck accidentally by a Hurricane flown by Sergeant Ray Holmes of 504 Squadron. The Dornier broke apart in mid-air, with debris falling in and around Victoria Station, and the Hurricane crashing into Buckingham Palace Road. Sergeant Holmes baled-out but had a lucky escape. Of the five men in the Dornier, two were killed and two were taken POW. Another was apparently so badly set about by a civilian mob when he landed at Kennington Oval that he later died of his injuries. As Hans Bertel had already discovered, feelings amongst some of the population were running high.

As for Ray Holmes, and after some difficulty getting out of his Hurricane, his adventure was not quite over after his parachute slammed him into the roof of a three-storey apartment:

"My parachute immediately collapsed, and I tried to grab something to halt my fall, but it was no good and I slithered down the tiles. Everybody knows you can't fall off a three-storey building and get away with it. As I slithered past the gutter, I thought: 'This is it. After all I've been through and I'm going to break my neck falling off a bloody roof!' Then, there was a terrible jolt and I came to a stop just off the ground, with my toes just touching the bottom of a dustbin with its lid off. My parachute had snagged and caught over the top of a down-pipe!"

Timeline: 13.45

The first raiders of a second assault then came into radar view, and by 14.15 hours RAF Fighter Command was able to

Top Left Over London, during the attacks on 15 September, gunners on board Luftwaffe bombers were hard pressed defending against RAF fighters. In this image, a Dornier 17-Z gunner scans the sky for fighters. During the noon attack that day, the escorting Messerschmitt 109s withdrew due to fuel shortage and the bombers had to make a fighting retreat under attack from twelve squadrons of RAF fighters.

Top One of the German fighters brought down that day was this Messerschmitt 109 flown by Unteroffizier August Klick of 3/LG2, which the pilot landed at Shell Ness on the Isle of Sheppey. It is pictured here in the aircraft scrap processing yard at Cowley, Oxfordshire.

Above One of the noon raiders, this Dornier 17-Z of 8/KG76, was shot down at Castle Farm, Lullingstone, Kent, with its four crew members captured. Three were wounded, one of them later succumbing to his injuries. The bomber is seen here being dismantled by a salvage gang. Fitted to the rear of the bomber, investigators found what has sometimes been described as a crude flame-thrower device fitted in the aircraft's tail, although official reports described it as: 'Smoke Producing Apparatus'.

DAYS OF BATTLE

This photographed was developed from a film taken from a camera owned by a captured Heinkel 111 crew member who was taken POW on 15 September 1940. It shows Heinkel 111 H-2, 3143, A1 + CC, of KG53, which made a crash landing at Vendeville, France, on 5 September 1940.

'FIRING LIKE SAVAGES...'

When a Heinkel from Stab II/KG53 was shot down over Kent on 15 September 1940, the Observer, Oberleutnant Hans Peter Schierning, was found in possession of a camera. When the film was developed, a photograph appeared of a belly landed Heinkel 111.

The photograph depicted an aircraft of II/KG53 which had crash landed at Vendeville, France, on 5 September 1940, after returning damaged from a reconnaissance sortie over RAF Hornchurch to check on the results of an attack on that airfield. Damaged by fighters, the Heinkel limped home and Oberleutnant Schierning snapped this photograph of the aftermath. Ten days later, he was shot down over England and captured.

The aircraft in which Schierning was shot down on 15 September 1940, came to earth at Frittenden, Kent, with five crew members POW and the gunner, Feldwebel Andreas Grassl, killed in the fighter attack which had downed them. The pilot was Oberfeldwebel Gunther Schmidt, the radio operator Feldwebel Max Nagl with Unteroffizier Eugen Schilling as flight engineer. On board was the Gruppenkommandeur, Major Max Gruber, who wrote an account in a diary whilst in a POW camp. It detailed the crew's sortie to attack the Victoria Docks, but it was found and passed to RAF Intelligence. Extracts of his diary give us some flavour of events:

"...we came out of the cloud again and a Spitfire chased us and attacked us from the front. One shot went through the glass nose, just missed me and went right through and hit the bomb chutes. At the same time, the flight engineer called out that the top rear gunner had been hit. I turned around to see him fall into the arms the flight engineer. His face was as white as chalk. He had every appearance of being dead. We could do nothing for him at the moment. A fire in the right engine had now gained hold...and the Spitfire was positioning for another attack. The only hope was to make a belly landing, and below us was a typical English hedged countryside"

Gruber went on to describe how the pilot selected a field for landing, and then:

"There was a jerk, a sound of rending and cracking and then a few moments of utter stillness. This was broken by the rattle of rifle fire which appeared to be coming from the Home Guard. The serious fire in the engine forced us to abandon the aircraft quickly. We pulled the windows open and climbed out but threw ourselves on the ground because of further shooting. Then about ten English soldiers came towards us at the double. We put our hands up while the men fired into the air like savages. The Spitfire circled around only 50 metres above the charred remains of our aircraft."

According to Gruber, the treatment initially meted out to them was "...entirely favourable". Only when they were taken away did things turn ugly. Like other shot down German airmen that day, they discovered that feelings in the civilian population were somewhat febrile:

"As we drove away, I saw a lot of men on either side of the road leaning on fences. As they caught sight of us, they gave vent to their feelings by shouting at us and shaking their fists – no doubt worked-up by propaganda."

For Gruber and his men, the war was over.

THE BATTLE OF BRITAIN IN COLOUR

Left Sergeant Ray Holmes of 504 Squadron with his Hurricane at RAF Hendon, summer 1940. On 15 September he was involved in a hair-raising collision with a Dornier 17-Z over central London and was lucky to escape with his life. The strange yellow square on the Hurricane's wing is a gas detector panel.
Below The stricken Dornier broke apart over central London with much of the wreckage falling into the forecourt of Victoria Station. The tail section, seen here, fell onto a rooftop in Vauxhall Bridge Road.
Facing page On 15 September 1940, a bomb which had failed to explode and buried itself under St Paul's Cathedral was eventually extricated safely. This is the view looking up Ludgate Hill as a Bomb Disposal team deals with the device. A solitary Policeman bars the way.

scramble 25 squadrons. Proof, if any were needed, that the RAF's fighter force was anything but done for.

Again, the bomber force and its fighter escort were intercepted before reaching the Capital, and heavy air fighting took place on the way to London, over the city and as the raiders withdrew. In contrast to the attack at noon, the Germans had rather more to show for their efforts with serious damage to rail, road, electricity and fuel infrastructure and other establishments. However, there was nothing even approaching the damage caused by an attack on 7 September, when three times the tonnage of bombs was dropped and when damage was concentrated in one area.

This time, the damage was scattered and *relatively* ineffective and if the weight of bombs dropped is to be reckoned as anything of an index of the German offensive, then it would be wrong to cite this day as either the culmination of attacks on London or as the crisis of battle as a whole.

Given the number of aircraft in the air, collisions were perhaps inevitable as Ray Holmes had already discovered. At least two, though, were deliberate. Pilot Officer 'Paddy' Stephenson in a 607 Squadron Hurricane had a choice: either hit a Dornier 17 he was closing on or else collide with another Hurricane that was blocking his escape route. He chose the

DAYS OF BATTLE

Below A Luftwaffe reconnaissance photo of central London dated September 1940. Whitehall is marked out as the War Ministry, and Buckingham Palace is also indicated.
Right A Heinkel 111 over the Isle of Dogs, London, and the dockland area which was heavily targeted throughout September 1940.

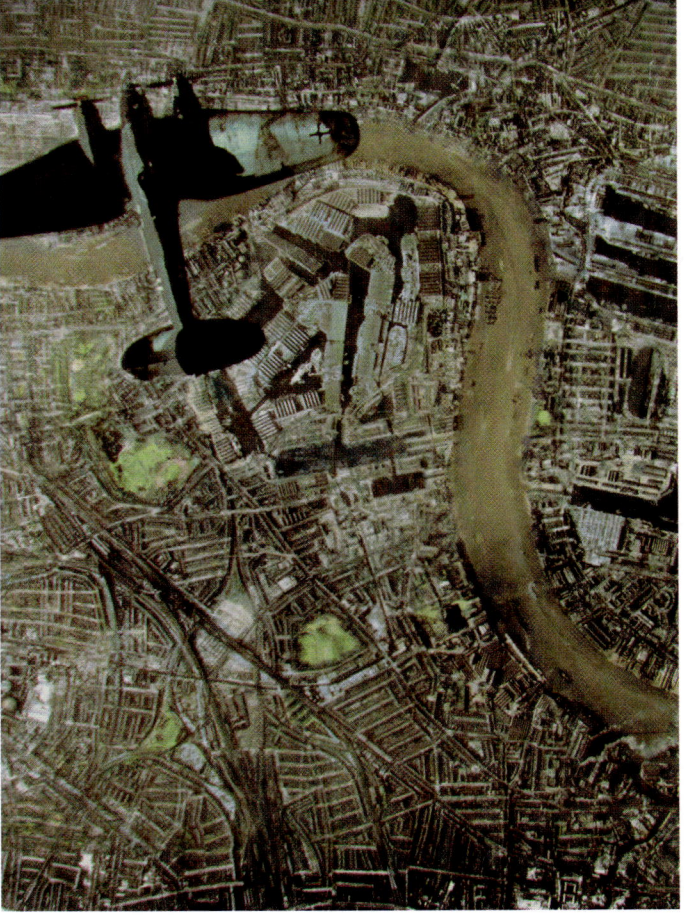

— 77 —

THE BATTLE OF BRITAIN IN COLOUR

DAYS OF BATTLE

Dornier, and survived. Chasing another Dornier 17, Pilot Officer Tom Cooper-Slipper was hit by gunfire and lost control as he closed on his quarry:

"I knew I was going to have to bale-out, so I decided to ram the Dornier first. I struck the bomber from three-quarters rear and saw it slew round in front of me. My overtaking advantage was only about 50 mph and I was surprised at the small force of impact. Nevertheless, I had to get out but have no recollection of actually pulling the ripcord. I'd been lucky."

It had certainly been a memorable day for many – including a considerable proportion of London's population who had witnessed the battle going on above their heads. ∎

Left Residential areas in London, particularly in the East End, came in for a hammering by the Luftwaffe during September 1940. This lucky pair were fortunately saved by their Anderson Air Raid Shelter.
Above Pilot Officer Tom Cooper-Slipper was another RAF pilot who had a lucky escape following a collision with a Dornier 17-Z on 15 September 1940.
Right On the ground in London, and across the south east of England, civilians had a grandstand view of the fighting. Here, children shelter in a trench but are mesmerised by the battles going on overhead.

THE DAY SUMMARISED

By the end of the fighting that day, the RAF had lost 28 fighters with twelve pilots killed, twelve wounded and one who had baled-out over the sea to be taken POW.

Against this total, the Luftwaffe lost 56 aircraft with 81 aircrew killed, 63 taken POW and 31 wounded. Additionally, large numbers of aircraft returned home damaged, although initial claims of 185 destroyed were certainly over inflated.

On this basis, the RAF had certainly scored a victory that day, although the Luftwaffe was far from a defeated or spent force. All the same, escorted daylight raids now declined as the bomber force began to restrict itself to largely nocturnal activities. Meanwhile, the Luftwaffe modified some Messerschmitt 109 fighters to carry bombs and continued with limited daylight raids.

Thus, 15 September 1940 was not the height of the battle nor was it entirely a turning point. But it was significant in many respects. And it was certainly one of the big days of the battle.

THE BATTLE OF BRITAIN IN COLOUR

Failed to Return

Losses of German aircraft over the British Isles during the Battle of Britain not only resulted in depletion of Luftwaffe materiel assets, but also pilots and aircrew. Whether killed or captured, German airmen who failed to return were a total loss to the Luftwaffe.

In total, the Luftwaffe lost some 1,887 aircraft and 2,662 aircrew across the whole period of air operations during the Battle of Britain. Of these, some were aircraft which managed to limp home with varying degrees of damage, their pilots or crew perhaps wounded, dead or dying. On the back of losses sustained during the 'Blitzkreig' across Europe, so the damage to the infrastructure of the Luftwaffe organisation was immense. Not only that, but the replacement of lost equipment was a constant struggle. In fact, re-supply did not keep pace with losses.

Of greater importance, though, was the loss of well trained and experienced aircrew. Making good the depletion of pilots and aircrew was the biggest challenge. And even when they had passed through the Luftwaffe's training system, so they arrived on front-line units as novices. Very often, these replacements were a hindrance rather than of being very much help.

Of the large number of Luftwaffe aircraft which fell across Britain during the summer and autumn of 1940, many were photographed – either illicitly and privately, or by accredited press

GERMAN AIRCRAFT LOSSES

Above RAF airmen remove a trophy in the form of a unit emblem from the engine cowling of a Messerschmitt 109 in a scrap processing yard during 1940. The aircraft had been shot down near Selmeston, East Sussex, on 12 August 1940, its pilot, Unteroffizier Leo Zaunbrecher of 2/JG52, was wounded and taken POW. He allegedly told his captors: "This is what you get for coming to England!"
Left A Policeman and an Army officer inspect a Heinkel 111 of 10/KG1 which had been shot down by a Hurricane at Haxted Mill, Lingfield, Surrey, on 30 August 1940. The bomber had just taken part in an attack on Farnborough aerodrome. Two crew members were captured unhurt, two were wounded and a fifth was killed. Bullet holes and oil stains tell their own story.

photographers. Today, those images are a rich source which give us an opportunity to have a window into events of the Battle of Britain. And in these pages, bringing many of those images to life in colour adds an entirely different dimension.

To the British public, spellbound by the fierce battles which raged above their heads, it almost became something of a 'spectator sport'. Albeit a deadly one. And when BBC radio journalist Charles Gardner gave a running commentary on an air battle from the White Cliffs of Dover, he was criticised for lines such as *"Oh Boy! I've never seen anything as good as this!"*, and for treating it all as if he were commenting on a cricket match, especially when men's lives were at stake.

Gardner's unbridled enthusiasm aside, the British public revelled in such drama. Particularly when it came to giving the enemy a thrashing, and to hearing his excitement as he yelled into the microphone:

"The pilot has baled out by parachute. It's a Junkers 87 and he's going slap into the sea...and there he goes now...SMASH! A terrific column of water, and there was a Junkers 87. Only one man got out by parachute, so presumably there was one crew member still in it."

A little more restrained, but perhaps still summing up the great British excitement at the prospect of mounting German losses, were the measured tones of the BBC Home Service newsreader on Sunday 15 September 1940:

'This is the BBC Midnight News read by Alvar Lidell. Up to ten o'clock, 185 German aircraft had been destroyed in today's raids over this country. Today was the most costly for the German air force for nearly a month. In daylight raids between 350 and 400 enemy aircraft were launched in two attacks against London and South-East England. About half of them were shot down.'

As we have already seen, Lidell's announcement was very much wide of the true figure of German losses for that day. But still, it wouldn't do to underplay things.

And as for British losses during the Battle of Britain, they were barely mentioned – and then only if the German losses far outweighed the RAF ones. And when announced, great emphasis was always placed on how many of 'our' pilots were safe.

As for photographing shot down British aircraft, this rarely happened. After all, it would be bad for morale to see wrecked Spitfires and Hurricanes in the newspapers.

All of this, then, gave rise to something of a widespread public perception that it was mostly German aircraft which were being shot down! ■

THE BATTLE OF BRITAIN IN COLOUR

Toy Pistol 'Capture'

When the crew of a shot down Heinkel 111 bomber landed right alongside an English pub, they were taken prisoner by the landlord, ably assisted by a painter and decorator. One of the pair was brandishing a 'pistol' in an episode making them both local heroes.

Pub landlord Percy Tibble, a First World War veteran of the trenches, was getting ready for evening opening time at the 'Horse and Jockey' in Hipley, Hampshire. It was a Friday, and very soon his thirsty customers would be flocking in for their pay-day drinks. War or no war, folk still wanted their beer!

A little earlier, there had been the distant sound of aero engines and machine gun fire and some far-away bursts of anti-aircraft fire over Portsmouth or Southampton. But he paid little attention. Such things were becoming the 'new normal', now. Slightly more concerning, though, was the closer crump of bomb explosions. He ducked his head, ever so slightly, as he counted them, judged how close they were and carried on polishing the glasses. Sixteen he counted. The last one not too far away – but far enough not to bother him greatly. Old instincts from hearing artillery bursts creeping ever closer in the trenches were instincts that never left you. Now, though, there was a growing commotion outside.

Aware of the sound of intermittent spluttering aircraft engines getting closer and louder, and then the shouting of a workman, Samuel Brown, who was busy painting the pub's front door.

"*Percy! Come quickly! There's a Jerry coming down!*"

Percy flung his glass cloth onto the bar and went to have a look. It was probably just a low-flying Blenheim from nearby RAF Thorney Island, he told Samuel. But the earlier gunfire and bomb explosions did make him wonder. Now, standing in the pub's forecourt, Percy and Samuel watched in amazement as the bulk of a low-flying Heinkel 111 hove into view, bannering smoke and with Hurricanes buzzing around it. Brushing the treetops beyond the pub, the bomber was down – bouncing, crunching and careering across the nearby meadow until it ended up, rather forlornly, on its belly, one wing in a hedge and about 50 yards from his pub.

"*If they want a drink, they've got another bloody think coming*" quipped Percy. "*It 'aint even opening time yet!*"

Then, pulling himself together, he shouted to Samuel: "*OK! Let's get those Jerries!*"

GERMAN AIRCRAFT LOSSES

Facing page Guarded by soldiers, the bullet riddled Heinkel 111 at the Horse and Jockey pub, Hipley.
Far left A view of the downed Heinkel with the Horse and Jockey visible in the background.
Left Feldwebel Jonny Möhn, pilot of the Heinkel 111.
Below Landlord Percy Tibble with the toy gun used to capture the Heinkel crew.

Imaginary Concealed Pistol

Grabbing a child's toy pistol, which he rather inexplicably kept in the saddlebag of his bicycle, Samuel sprinted to the bomber with Percy close on his heel. Feeling rather less well defended than Samuel, who was 'armed' with his tinplate cap-gun, Percy ran with one hand in his back pocket as if to feign a hand on an imaginary concealed pistol. That, thought Percy, would worry the Germans! But neither he nor Percy needed to have worried about the German airmen doing anything other than willingly giving up. On the other hand, though, Samuel was taking no chances. And as Percy had spent time during the First World War as a POW, he had his 'views' about the Germans! Only that morning, according to a rather colourful report in the *Portsmouth Evening News*, published the next day, Percy had told his wife:

"If any Jerries come down near here, I'd shoot them if I had a gun!"

It was a good line for the newspapers. And the events that day also ensured it was good for pub business, too. That day saw a steady stream of visitors to the 'Horse and Jockey' to gaze at the bomber and for both regulars and others to hear, over and over, the tale repeated by Percy and Samuel – such that the pub had sold a fortnight's worth of beer before closing time. No doubt, either, that the tale became more embroidered with the telling and re-telling, and with each pint pulled.

Arriving at the bomber, Percy and Samuel had found four of the occupants already out of the aircraft and helping another man who was laying on the grass in a crouching position. All but one of the men was wounded. At once, Samuel shouted:

"Give me your guns – quick as you like!"

Almost immediately, the Germans complied with the demand and Percy, taking one of the Luger pistols, covered the men while Samuel raced back to the pub to fetch water to help the wounded men. Fortunately for the crew, though, Percy clearly had second thoughts about the earlier boast to his wife – especially now that he unexpectedly had real 'Jerries' in front of him and, equally unexpectedly, was holding a real pistol!

Dumped Its Bombs

Eventually, the Police and military turned up and took charge, relieving the two men of their prisoners before they discovered a fifth man dead in the fuselage. He was the observer, slumped over the bombsight in a growing pool of blood.

The aircraft was a Heinkel III P of Stab./KG55 which had been engaged on a risky lone reconnaissance mission to the Fawley oil refinery and storage depot when it encountered six Hurricanes from 43 Squadron, RAF Tangmere, which had been sent out to intercept the solitary enemy aircraft as it came in across the Isle of Wight. On board was the pilot, Feldwebel Jonny Möhn, radio operator Feldwebel Heinz Kalina, flight engineer Oberfeldwebel Oberfeldwebel Fritz Knecht and air gunner Oberfeldwebel Philipp Müller – together with the observer and captain of the aircraft, Oberleutnant Walter Kleinhans.

Almost immediately, on sighting the Hurricanes, the aircraft dumped its sixteen 50kg bombs as the first Hurricane closed in. Starting to run for home, the Heinkel was now a sitting duck and the Hurricanes almost took it in turns to line up for attacks. A Combat Report from Flight Lieutenant 'Tom' Dalton-Morgan told the story:

"I saw enemy aircraft on the port side below me at 8,000 ft. I turned on his tail and came in to attack. I opened fire at 200 yards and closed to 100 yards. During this attack, the starboard wing started to break up and the starboard engine blew up. I was enveloped in smoke and fragments for a few seconds. I broke away and followed him through cloud. I made a second attack and opened fire at 200 yards and closed to 100 yards. This time, fragments and smoke came from the port engine. The enemy aircraft then commenced a glide towards the ground. I followed him down. He selected a field four miles north of Fort Nelson and landed in a northerly direction, finishing up in a hedge near a farmhouse. [*sic.*]'

While all six of the attacking Hurricane pilots took an official share in the destruction of the Heinkel, the public glory went wholly to Percy Tibble and Samuel Brown. At the *Horse and Jockey*, they were the undisputed 'heroes' of the day. Although perhaps the regulars grudgingly agreed that the RAF had had a small part to play. ∎

THE BATTLE OF BRITAIN IN COLOUR

Above This Junkers 87 Stuka, downed at South Mundham on 16 August 1940, draws a crowd of interested onlookers. It came to rest after crashing through trees and a hedge, with its gunner dead and its pilot mortally wounded.
Inset Flying Officer Carl Davis.

Incident Report

On 16 August 1940, 29 'Stukas' of Stukageschwader 2 carried out a dive-bombing attack on RAF Tangmere. Although considerable damage to the airfield was sustained, a number of the raiders were either shot down or damaged. One of the losses was a Junkers 87 which came to earth at Bowley Farm, South Mundham, near Bognor Regis and to the south of Chichester in West Sussex. The aircraft was shot down by Flying Officer Carl Davis of the Tangmere-based 601 Squadron. He filed the following Combat Report:

"We took off and patrolled base at 10,000 ft and then were ordered to Bembridge at 20,000 ft. We were then told there were bandits coming from the south and to take the top layer. Bandits were seen below coming in at about 10,000 ft but we could see no escort, so dived to attack.

"Just at this point, the enemy aircraft dived for Tangmere. By the time I reached them they were at about 2,000 ft, had delivered their attack and were making for the south.

"I closed with one Ju 87 and after several bursts he went down under control and landed between Pagham and Bognor, crashing through some trees and a hedge. No one got out.

Date	16 August 1940
Location	South Mundham
Aircraft	Junkers 87 B-1, 3/StG2
Crew	Pilot: Feldwebel Heinz Rocktaschel (wounded, died later); Gunner: Oberfeldwebel Willi Witt (killed)

"Heavy fire, fairly accurate, and violent evasive actions were employed by the Ju 87. My aircraft was hit in the radiator, so I returned to Tangmere and landed at about 13.05 hours." ■

- 84 -

GERMAN AIRCRAFT LOSSES

AN AMERICAN ACE IN 'THE MILLIONAIRES' SQUADRON

Carl Raymond Davis, the pilot who brought down the Junkers 87, was an American citizen serving with 601 Squadron. The squadron, an Auxilary Air Force unit, was often called 'The Millionaires Squadron' as its officer cadre comprised largelyaffluent young men; wealthy, privileged and well connected.

Carl Davis claimed several aircraft shot down during the Battle of Britain: a Messerschmitt 110 on 11 July, on 11 August another 110 destroyed. Then, three more probably destroyed, and another damaged, on 13 August, when he also destroyed a Junkers 88 and shared in another. On 15 and 16 August, he destroyed two '88s, along with a '109 and an '87 on 18 August, sharing in another '87.

He was awarded the DFC on 30 August, and shot down another Messerschmitt 110 on 4 September, the day after promotion to Flight Lieutenant.

On 6 September, his Hurricane was shot down and he was killed over Tunbridge Wells, crashing in a garden at Matfield.

He was buried at Storrington, West Sussex, not far from his Tangmere base and close to where his parents were then living.

THE BATTLE OF BRITAIN IN COLOUR

'Brief Visit to Hell'

As a Luftwaffe bomber pilot crash landed his bullet-riddled Heinkel 111 on the South Coast, he believed he had been spared further attacks by chivalrous RAF fighter pilots. In fact, they were simply out of ammunition.

On 26 August 1940, a large number of enemy aircraft had been picked up on radar and were heading for The Solent across a twenty-mile front. Converging into one force as they neared the English coast, the formation comprised 50 He 111 aircraft flying at 15,000 ft, escorted by up to 100 Me 109s and Me 110s flying some 5,000 ft above them.

Three squadrons were scrambled to intercept: 43 Squadron's Hurricanes from Tangmere, 602 Squadron's Spitfires from Westhampnett and 615 Squadron's Hurricanes from Kenley.

Piloting one of the participating Heinkels of StabI/KG55 was an Austrian officer, Oblt Ignatz Krenn:

"On 26 August 1940, we got the order to launch a daylight attack against the docks at Portsmouth. Me 109 and Me 110 cover was to be provided and our I Gruppe set out from Dreux, near Paris. We assembled over Normandy, then crossed the Channel. We had been ordered to fly north, avoiding the Isle of Wight, and on a track for London in order to trick the defending fighters. Then, we would turn south and come down on Portsmouth from the landward side. As we turned, suddenly over the intercom came the words: 'Achtung! Spitfire!' There was no point in asking where the fighters had come from, because suddenly it was as if thousands of stones were being thrown at the fuselage."

The official RAF narrative of the Battle of Britain related the events that unfolded:

"43 Squadron were the first to attack, followed a moment or two later by 602 Squadron. A head-on attack was delivered and while this did not force the enemy aircraft to break formation many of them jettisoned their bombs in the sea near Hayling Island. Signal cartridges were fired by the bombers to bring down the escorting fighters."

Above The Heinkel 111 P bomber which was crash landed by Oberleutnant Ignatz Krenn at Wick, near Littlehampton, on 26 August 1940.
Right One of a set of cartoons depicting the downing of Ignatz Krenn's Heinkel on 26 August 1940, painted by him in his Prisoner of War camp. This cartoon, called '14 against 1 sick', carries a number of amusing details, including startled cherubs peeping from behind clouds, Spitfires colliding head-on, a crew member being airsick and another throwing an empty ammunition drum at a pursuer, while using his thumb for sighting purposes!

'BRIEF VISIT TO HELL'

THE BATTLE OF BRITAIN IN COLOUR

Right Luftwaffe unit emblems were often colourful or gaudy, and the example carried on Ignatz Krenn's Heinkel 111 was no exception. The badge of Kampfgeschwader 55 depicted a red griffon with blue wings set on a gold shield.
Far Right A self-portrait painted by Ignatz Krenn whilst Prisoner of War.
Below Oberleutnant Ignatz Krenn is marched to a train at Littlehampton Railway Station, on his way to be interrogated in London and before his long incarceration in a POW camp.

Flashes and Explosions

As the bomber formation changed track onto a heading for the intended target, Ignatz Krenn picks up the story:

"Tracers came from behind and went over the cockpit and disappeared into the sky. From the left, a shadow shot past and plunged down – the enemy fighter! I noticed with horror that my starboard engine was trailing smoke. I knew that I had an armoured sheet behind me, but the 'plane had been badly hit. Suddenly, I heard the uneven juddering of the engine. Just so long as it didn't catch fire! But the spluttering engine gave up the ghost, the propeller made a few last jerky movements and then stopped.

"Turning off the ignition, I also jettisoned the bombs. I glanced around. Where were the other chaps? They were nowhere in sight and I was alone and now at the mercy of a pack of fighters. I glanced at the still intact port engine, and then suddenly saw an enemy fighter coming straight for me. I broke out in a cold sweat as I saw the flashes of light at the mouths of the guns in the fighter's wings.

"More crashes and explosions as we took more hits. I put the Heinkel into a steep dive, looking for a cloud to hide in. There were none, just flashes and explosions all around us. This is it, I thought. The famous 'death-hunt' is on, but to my astonishment the fighters chivalrously held back. I scanned the instrument panel as I didn't want to land in the Channel, but now the second engine began to splutter and gradually slowed.

"By now, I was at less than 1,000 ft and I looked for, and found, a suitable landing place. Then, a village and a row of trees. With all my might I pulled back the stick, skimmed over the top, and careered over a grassy field, throwing up earth and stones with a terrible noise and finally coming to rest just in front of stream.

Now, peace and quiet all around, and I just sat in the cockpit, my eyes smarting from the sweat running into them. Then, I was startled out of stunned silence by my flight engineer tapping me on the shoulder: 'All change, Oberleutnant. This is the end of the line!'

"As we helped each other clamber out onto the grass, a gentleman came up with a walking stick and arrested us. 'I suppose this is my Waterloo?' I asked him. 'Yes, it is' he replied. He asked if we had any pistols. I said we did, and he look alarmed. I said: 'Don't worry, I've no intention of waging a personal war!' and handed them all over to him.

"An Army truck very quickly arrived, and that was it. My war was over. My own part in the Battle of Britain had been depressingly brief; it was just a brief visit to Hell."

Mock Attacks

Ignatz Krenn and his crew had been attacked and harried along the south coast by 43 Squadron's Squadron Leader 'Tubby' Badger and Sergeant Hubert 'Jim' Hallowes, who had raked it relentlessly with fire until they ran out of ammunition. Nevertheless, they continued to carry out mock attacks on the bomber in order to persuade the pilot that continuing was futile. They could not know, of course, that the bomber was already 'done for', anyway.

On board the Heinkel, Krenn had taken the failure of the Hurricanes to make any further attack as an act of chivalry. In fact, he had been very lucky; were it not

'BRIEF VISIT TO HELL'

Left The second of Ignatz Krenn's cartoons depicts his arrival on British soil – although he allows himself some artistic licence in its execution. For example, he didn't abandon the aircraft by parachute and the Heinkel didn't flatten a cow in its landing. The cartoons are a wonderful study of Krenn's perception of 1940 England.

THE INTELLIGENCE REPORT

Each crashed enemy aircraft, and every captured airman, was subject to intelligence reports. This is an extract of what the RAF's Air Intelligence Branch had to say about Ignatz Krenn's aircraft and crew:

Tracks marked on a map found in the aircraft were Rembouillet/Dreux/Portsmouth.

Before reaching its objective, this aircraft was shot at by six or seven fighters which shot at and first stopped one engine and then the other engine. The bombs were scuttled shortly before the aircraft made a good forced landing beside the River Arun.

The aircraft carried a badge showing a shield in gold bearing a red dragon with blue wings.

Armament: MG15 machine guns in nose, top rear, lower rear, one each side and a single MG15 firing out of the extreme of the tail, operated by a simple cable-operated trigger release.

Crew:
- Pilot – Oberleutnant Ignatz Krenn (unwounded)
- Observer – Unteroffizier Helmut Morrack (unwounded)
- Radio Operator – Unteroffizier Hans Degen (slightly wounded)
- Flight Engineer – Unteroffizier Willi Shneiders (slightly wounded)
- Air Gunner – Feldwebel Alois Schreck (seriously wounded)

---

for their lack of bullets then it is almost certain that the two pilots would have delivered a fatal *coup-de-grace* before Oberleutnant Krenn was forced to bring his crippled aircraft down at Helyers Farm, Wick, near Littlehampton in West Sussex.

As an operation, however, the raid of 26 August 1940 was as surprising as it was futile. Surprising in that this was something of a departure from the concentrated airfield attacks which the Luftwaffe were then undertaking. This time, the intended target had been dockyards – although the objective wasn't even hit. Random bombs were scattered far and wide, with some hitting Fort Cumberland where six Royal Marines were killed, and others causing a small fire at a gas works.

Given the scale of this operation, coupled with the losses, it was an entirely wasted effort. But for Krenn and his crew, their captivity would at least ensure their survival – even though they couldn't have seen it that way at the time.

The fact of the matter, quite simply, was that their chances of continuing alive until the end of the war would have been quite slim had they not been taken POW during the Battle of Britain. ■

> "I glanced at the still intact port engine, and then suddenly saw an enemy fighter coming straight for me. I broke out in a cold sweat as I saw the flashes of light at the mouths of the guns in the fighter's wings."
>
> Oberleutnant Ignatz Krenn, Stab.I/KG55

THE BATTLE OF BRITAIN IN COLOUR

The Lost Post

When a small German biplane landed on the South Downs during the Battle of Britain, it brought with it an unexpected intelligence windfall.

During the sunny late afternoon of 28 August 1940, schoolmaster George Bennett and surveyor James Palmer were walking on the South Downs at Lewes, East Sussex, when they heard approaching aircraft and were surprised to see a small biplane in German markings circle twice and then come in to land. Overhead, two Hurricanes circled the scene before flying away to the west as Bennett, Palmer and a number of other civilians ran towards the biplane, now sitting on the Lewes Racecourse gallops with its engine still running. Almost immediately, the pilot climbed from the aircraft and was approached by the two startled civilians.

As Bennett was fluent in German, he asked the pilot if he was alone. Palmer then asked Bennett to enquire how the engine could be switched off, and after the pilot indicated how, Palmer leaned into the cockpit and turned off the idling motor. By now, other civilians and the Home Guard were arriving on the scene and Bennett only had time to ask the pilot one more thing: *"Where are you from?".* The reply, *"Stuttgart",* was all the German was able to say before members of the Home Guard arrived on the scene and arrested the agitated pilot.

Taking charge, Superintendent Holloway detailed Police Sergeant Simmonds and other officers to guard the aeroplane from the growing crowd before marching his prisoner down the hill to a waiting car and off to Lewes Police Station. Here, the prisoner expressed concern as to what his CO would say about things. The Policemen tried to allay his fears, telling him that he would not be seeing his CO for some while. However, the pilot replied: *"Well, that's all very well so long as he doesn't get shot down and taken prisoner too!"*

The aeroplane was a Gotha Go 145B training and communications aircraft from Stab/JG 27 based on the Cherbourg peninsula. This Messerschmitt 109 E fighter unit was using the Go 145 as its communications aircraft, and on the day in question, Unteroffizier Leonhard Buckle was detailed to carry out a routine mail delivery flight between the Channel Islands and JG 27s bases around Cherbourg. Unfortunately for Buckle, he became lost over France and unwittingly wandered out over the Channel. Here, a sea fog had come up and the frightened pilot became completely disorientated. Eventually, he found himself a long way out to sea with no land in sight.

GERMAN AIRCRAFT LOSSES

Above Unteroffizier Leonhard Buckle, the hapless pilot of the Gotha 145.
Left The Gotha 145 training and communications aircraft which made a landing on the South Downs at Lewes in East Sussex on 28 August 1940, becoming the most unusual Luftwaffe arrival in the country during the Battle of Britain. The aircraft drew crowds of sightseers before it was eventually flown away by the RAF.

Quite what happened as the young pilot contemplated his certain and looming fate in the English Channel is unclear, but somewhere off the Sussex coast a pair of Hurricanes chanced across the meandering biplane and escorted it back towards land, eventually encouraging it to land at Lewes.

Valuable Intelligence Tool

For British Intelligence, a substantial coup lay in the bulging sacks of mail found in the Gotha, and both Buckle and his aeroplane came under considerable scrutiny. Having been searched at the Police station, Buckle was locked up in the cell block while Sergeant Simmonds telephoned to RAF Biggin Hill requesting an interrogation officer be sent urgently.

Returning to the aircraft (now guarded by men of 325 Company, Royal Engineers) Superintendent Holloway found a Pilot Officer Gibbs and three RAF officers were present, being told by Gibbs he had been sent to interrogate the prisoner.

Later that evening, Gibbs interrogated Buckle but was then notified by superior officers that he should cease and that another officer, Pilot Officer Sankey, was on his way to carry out the interrogation instead. Sankey duly arrived late in the evening and started his interrogation of the prisoner, only to be interrupted some three quarters of an hour later by the arrival of a Pilot Officer Birch. He too had been detailed to interrogate Buckle in an apparent race by different RAF intelligence branches to extract what information they could from the prisoner and his unusual cargo.

Birch demanded that he be given the letters and documents found in the Gotha, but an irritated and reluctant Sankey declined to hand them over. It was not until 2am that an exhausted Buckle was finally allowed to get some rest in his cell, while Birch and Sankey continued to argue about who was in charge of the recovered documents.

Either way, the windfall of letters would allow a great deal to be learned about personnel in that unit, and even details of relatives of these men. Such information could be an extremely valuable intelligence tool during interrogation if, for example, pilots of that unit should later be captured. That the enemy should be in possession of such personal information would be puzzling and incomprehensible, and would be likely to considerably undermine the morale of prisoners when under interrogation.

Under New Management

As for the aeroplane, this was left under Army guard until 31 August, when it was flown to the Royal Aircraft Establishment at Farnborough by Squadron Leader H J Wilson after RAF roundels were painted on the wings and fuselage, denoting that it was now under new management.

Brief test flights were made at Farnborough on 6 and 10 September, but the Gotha did not fly again until 12 December when it was flown to the RAF's No. 20 Maintenance Unit at RAF Cosford on 1 January 1941, after another brief test flight.

It was used for technical training at Cosford, but by 1 April 1942, its usefulness was exhausted and it was scrapped.

Whilst Buckle languished in a Prisoner of War Camp, reflecting on a disastrous postal delivery flight, his aeroplane was eventually broken up, its meagre useful parts joining the scrap mountain of wrecked airframes feeding raw material to the British aircraft industry.

It had not exactly been the most potent of Luftwaffe aircraft captured during the period, but the arrival of Leonhard Buckle and his Gotha biplane had arguably been one of the more unusual episodes of the Battle of Britain. ■

THE BATTLE OF BRITAIN IN COLOUR

'British Air Victories Over German Raiders'

In the autumn of 1940, Odhams Printers of Watford printed a large wall chart depicting dozens of images of German aircraft downed over the British Isles during the Battle of Britain. This private venture publication was called 'British Air Victories Over German Raiders'. We can now look at some of those images in a new light through the colourisation techniques of our digital colour artist for this publication, Richard J Molloy.

Above Early in the morning of 28 July 1940, a Junkers 88 A-1 circled the south coast town of Bexhill-on-Sea, East Sussex, causing consternation with some of the population who thought they were about to come under attack. In fact, the aircraft was lost and low on fuel after a sortie to Crewe, and the pilot, Oberfeldwebel Josef Bier, was searching for a landing place. He eventually found a suitable spot in a clover field at Buckholt Farm on the outskirts of the town. As it came in for a belly landing, it was fired on by a Lewis gun manned by members of 302 Searchlight Battery, Royal Engineers. At least one round hit the bomber, and this resulted in the jubilant soldiers claiming to have shot it down! All four crew members were captured unhurt and the aircraft was only slightly damaged, later being repaired and test flown by the RAF. The aircraft belonged to 3/KG51, the 'Edelweiss' Geschwader, and it carried a colourful badge depicting the Edelweiss flower beneath the cockpit.

Right RAF airmen pose with the wrecked starboard wing of a Messerschmitt 109 E-1 of 7/JG26, which was brought down at Knatts Valley, near West Kingsdown, Kent, on 31 August 1940. The aircraft had been shot down by Flying Officer Beverley Christmas in a Hurricane of 1 (RCAF) Squadron during the late afternoon as it was flying an escort mission to cover bombers attacking RAF Hornchurch. The aircraft broke up in mid-air, with Unteroffizier Horst Liebeck being lucky to escape by parachute, albeit injured.

GERMAN AIRCRAFT LOSSES

Left On 14 August 1940, this Heinkel 111 P-2 of 8/KG27 was engaged on a reconnaissance sortie to the north-west of the Bristol Channel area when it was intercepted by three Spitfires of No.7 Operational Training Unit, RAF Hawarden, flown by Wing Commander J Hallings-Potts, Squadron Leader J McLean and Pilot Officer P Ayerst, who jointly shot the bomber down. However, and although they succeeded in downing an enemy aircraft, they are not regarded as Battle of Britain pilots because they were not serving on a Fighter Command squadron. The aircraft landed at Border House Farm near Chester, where the crew set fire to the bomber before giving themselves up to the farmer, a Mr Anderton, and a local butcher, Mr Llewelyn Jones. They were then taken into the farmhouse where Wendy Anderton (left) and Cathie Jones made tea for the German crew before the airmen were taken away by Police. Here, the girls point out the bullet holes in the bomber.

Right Two soldiers pose with a souvenir cut from the cowling of a Messerschmitt 109 E-1 of 1/JG52 shot down on 24 August 1940 by Flight Lieutenant Gribble in a Spitfire of 54 Squadron. Feldwebel Herbert Bischoff was surprised from behind at 18,000 ft over London, and his aircraft hit in the engine and radiator. Making a landing near Westgate, Bischoff's Messerschmitt lost the outer section of its port wing after striking an electricity pylon.

Right On 27 October 1940, Messerschmitt 109 E-1 pilot Unteroffizier Arno Zimmermann, of 7/JG54, was on a patrol over London at 23,000 ft, his 34th sortie over the city. Then, his unit spotted Hurricanes below and dived to attack. Climbing back up, a Hurricane got on his tail and fired a burst into his engine. Zimmermann made for the coast, but his cockpit filled with smoke. He made a successful belly landing on the beach near Lydd Water Tower and was captured with slight wounds.

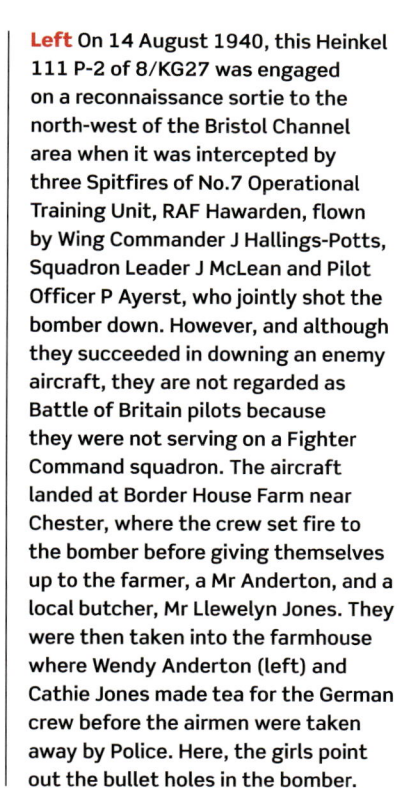

Left Whilst on the way to its target in the London Docks on 11 September 1940, in a formation of some 30 bombers, this Heinkel He 111 H-2 of 6/KG1 was attacked by Spitfires which stopped both engines. Ditching the bomb load, the pilot, Unteroffizier Bernhard Hansen, glided down to make a good forced landing at Camber, East Sussex, with just one member of the crew wounded. Climbing out, the crew set fire to their aircraft to prevent anything of value falling into the hands of the enemy.

GERMAN AIRCRAFT LOSSES

Incident Report

James Wadman was a farmer and Home Guardsman living near Westham, East Sussex, during the Battle of Britain. He was one of the first on the scene when a Messerschmitt 109 made a force-landing at Langney, on the eastern outskirts of Eastbourne, on 30 September 1940.

"At about 2 o'clock that day, I saw this yellow-nosed Jerry fighter circle and get lower as I was working in the fields and I could see that he was coming down over Langney way. I lost sight of him behind trees and buildings, but soon realised he was down.

I had worked out pretty much where he must have fetched-up and knowing how the tracks and ditches ran in those parts, and where the bridges and gates were, I made for the spot on the run. Soon, I could see the aircraft sitting in a field and as I got close, I realised the pilot was standing alongside. As I got to him, he tore off his flying helmet and flung it onto the wing and put his hands up.

I said: "It's OK mate, you're my prisoner now. Wait here until somebody else comes along."

I didn't know quite what else to do. In truth, I was a little bit scared. Worried, at least. What if he cut up rough? Or legged it?

I don't think he understood anything I said, though, as he just blankly stared at me. Suddenly, he handed me something which I realised was his holstered pistol. I tried to make a joke of the fact that the number on his 'plane was '13'. "Unlucky for some!" I said. He understood that, and nervously laughed with me.

It was all a bit awkward for a while, but then I noticed a War Reserve Constable heading across from the cottages nearby. I watched as the rather overweight Bobby scrambled through

Date	30 September 1940
Location	Langney, near Eastbourne
Aircraft	Messerschmitt 109 E - 4
Pilot	Feldwebel Walter Scholz, 3/JG53

water-filled ditches, and tip-toed through cow pancakes to finally reach us. He was out of breath, wet up to his waist and puce in the face - but carrying a first aid satchel. He could hardly speak, but gasped: "Anyone need First Aid?" He seemed rather disappointed that nobody was hurt, although I thought I may need to give him first aid. He looked about to have a heart attack.

Then I thought I'd offer the pilot a cigarette. He took it, and I lit it for him but noticed how he was trembling and his hands shaking violently. He looked pale and frightened. I thought he was going to be sick.

More and more people then turned up, along with the Police and military. I left after a while but came back with my unit later that evening when we were photographed with the 'plane by local photographer, Harry Deal."

If James Wadman had sensed the pilot was anxious and shaken, this might be borne out by the report of his RAF interrogator who noted his morale was poor and that "…he is rather depressed about the war."

The report went on to state that the 27-year-old pilot had left his home airfield at Etaples, France, shortly after lunchtime on a mission to escort bombers to London, which they had joined up with near the English coast, the escorting fighters flying at between 18,000 and 19,000 ft.

According to his interrogation report, he was not in combat prior to having to make a force-landing but had simply run out of fuel*. However, it was also reported that there were several bullet strikes in the cooling system and engine.

The aircraft was eventually taken away by a salvage gang but is known to have been placed on public display in Piccadilly on 24 October 1940, to raise money for the 'Spitfire Fund', before it was sent to the scrapyard. ∎

*Note: the Messerschmitt 109 had a very limited range and effective operational radius when engaged on sorties over Britain. Running low on fuel was not an uncommon cause of losses.

Top Feldwebel Walter Scholz's Messerschmitt 109 after its force-landing at Langney, Eastbourne, on 30 September 1940.
Above Walter Scholz's pilot's flying licence.

GERMAN AIRCRAFT LOSSES

The One That Got Away

The story of Oberleutnant Franz von Werra, shot down over Kent in 1940, is one of the most colourful tales of the Battle of Britain.

Oberleutnant Franz von Werra, the adjutant with Stab.II/JG3, had already made his mark racking up victories across Europe in the spring of 1940. But when he landed his battle-damaged Messerschmitt 109 at Marden on 5 September 1940, von Werra was just another captured enemy pilot. However, blusteringly confident, he was apparently unfazed by his predicament and unconcerned about captivity. Immediately, he became something of an enigma to his captors. Already, von Werra was known to the British – not least of all through boastful claims of victories and a penchant for being photographed with his pet lion cub, 'Simba'.

The RAF Intelligence Report on von Werra's interrogation makes reference to an interview that had recently been broadcast on German radio when he talked about an attack on an airfield 'near Rochester', claiming to have shot down four Hurricanes which were coming in to land, shot up and set fire to a hangar and destroyed five Hurricanes on the ground. This supposedly occurred on 28 August 1940, although it is difficult if not impossible to substantiate these extravagant claims.

Nevertheless, other officers from his unit described him as: *'One Hell of a fellow'*. Indeed, he was.

To Steal a Hurricane

Incarcerated in a POW camp in the north of England, von Werra immediately and obsessively set about planning an escape. His first break for freedom saw him jump over a dry-stone wall while out on a route march with fellow prisoners. However, it was an ill-conceived and badly planned venture, with von Werra being recaptured after a couple of days.

A move to another camp, however, saw von Werra's involvement in a tunnel escape. Ultimately successful, von Werra got away from the camp and bluffed his way onto Hucknall airfield where, audaciously, he nearly managed to steal a Hurricane. He was arrested at pistol point as he sat in the cockpit.

Above The tail of Oberleutnant Franz von Werra's Messerschmitt 109 is examined by a British soldier after it was shot down at Marden, Kent, on 5 September 1940. It carries an impressive tally of 'kills', with the five downward pointing arrows representing the Hurricanes he claimed to have destroyed on the ground on 28 August 1940.

Right Franz von Werra's pet lion cub, 'Simba', plays in the cockpit of the Oberleutnant's Messerschmitt 109 on a French airfield during the summer of 1940.

In January 1941, German POWs were transferred to camps in Canada, but when being transported across the country on arrival, von Werra jumped from a speeding train. Unhurt, he made his way to the frozen St Lawrence River and walked across the ice to neutral America. From here, he was repatriated to Germany.

Feted as a hero, von Werra was awarded the Knight's Cross and went back to operational flying, achieving more success on the Eastern Front before being killed in a flying accident on 25 October 1941 when his Messerschmitt crashed into the sea off Vlissingen.

Post-war, his story was told in the 1956 book *'The One That Got Away'* by Kendal Burt and James Leasor. A film by the same name followed in 1956, with Hardy Krüger playing the lead.

His comrades on II/JG3 were undoubtedly correct. He was certainly a *'Hell of a fellow'*! ∎

THE BATTLE OF BRITAIN IN COLOUR

The King's Messerschmitt

When Buckingham Palace was hit by bombs on 15 September 1940, it brought the war to the very front door of The King and Queen. And just over two weeks later, the war also came to their back garden at Windsor Castle with the 'arrival' of a Messerschmitt 109 E-1.

Although the Battle of Britain is officially recognised as having ended on 31 October 1940, German daylight attacks had certainly started to diminish as September moved into October. However, it could be said that Luftwaffe air operations over Britain on 30 September were, perhaps, one of the 'last gasps' of major daylight offensive operations. In the context of this account, we are concerned only with Luftwaffe operations during the latter part of the day. The narrative of events was later set out by the RAF's Air Historical Branch:

"30 September 1940. Operations Against London, 15.45 – 17.15 hours

The main body of the enemy moved towards Biggin Hill, where most of them then turned west towards the Thames Valley. As before, the bombers failed to find their objective (there was still much cloud at about 6,000 feet) and no serious damage was done. There was, however, even shorter warning than before, and the first defending squadrons only left the ground as the Germans crossed the coast. They were 603 and 41 from Hornchurch, and their orders were to patrol Maidstone at 25,000 feet.

Shortly afterwards, the controller realised that they would be in grave danger of being attacked while still climbing. He therefore ordered them to reach their operating height over their own base.

The next British squadrons to take off did not do so until 16.15 hours, by which time the first of the German forces were near Tonbridge. *(No 1 RCAF Squadron, 303 (Polish) Squadron and 229 Squadron – all of them Hurricane squadrons - were ordered to patrol Northolt at 20,000 feet.)*

The chief burden of the combat fell upon the Hornchurch and Northolt squadrons, especially the latter. The former were ordered west from Hornchurch, and came upon a large number of fighters, including He 113s [sic.] *(see also page 43)*, near Biggin Hill.

By the time this combat was joined (16.35 hours), the main enemy force was approaching Brooklands where it was sighted by the Northolt Wing. Our pilots reported about 18 bombers flying at 17,000 feet, with a large number of Me 109s on each flank and behind the

– 96 –

THE KING'S MESSERSCHMITT

Left The wreck of Oberleutnant Karl Fischer's Messerschmitt 109 E-1 of 7/JG 27 in Windsor Great Park after it had been righted by crane. It had overturned during its crash-landing on 30 September 1940, its pilot miraculously surviving unscathed. Civilians, including a liveried member of the Windsor Castle staff, are kept at a distance, although the trilby-hatted individual peering into the gun compartment in the wing is the war artist, Paul Nash.

Above This was the scene painted by Paul Nash and depicted the moment the German fighter was righted by crane. Called 'The Messerschmitt in Windsor Great Park', it became one of the best-known paintings depicting events during the Battle of Britain.

Above Right The scene as Oberleutnant Karl Fischer's Messerschmitt was righted in Windsor Great Park. It was this moment that was later captured by Paul Nash. The war artist must have witnessed the operation from the same viewpoint as the photographer.

bombers, as well as some 2,000 feet above them.

The Germans continued to press on to the north-west and were sighted at 16.45 hours near Windsor by the RAF Northolt station commander (Group Captain Stanley Vincent) who had taken off "to watch the Northolt Wing in action" and was flying at 20,000 feet when he saw the whole enemy formation approaching from the south. One attack was made head-on against the bombers and a second from below. Shortly afterwards, the whole force was seen to swing round to the south."

Victories in Both World Wars

Group Captain Vincent, who had been a fighter pilot in the Royal Flying Corps during the First World War, made a claim for two Messerschmitt 109s destroyed during this engagement – adding these to three victories claimed over France between 1916 and 1917, which included an LVG and Albatross. He was the only RAF fighter pilot to claim victories during the Battle of Britain over the Western Front.

In its conclusion, the official narrative of events during the late afternoon went on to state:

"Only eight Me 109s were claimed as destroyed, in addition to one Junkers 88, and five crashed on land. These were from JG 26, JG 27 and JG 52. This confirmed that the Germans had used powerful forces of fighters to protect less than one Gruppe of bombers."

Interestingly, during Vincent's flight, he observed two Messerschmitt 109s engaged in mortal combat.

What Vincent had seen was a Messerschmitt 109 engaging another flown by Unteroffizier Herbert Schmid, of 6./JG 27, who was ultimately shot down wounded and taken prisoner when a single 20mm cannon shell exploded and blew his starboard tail plane clean away.

Above Windsor, though, and as Vincent circled and attacked, one particular Messerschmitt 109 pilot was running into problems as he took hits from behind in his aircraft's fuel tank. In the event, though, Vincent was not the attacker. In this particular instance, the 'victory' can most likely be attributed to Pilot Officer P G Dexter, flying a Spitfire of the Hornchurch based 603 Squadron.

The pilot of the Messerschmitt 109 in question, Oberleutnant Karl Fischer of 7/JG 27, had taken off earlier that

FRIENDLY FIRE

During the air battle in which Oberleutnant Karl Fischer was shot down, another Messerschmitt 109 was brought down some miles to the south, over Haslemere, Surrey. RAF pilot Group Captain Stanley Vincent had seen two Messerschmitts locked in combat in a 'friendly fire' situation. Ultimately, Leutnant Herbert Schmidt's aircraft was hit and he baled-out and was taken POW.

The starboard tail plane of his aircraft had been blown off as a result of a direct hit from dead astern by a 20mm cannon shell which can only have been fired from a German aircraft. The evidence can be clearly seen in the preserved tail plane.

THE BATTLE OF BRITAIN IN COLOUR

Left An RAF Coles crane prepares to lift the crashed Messerschmitt 109 from the spot where it had come to rest.
Right Paul Nash's famous painting, 'Totes Meer', depicting a graveyard of crashed German aircraft at Cowley, Oxfordshire, during the Battle of Britain.
Below Right The artist, Paul Nash.

afternoon from his base at Guines in the Pas-de-Calais for yet another mentally and physically exhausting cross-Channel bomber escort sortie that defined that summer for the Luftwaffe's fighter pilots. And as his crew chief closed the cockpit canopy on the 27-year-old pilot, he joked: "Take care not to become a guest of His Majesty, Herr Oberleutnant!"

Bone-jarring Crunch

Exactly what happened above Windsor Castle that afternoon is unclear in any detail. However, we do know that Pilot Officer Dexter hit and damaged a Messerschmitt 109 in a dogfight under circumstances and in a geographical location which make it highly likely that his victim was Karl Fischer.

For his part, Fischer gave little away under interrogation by RAF Intelligence Officers, save for the fact that he had got into a dogfight but that the combat was broken off and he thought he hadn't been hit. That belief, though, was soon shattered by a call from Fischer's 'No.2' who reported that his leader's aircraft had a white petrol plume bannering out behind. Glancing down at his fuel gauge, he realised that his tank was almost on empty.

Fischer still had the advantage of height, and although his engine was still running it clearly wouldn't do so for very long. The question, now, was whether to bale-out or make a force landing. Preferring the latter option, he had time to select a wide-open, flat and grassy area that would suit the emergency perfectly. Thus, peeling reluctantly away from his home-bound colleagues, Karl Fischer set his aircraft up for what should have been a relatively easy belly-landing – albeit he was heading into the unknown.

On 'finals', and just as the experienced pilot was literally about to touch-down, something happened causing the starboard wing to dip and dig into the turf, just as the aircraft was about to settle. In a bone-jarring crunch, the aircraft pirouetted around, tipped, and then slammed violently down onto its back as the propeller blades curled themselves around the cowling and the engine was forced to an abrupt stop.

Upside down, and hanging by his

THE KING'S MESSERSCHMITT

straps, Fischer was lucky to have survived unharmed in his crushed cockpit but had instinctively curled into a ball to protect himself from what seemed a likely fatal impact. Now, as a dust cloud settled around the Messerschmitt, he scrambled to get out through a tiny gap – his exit no doubt hastened by the smell of the remaining fuel as it drained and pooled around his wildly scrambling limbs.

Emerging just as startled locals raced to the scene - who collectively paused as they neared the wreckage uncertain as to what they faced - Fischer brushed himself down and enquired, in halting English, as to where he was. "You are in the grounds of the Windsor Castle estate" he was told.

Smiling, Fischer is said to have coolly remarked: "So, I really am a guest of His Majesty, then?"

Indeed, his demeanour was remarked on by the RAF interrogator who noted: "His morale is good, and he takes the whole matter very calmly."

Spitfire Fund

For a day or so, the Messerschmitt lay on its back in the middle of the greensward, very close to Queen Anne's Gate in Windsor Great Park. Meanwhile, locals came to gape from behind a rope barrier guarded by soldiers. Before long, however, an RAF salvage party arrived with a low-loader, together with a Coles crane, to lift and recover the wreck from where it incongruously lay, almost under the imposing ramparts of Windsor Castle and its famous Round Tower.

As the salvage party lifted and then righted the Messerschmitt, civilians were kept their distance. All except one, that is. Noted artist, Paul Nash, was then working as a war artist attached to the RAF to paint scenes that would later become redolent of the Battle of Britain. In this capacity, he was invited to view the Messerschmitt and watch its recovery. Ultimately, the whole operation would be captured in one of his famous paintings of the period.

Recovered from its crash site, the aircraft was initially placed on display outside the walls of Windsor Castle where it became a short-term attraction to raise funds for the local 'Spitfire Fund.' Whilst there, it is said that the young Princess Elizabeth visited and sat in Karl Fischer's rather crumpled cockpit.

Meanwhile, not far away at Cockfosters interrogation centre in London, Oberleutnant Fischer was starting what would become some six years as a 'guest' of Princess Elizabeth's father. ∎

Paul Nash

Paul Nash (1889 - 1946) is one of Britain's best-known war artists, and when he arrived at the Ypres Salient in March 1917, as an officer in the Hampshire Regiment, he was initially struck by the ability of nature to regenerate the battlefield, something featured in his many war paintings.

After breaking a rib through falling into a trench, Nash was sent back to England to convalesce during May 1917; only a week later, his division was all but annihilated in an assault on Hill 60. His homage to his comrades in arms, The Landscape Hill 60 (1918), depicts a scarred landscape of earth and water ravaged by shellfire, with dogfighting aeroplanes and explosions in the sky.

Nash returned to Belgium as an official war artist in October 1917, complete with batman and chauffeur, but facing an alien environment of craters, shattered trees and mud in the aftermath of the Battle of Passchendaele. Nash was outraged at this desecration of nature, producing a frenzy of '50 drawings of muddy places', as he called them.

Nash provided a new and startling vision of war, although few of his war paintings depict dead soldiers or bodies; his outrage at the waste of life was expressed more through portraying the violation of nature.

In the aftermath of war, Nash was diagnosed with 'emotional shock', but throughout the 1930s he became a pioneer of modernism, promoting abstraction and surrealism.

In 1940 he was appointed as a war artist by the War Artists' Advisory Committee (WAAC), attached to the RAF and Air Ministry.

He was unpopular within the WAAC, because of his modernist work and because the RAF wanted him to concentrate on producing portraits of aircrew and pilots. Nash went some way to appeasing them by painting a series of watercolours of various events of 1940, such as The Messerschmitt in Windsor Great Park (1940) and Battle of Britain (1941).

His extraordinary creation, Totes Meer (Dead Sea) (1940-1), an allegorical depiction of tangled wrecks of German aircraft, is considered one of the greatest evocations of the futility of war.

Paul Nash died on 11 July 1946 and lies buried in Langley, Bucks.

THE BATTLE OF BRITAIN IN COLOUR

Dogfights to Blitz Nights

Although the Blitz might be regarded as a stand-alone event, it was initially an integral part of the Battle of Britain and is an important part of the 1940 story. Unfortunately, RAF Fighter Command were all but powerless to protect Londoners from the devastating night raids.

During the afternoon of 7 September 1940, one of the heaviest fought days of the Battle of Britain, the Luftwaffe launched massive air attacks which were directed at the dockland area and East End of London. That night, Luftwaffe bombers returned to the blazing docks and continued to rain high explosive and incendiary bombs onto the inferno. Such was the intensity of the blaze, and such was its duration, that it became known as the 'Second Fire of London'. The next day, and then the next night...and then night after night, the Luftwaffe returned.

In total, the Blitz on London is considered to have lasted from 7 September 1940, right through to 11 May 1941. However, air attacks against the Capital continued sporadically after 11 May 1941, almost through to the end of the war. Equally, other cities and towns came in for the attention of the Luftwaffe during the Battle of Britain period and beyond – notably Coventry on the night of 14 November 1940.

As the Blitz wore on, the Luftwaffe also attacked the main Atlantic sea port of Liverpool in the Liverpool Blitz. The North Sea port of Hull, a convenient and easily found target - or a secondary target for bombers unable to locate their primary targets - suffered the Hull Blitz. Bristol, Cardiff, Portsmouth, Plymouth, Southampton and Swansea were also bombed, as were the industrial cities of Birmingham, Belfast, Coventry, Glasgow, Manchester and Sheffield.

Very often, the Luftwaffe would drop mixtures of high explosive and incendiary bombs. These both blasted and laid waste to factories and other buildings, but then potentially ignited large swathes of buildings such that virtual fire storms quickly began to rage.

THE BLITZ

Facing page London's Burning! Surrey Docks ablaze on 7 September 1940, the first day of the Blitz. It was the start of a dark period in London's history.
Above right As the fires in Surrey docks took a hold, so more high explosive and incendiary bombs were rained onto the area by the Luftwaffe throughout the night.
Below right On the night of 14 October 1940, a bomb penetrated the road and exploded in Balham Underground station, killing 68 people. A No 88 bus travelling in black-out conditions then fell into the crater.

On 7 September 1940, for example, the bombers which came after dusk were quite easily guided to their target by what was now a flaming inferno. A cauldron of fire.

British Air Defence Weaknesses

At first, and certainly across much of September 1940, the Luftwaffe bombed London by day and by night when conditions were favourable. However, as the autumn drew on, so the daylight air attacks against London drew down and as October came, so the mass daylight attacks on the city ceased. However, not so the nocturnal attacks.

By attacking at night, the Luftwaffe were exploiting British air defence weaknesses and the RAF's distinct deficiency in its lack of any effective night-fighter force. It was not until after the Battle of Britain, and indeed after the main thrust of the Blitz, that the RAF's night fighter force was developed and strengthened with new aircraft such as the Mosquito and updated radar and other countermeasures.

During the Battle of Britain, night-fighting was very much in its infancy, although the earliest installation of Airborne Interception (AI) radar was already being trialled. However, single-seat fighters were frequently detailed to carry out night patrols. This was a terrifying experience for pilots inexperienced in night flying and the glare from the exhaust was such that a special shield had to fitted between the exhaust ports and the cockpit for night flying purposes.

Of the attacks on London, Prime Minister Winston Churchill had this to say on 11 September, just as the Blitz was getting underway:

"These cruel, wanton, indiscriminate bombings of London are, of course, a part of Hitler's invasion plans. He hopes, by killing large numbers of civilians, and women and children, that he will terrorise and cow the people of this mighty Imperial city, and make them a burden and an anxiety to the Government and thus distract our attention unduly from the ferocious onslaught he is preparing.

"Little does he know the spirit of the British nation, or the tough fibre of the Londoners, whose forbears played a leading part in the establishment of Parliamentary institutions, and who have been bred to value freedom far above their lives. This wicked man, the repository and embodiment of many forms of soul-destroying hatred, this monstrous product of former wrongs and shame, has now resolved to try to break our famous island race by a process of indiscriminate slaughter and destruction.

"What he has done is to kindle a fire in British hearts, here and all over the world, which will glow long after all traces of the conflagration he has caused in London have been removed."

Although the Battle of Britain was later deemed to have ended on 31 October, the Blitz carried on beyond that date. However, the Blitz was very much a part of the Battle of Britain for the last three weeks of September 1940, and through to the end of October.

Generally, it is accepted that the Blitz ended on 11 May 1941, and this coincided with the German build-up for an assault on Russia. A consequence of the Germans turning their attention eastwards was that the Luftwaffe were no longer able to sustain the intensity of the air attacks it had been making on British towns and cities. Rather like the Battle of Britain some seven months earlier, the Blitz finally petered out. But not before eight months and five days of terror.

THE BATTLE OF BRITAIN IN COLOUR

Above Oil storage tanks set ablaze at Thames Haven, Essex, during September 1940 are photographed by a Luftwaffe reconnaissance aircraft.

Wholesale Destruction

Although the night blitz on Britain had failed to bring about the collapse that the Germans had anticipated, it had not been unprofitable for them. Most rewarding had been the adverse effect on British aircraft production which had been seriously impaired by the destruction of factories manufacturing components and equipment, and by the enforced dispersal of plant. The Germans had also inflicted heavy commercial and residential damage on the towns and cities which they attacked. More than one million houses were damaged or destroyed, and casualties sustained by the civilian population were nearly 45,000 killed and some 50,000 injured. However, the Blitz was far from being a strategic victory.

Widespread as damage undoubtedly was, its effect on the country's overall production was not serious, and in the onslaught on the ports, only approximately 70,000 tonnes of food stocks were destroyed, oil stocks were depleted by less than 1/2 of 1%. Damage to communications, road, rail and telephone services were serious at times, but in every case repairs were quickly effected. At no stage of the German offensive did it appear that permanent irreparable damage was being done to industry, or that the ability of the country to wage war would be impaired. Nor was there any real likelihood of morale reaching the point where the population would force the government to sue for peace as the Germans had hoped.

It must be conceded, though, that the Germans achieved a considerable amount of damage for an almost insignificant loss rate in aircraft and crews. Wholesale destruction and disruption had been achieved for the loss on night operations of a few hundred bomber aircraft - or approximately 1.5% of the sorties flown. Thus, the campaign had been conducted at no great expense to the Luftwaffe, but militarily it had achieved little more than forcing the RAF and the Army to retain large numbers of men and equipment in the United Kingdom when they were sorely needed in other parts of the world.

However, the Luftwaffe turning its attention on London at a critical point in the Battle of Britain at least gave some respite to RAF Fighter Command, through the cessation of attacks on its airfields. Additionally, the gradual drawdown of German daylight activity gave the RAF's day fighter force a chance to catch its breath and lick its wounds.

The Blitz taught much to both the British and the Germans. But one thing was particularly clear. Truly effective strategic bombing could only be achieved by directing an enormous weight of bombs at vital objectives, such as power installations, the aircraft industry and ports. And for much of the Second World War, this was beyond the capability of any nation.

It was certainly beyond the capability of Nazi Germany in the period from September 1940 through to the spring of 1941. ■

THE BLITZ

NIGHT FIGHTING

With the paucity of any effective night-fighting capability during the Battle of Britain and the Blitz, RAF day fighter pilots were often called upon to provide night-fighter patrols in their Hurricanes or Spitfires. It was a nerve-wracking experience. Of the Hurricane pilots called upon to carry out this duty, one was Pilot Officer Peter Parrott of 145 Squadron based at RAF Westhampnett:

"We were more than a little surprised to be ordered to send three of our number over to Tangmere on the evening of 8 August 1940 for night readiness – the first time that we had been called for this duty. I was one of the three selected to go. It so happened that I had never flown a Hurricane at night, but I deemed it politic not to reveal this fact at such a late stage. It was, I suppose, inevitable that I should draw the short straw and thus be the first to go if we were scrambled. And I was.

Taxiing out to the flarepath was another new innovation for me, and was at walking speed with an airman on each wing tip to guide me. As I took off, there was no visible horizon, so I was forced to concentrate on the blind flying instruments. As I climbed, I could see searchlight beams ahead seeking targets. Over Portsmouth, there were the flashes of ant-aircraft shells bursting. I next noticed that the Hurricane seemed to be gaining height rather more slowly than usual. I scanned the instruments, and all was reassuringly normal with no red lights. Wait a minute! In concentrating on the flying instruments of the blind flying panel, I had omitted to raise the undercarriage. Rectifying this improved the rate of climb considerably and having reached the height ordered by the controller I levelled off and headed towards the action.

Then, I was almost immediately caught, and totally blinded, by a searchlight beam. No matter what evasive action I took I was held in the beam. I asked the controller to have the light doused, but to no avail. To lose the beam, I had to get out of its range, and this I eventually did whilst worrying that I would very soon become a target for the anti-aircraft gunners as I was very nicely illuminated for them, thank you very much.

Recovering my night vision took some little while, and as the controller had no targets for me I was recalled after a fruitless hour. Coming into land, the Merlin coughed and crackled in the throttle-back with great glaring bright jets of bluish flame issuing from the exhaust stacks. A judicious adjustment of opening the throttle a tad, and I got the same result again. It played havoc with your night vision - and just at the point when you needed it most to concentrate on a pretty hairy landing in the dark. Great!

I had never enjoyed night flying, and this episode confirmed my opinion that I was not cut out to be a night-fighter pilot. Frankly, I had had some scares and excitement, but my flying that night certainly topped them all. It was a far more worrying and nerve-wracking experience than fighting the Luftwaffe had ever been!"

Top Rescuers attempt to dig out a victim of the Blitz during the autumn of 1940 who has been trapped in the rubble of their collapsed home. In total, 45,000 people were killed during the Blitz and 50,000 injured, while over one million houses were damaged or destroyed.
Centre Luftwaffe ground crew chalk slogans onto the bomb load of a Junkers 88 before loading the weapons prior to an attack on Britain in the autumn of 1940.
Above One of the great hazards of the Blitz was the incendiary bomb. This was a commonly seen public information poster from the period.
Above right A Hurricane taxies out for a night sortie.

THE BATTLE OF BRITAIN IN COLOUR

Above London's courageous firefighters were hard pressed to deal with some of the blazes caused during the Blitz. Often, fires raged out of control as water mains were fractured or water pressure dropped.
Right On the night of 13/14 September 1940, during an attack on London, a Heinkel 111 from 3/KG4 was caught and shot down by a Blenheim of 25 Squadron, crashing at Down Hall Farm, Sheering. Two of the crew were killed, the other two captured. Here, military personnel and ARP wardens pick over the wreckage.
Below During the height of the Blitz, Londoners took to sleeping in London Underground stations as they perceived these to be the safest places to be.
Below right ARP dispatch cyclist, Charity Anne Bick, GM.

THEY ALSO SERVED

Civilians were very much on the front line during the Battle of Britain and the Blitz, including those who volunteered for Air Raid Precautions duties.

Charity Anne Bick was a dispatch cyclist in the ARP, and at the age of 16 became the youngest recipient of the George Medal for her bravery. This was during an air raid on West Bromwich in 1940. The citation for her George Medal set out the details:

'During a very heavy air raid, Miss Bick played an heroic part under nerve-racking conditions. At the outset, when incendiary bombs began to fall, she assisted her father, a Post Warden, to put out one of the fires in the roof of a shop, with the aid of a stirrup pump and bucket of water. The pump proved to be out of order, but nothing daunted she proceeded to splash the water with her hands and eventually put out the fire. While endeavouring to get out of the roof, the charred rafters gave way and she fell through to the room below and sustained minor injuries.

Miss Bick and her father then returned to the ARP Post. Almost immediately, high explosive bombs began to fall and a terrific explosion nearly shook them off their feet. They discovered that a bomb had destroyed two houses opposite and another one nearby. The Wardens attached to the Post were all on duty, so she borrowed a bicycle and rushed out to take a message to the Control Room amidst shrapnel from guns and falling bombs. She made repeated attempts to get through and several times had to dismount and fall flat on the ground for safety. Covered with dirt and grime she eventually delivered the message.

She made three journeys from her Post to the Control Room, a distance of approximately one and a quarter miles, during the height of the raid, and made further journeys afterwards.

Miss Bick, by acting as a means of communication between the Wardens' Post to which she was attached and the Control Room, did very valuable work and released other Wardens for duty. She displayed outstanding courage and coolness in very trying circumstances.'

Her portrait was later painted by Alfred Thomson.

3 ISSUES FOR £5

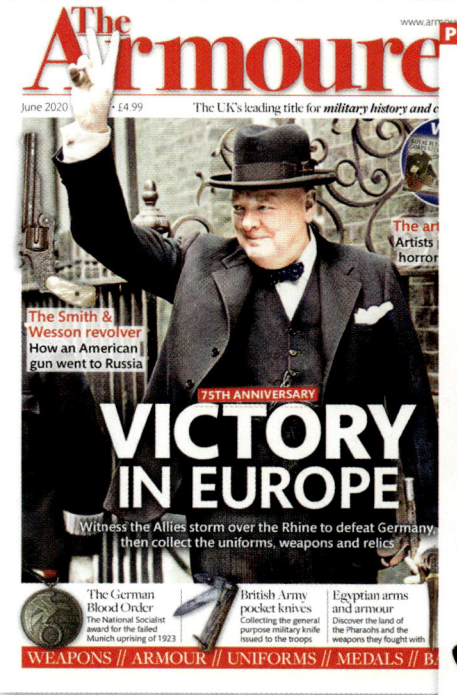

Saving almost £10

INSIDE EVERY MONTHLY ISSUE

- Discover the people, uniforms, medals and the weapons behind the stories
- The latest militaria news, re-enactments and event reports
- Prices, rare item finds, auctions and fair guides

Subscribe today

Visit **www.militaria.ma/arm_sub** or call **01778 392489** quoting ARM/BOB2020

Read the magazine anywhere!

Did you know... *The Armourer* is also available as a digital edition! Download issues directly to your devices and read wherever you are. Visit www.pktmags.com/arm_bobic to find out more!

Small print: Offer only available on direct debit to the printed edition and expires on 31 December 2020. For international subscription offers, please visit our website.

The Italian Job

During the latter part of the Battle of Britain, a small contingent of Italian air force bombers and fighters took part in air operations over Britain. Their involvement was not a successful one.

For the sake of national pride and political necessity, the Italian Air Force (Regia Aeronautica) was instructed by the Italian leader, Benito Mussolini, to send a force to northern Europe to 'assist' the Luftwaffe in its campaign against Britain. Göring, however, and the Luftwaffe High Command were not exactly enthusiastic, reasoning that they could probably manage without them. Nevertheless, a force named Corpo Aereo Italiano was formed under the command of Generale sa Rino Corso-Fougier in September 1940, its express purpose being to join in the air assault against Britain.

The organisational structure of the Regia Aeronautica broadly comprised 'Stormo' (Wings) which had a number of 'Gruppo' (Groups) which in turn comprised several 'Squadriglia' (Squadrons).

There were two 'Stormo' of Fiat BR.20 twin-engine bombers: the 13th and 43rd. There was also one 'Stormo' of fighters, the 56th, which had two 'Gruppo': the 18th 'Gruppo' made up of three 'Squadriglia', equipped with Fiat CR.42 bi-planes, and the 20th 'Gruppo' with three 'Squadriglia' of Fiat G.50 all-metal monoplanes. Finally, there was an assortment of transport, communications and reconnaissance machines. In total, a force of around 200 aircraft.

Crossing the Alps

In late September, the Corpo Aereo Italiano headed north to their allotted bases in Belgium. First to leave Italy were the Fiat G.50 fighters. After heading off on 22 September, they landed at their first stop-over in Treviso – where they remained until 6 October, delayed by fog. Next stop was Bolzano, where they spent 11 days waiting for suitable weather to attempt a crossing of the Alps. Then, on to Munich, Frankfurt and finally Ursel.

The Fiat CR.42 biplanes made the journey with comparative ease, although of the 77 Fiat BR.20 bombers attempting the four-hour flight over the Alps on 27 September, only 60 made it all the way. Two aircraft were destroyed, with the remaining 15 scattered along the route due to mechanical failures.

On arrival in Belgium, the men and machines presented a strange sight to their German allies, the men having been issued with newly designed Luftwaffe-esque uniforms to replace their First World War style breeches, although their machines retained bright camouflage which was far better suited to the sunnier climes of the Mediterranean.

When news of Corpo Aereo Italiano's arrival reached the Belgian Government,

ITALIAN AIR FORCE PARTICIPATION

Left Fiat BR 20 bombers of the Corpo Aereo Italiano arrived at Chièvres, Belgium, at the end of September 1940 to take part in the air assault against Britain, together with CR.42 and G.50 fighters. This particular crew had Disney's Peg-leg-Pete as their mascot ahead of the first Italian sortie over Britain – a raid against Felixstowe and Harwich on the night of 24/25 October.

Right Pilots of 257 Squadron after the action against the Corpo Aereo Italiano raiders on 11 November 1940. Some of the pilots have souvenirs gathered from one of the downed Italian bombers: a steel helmet, a bottle of Chianti and the Italian coat of arms cut from the aircraft's rudder. In the background stands the Hurricane of Squadron Leader 'Bob' R R S Tuck, marked with its impressive tally of swastika 'kill' markings. Tuck was medically unfit for flying that day and missed the action.

Below One of the Fiat CR.42 biplane fighters downed in the action on 11 November 1940 was this aircraft, flown by Sergente Pilota Pietro Salvadori, which tipped onto its nose during a force-landing in the shingle at Orfordness Ranges.

exiled in London, they symbolically declared war on Italy since the forces of that country were now using sovereign Belgian soil from which to wage war.

The First Attacks

The Corpo Aereo Italiano operationally came under the command of the Luftwaffe's Fliegerkorps 2 and was allocated an operating area from Ramsgate to Harwich. On the evening of 24 October, the first attack was launched – a night raid by 18 BR.20 bombers on Harwich and Felixstowe. Only minutes after take-off, one of the BR.20s crashed and killed its six crew. Ten crews reported that they had successfully bombed the target, but on their return, two of the aircraft were wrecked and one badly damaged when landing.

The first daylight raid was made on 29 October and was an elaborate and large-scale raid against Ramsgate in Kent by 15 BR.20 bombers with a fighter escort of 39 CR.42s, 34 G.50s and a few Luftwaffe Messerschmitt 109s offering some further token cover.

The armada flew along the Channel and then swung in over the coast at 10,000 feet near Ramsgate – all in neat formation. On the ground, the anti-aircraft gunners were baffled by the sight and sound the spectacle presented and the unusual rattling noise that the engines made. The sound was quite unlike RAF or Luftwaffe aircraft, but after further deliberation as to the identity of the aircraft, the guns began firing, anyway.

In total, 75 bombs fell in the area and the Italian press could truthfully proclaim that the Corpo Aereo Italiano had indeed attacked England. Remarkably, and most fortuitously for the Italians, RAF Fighter Command did not manage to intercept the raiders. However, five bombers were hit by the gunners, but all returned to Belgium. It would, though, be a different story two weeks later – albeit that this fell outside the period now generally accepted to have been the Battle of Britain.

Failure and Rout

At around mid-day on 11 November, ten BR.20s - each loaded with three 250kg bombs - took off from Chièvres, Belgium, with the intention of attacking Harwich. They were escorted by a strong fighter force of 42 CR.42s, 46 G.50s and a few Luftwaffe Messerschmitt 109s, but almost immediately the G.50s and Messerschmitt 109s turned back in the face of bad weather, leaving the ten bombers and the 42 bi-planes to carry on.

- 107 -

THE BATTLE OF BRITAIN IN COLOUR

A flight of BR.20 bombers of the Corpo Aereo Italiano, operating from Belgium, October 1940.

By the time the raid was nearing the English coast, heavy cloud and poor visibility had caused the aircraft to be scattered in small groups spread over several miles, each unable to see the others.

In England, the coastal Radar stations had picked up the incoming raid and the Hurricanes of 17 and 257 Squadrons were scrambled. Flights from two further squadrons, 46 and 249, were already airborne and were also vectored towards the raiders. What ensued appeared to be a relative massacre of the attacking Italian force – although it was perhaps more of a rout than a massacre.

The final tally of the engaging RAF fighter pilot's claims amounted to seven BR.20s destroyed, five CR.42s destroyed, three probably destroyed and one damaged. In fact, actual losses amounted to three BR.20s and three CR.42s.

As was usually the case in air fighting, there was some over-claiming. Under the circumstances, given the numbers of RAF fighters that got amongst the technically outclassed bombers and fighters, the Italians got away relatively lightly. But the force had been split up and the worsening weather caused further losses on their return to Belgium: four BR.20s crash landing near the coast and 18 CR.42s making emergency landings with varying degrees of damage. Another CR.42 wandered off course and ended up over Amsterdam where it crashed into a town square, its pilot being killed.

One of the Fiat CR-42 fighters from the 95 Squadriglia /18 Gruppo /56 Stormo was piloted by Sergente Pilota Pietro Salvadori who made a forced-landing at Orfordness Ranges, Suffolk. Taken prisoner, he sullenly told his interrogators:

"I didn't want to fight and I'm really glad to be out of the war. I was very dissatisfied with my Officers and I loathed the Belgium climate. And I couldn't stand the food - or the Germans."

However, whether he found the food as a POW any more appetising, the climate any more appealing or his captors any more tolerable, is not recorded!

On landing, he said that had been rather worried because a Hurricane had flown over to have a close look, but in response to his frantic waving the RAF pilot simply waved back and flew off. Today, the aircraft in which he landed is preserved by the Royal Air Force Museum.

Inglorious Participation

Coincidentally, and just a few hours after the Italians had ventured to attack Harwich, the Fleet Air Arm launched an attack on shipping in an Italian port - also using bi-planes. The port was Taranto, which was attacked by Fairey Swordfish torpedo bombers. Three Italian battleships were put out of action and in one night the Italian fleet had lost half its capital ships.

Prime Minister Winston Churchill was later prompted to comment of the Corpo Aereo Italiano:

"They might have found better employment defending their fleet at Taranto."

It wasn't quite the end, though, of the Italian air force's somewhat inglorious participation in the Battle of Britain and the air war against the British Isles. Another twelve operations were flown with limited success against Britain after 11 November, mostly by night, before the force made its last raid on 2 January 1941.

What can be said, though, is that the Italian pilots and aircrew fought bravely and tenaciously given the task they were set and the difficult conditions under which they had operated. ■

Operations Flown by the Corpo Aereo Italiano

24 October	Night raid - Felixstowe & Harwich
27 October	Night raid – Ramsgate
29 October	Daylight raid – Ramsgate
1 November	Daylight fighter sweep over Kent
5 November	Night raid – Felixstowe & Ipswich
8 November	Daylight fighter sweep over Kent
10 November	Night raid – Ramsgate
11 November	Daylight raid - Harwich
17 November	Night raid – Harwich
20th November	Night raid – Norwich
23rd November	Daylight fighter sweep over Kent *
25th November	Daylight fighter sweep over Kent
27th November	Night raid – Ipswich
28th November	Daylight fighter sweep over Kent
29th November	Night raid – Ipswich and Harwich
5 December	Night raid – Ipswich
13 December	Night raid – Harwich
21 December	Night raid – Harwich
22 December	Night raid – Harwich
2 January 1941	Night raid – Harwich

*This was the only other raid intercepted in strength by RAF Fighter Command. Twelve Spitfires of 603 Squadron attacked the Italian formation off Folkestone and claimed seven CR.42s shot down with two more claimed as probably destroyed. In fact, only two CR.42s were shot down. Several others were damaged.

DOUGLAS C. DILDY & PAUL F. CRICKMORE

TO DEFEAT THE FEW

THE LUFTWAFFE'S CAMPAIGN TO DESTROY RAF FIGHTER COMMAND

AUGUST–SEPTEMBER 1940

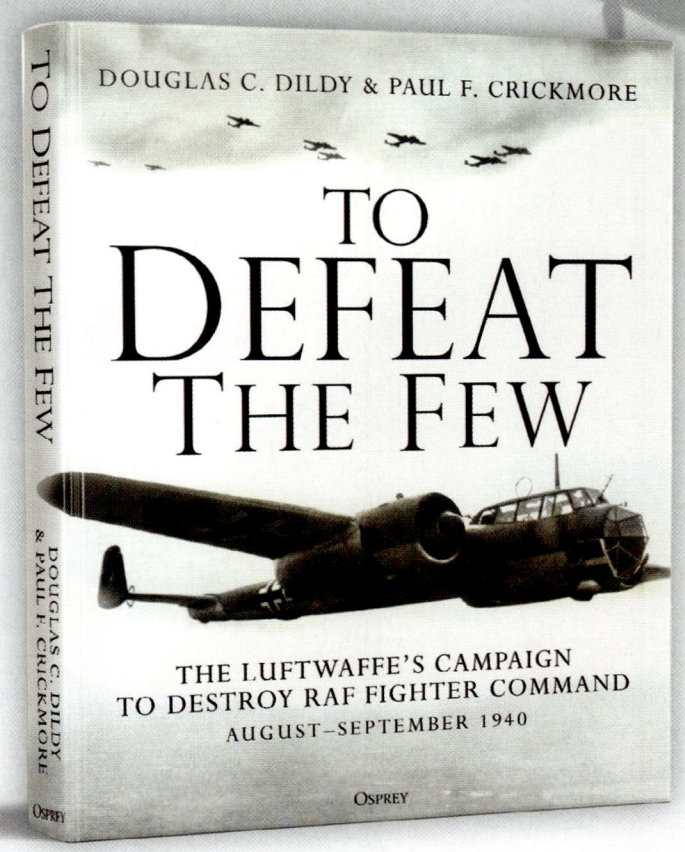

'In order to establish the necessary conditions for the final conquest of England… I therefore order the Luftwaffe to overpower the English air force with all the forces at its command, in the shortest possible time.'

FÜHRER DIRECTIVE NR. 17

The Battle of Britain has acquired near-legendary status as one of the most iconic events of the 20th century. This new history, based on an exhaustive study of German records, explores the battle through the eyes of the Luftwaffe.

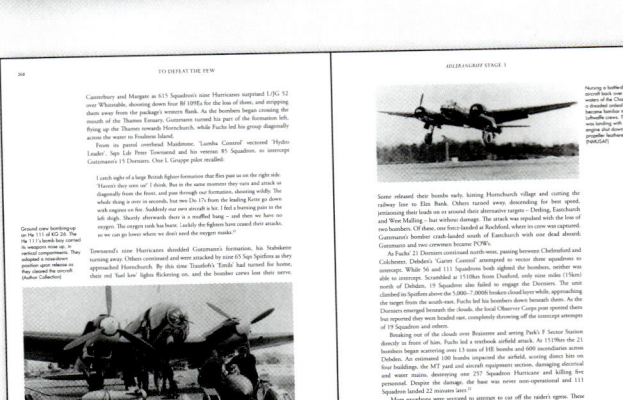

AVAILABLE NOW FROM
WWW.OSPREYPUBLISHING.COM

OSPREY PUBLISHING

THE BATTLE OF BRITAIN IN COLOUR

The Fearsome Channel

For the Luftwaffe fighter pilot or bomber crew during the Battle of Britain, the enemy was not just the Royal Air Force. Each air operation against the British Isles necessitated hazardous crossings of the English Channel or North Sea.

Although the Luftwaffe airman during the Battle of Britain did not face quite the same nervous tensions as their RAF counterparts, who waited uncertainly for action not knowing when or if it would come, the German flier still had worries a-plenty. For fighter pilots, on each day when the weather was suitable for air operations, they could potentially fly at least three or four stressful sorties. As the days wore on through the summer, and into autumn, the losses rose.

For the bomber crews, each sortie was a lottery. Would the target be relatively undefended? Or would they encounter flak and fighters? Worrying, too, was the question of their own fighter escorts. Would they keep the rendezvous? If they did, would they be able to defend the bombers against determined enemy fighters? And what would happen if their own fighter screen had to withdraw? And that was often the case – especially if the Messerschmitt 109s ran low on fuel. Next, there was the worry about getting home across the Channel or North Sea. And that was a huge concern for both bomber and fighter boys.

Out over the water, and separated

Above Oberfeldwebel Artur Dau, a Messerschmitt 109 pilot with 7/JG51, was already the veteran of 140 operational sorties when his aircraft was hit by ant-aircraft fire and he was forced to bale-out over Alkham, Kent, on 28 August 1940. The local Police Constable takes down particulars as other locals gather – including a Home Guardsman who seems to have got dressed in rather a hurry! For the most part, Luftwaffe airmen taken prisoner in Britain were treated fairly, although there were exceptions.
Facing Page Major (later Generalleutnant) Adolf Galland.

LUFTWAFFE AIRCREW DAY

THE BATTLE OF BRITAIN IN COLOUR

because of battle from the protection afforded in their formations, the RAF would pick-off stragglers: aircraft that were already damaged or fighters that were having to run for home because of low fuel states and who couldn't stay to fight. In fact, lone German aircraft struggling to return to France were easy prey and the Germans called the attackers 'leichenfledderer' – or corpse attackers. Sometimes, pilots or aircrew might already be wounded. And now they had to run the gauntlet of the cruel sea, too. While the air campaigns in Poland, France and the Low Countries had not been without cost, at least there was little prospect of coming down over water.

Another factor was the unwelcome prospect of being brought down over Britain and captured. And that was quite apart from the prospect of death, of course. And while potential death or injury in battle was a common denominator for either side, the Luftwaffe airman suffered another distinct disadvantage over his RAF counterpart: the possibility of capture. For the German airman brought down alive over Britain, the uncertainty of what it would mean to be captured also weighed heavily: how he would be treated, how long his captivity would last and the anxiety of separation from home and family all affected his mental state. Especially as men around him did not come back from operations over Britain.

Physical Strain

One of the best-known 'aces' on the Channel front in 1940 was Generalleutnant Adolf Galland who conveyed what it meant to be a Luftwaffe fighter pilot during the Battle of Britain:

"During the summer of 1940, I served as Kommodore of Jagdgeschwader 26. Normally, each unit made three sorties per day and the physical strain on pilots was heavy. Airframes and engines also suffered in these efforts. On occasions, we would be called on to carry out up to four freelance fighter sweeps (Freijagd) over England in a single day.

"Our missions were carried out in the following manner: once airborne, we assembled as quickly as possible at an altitude of more than 5,000 metres over the Continent. The approach flight began from this height, the altitude being gradually increased to between 6,500 to 8,000 metres.

"It took an average of 30 minutes to reach the English coast from take-off, and this left no more than 20 minutes for penetration into enemy airspace. To be able to attack British fighters from higher altitude, this meant that our time over England was reduced by fuel consumption during the act of climbing. Combats would then take place, progressively downwards, from our maximum altitude. The disadvantage of not having drop tanks on the Messerschmitt 109s also became apparent. Had they been so equipped, then endurance would have been increased by some 30 or 40 minutes and may have had a significant impact on eventual outcomes."

Galland also explained tactical issues in relation to German fighter operations in the Battle of Britain, and the stresses placed on the fighter pilots and the bomber crews they were escorting:

"Insofar as it worked at all, the system of escorting bombers functioned very poorly. There were neither special tactical rules nor uniformity of any concept; each fighter squadron carried out operations as it thought best. Hence, the quality of performance attained on these sorties was extremely variable. Some squadrons executed their missions in a highly efficient manner. Others did badly.

"Over Britain, we either flew as direct escort, indirect or deployed escort, freelance patrols, supplementary escorts to pick up and cover returning formations or protection for air-sea rescue operations. The most difficult mission was direct escort when we were tied closely to the bombers.

"In order to avoid British anti-aircraft fire, which was generally effective, bomber units flew higher than their ideal service ceiling and were thus much slower than they should have been. This compounded the problem for the escorting fighters who had to reduce speed to correspond with the bombers and, at the same time, try to retain manoeuvrability. It also further limited time the fighters had over England.

"Whenever possible, the leaders of the fighter escorts and leaders of the bomber formations would confer beforehand –

Above Airframes and engines suffered as the result of sustained operations, as did the men who flew them. Here, a Messerschmitt 109 undergoes maintenance at a French airfield.

Right For Luftwaffe fighter pilots in 1940, flying over the English Channel was an anxious time. On the outward journey, there was the stress of impending contact with the RAF. On the way home, the worry of low fuel levels.

LUFTWAFFE AIRCREW DAY

Above Paul Lege's logbook, showing his final sorties on 7 October 1940. In total, he had flown 48 operational flights during the Battle of Britain.
Top left Unteroffizier Paul Lege of 5/JG27 with his Messerschmitt 109 and ground crew in northern France, October 1940. Lege flew relentlessly during the Battle of Britain, including three sorties on 7 October. On the second operation that day he shot down a Hurricane but failed to return from the third sortie. He was killed when he was shot down near Heathfield, East Sussex.
Left A good many Messerschmitt 109 pilots literally just made it to the French coast.

usually by telephone. This was important, because in most cases any radio contact between fighters and bombers was not possible owing to dissimilarity of equipment in the two types of aircraft. And this caused big problems for the fighters and bombers."

But it was also the English Channel which was a fearsome enemy. Not just the RAF.

'Bobbing Across The Channel'

Again, Adolf Galland was clear about the problems presented by that narrow strip of water which took just a matter of minutes to cross. Invariably, though, they were long and anxious minutes for the German flier of 1940:

"In the course of a mission to London from the Pas-de-Calais, for example, a bomber formation with its escort could be in the air for two hours and had to return by the most direct route. If not, the escorting fighters would be short of fuel and would have to abandon the bombers or risk coming down in the Channel. And that was a huge worry."

It was certainly the case that coming down in the English Channel was the cause of great concern for all Luftwaffe airmen, but it was especially worrisome for the Messerschmitt 109 pilot, almost invariably returning with little fuel. One pilot, Oberleutnant Hans-Ekkehard Bob of 7/JG54, invented a method of getting home across the Channel if the tank was running low. However, it only worked if the pilot had sufficient altitude to play with.

The process involved switching off the engine and gliding for as long as possible before restarting the motor briefly to climb, and then to re-commence the process. With each glide and climb, overall altitude was gradually reduced, the pilot needing to judge things carefully to make sure he still had sufficient fuel and height to make it. If RAF fighters were still following, then it became impossible. But if circumstances were favourable, it could be the only way to get home without getting wet. Inevitably, it became known as 'Bobbing across the Channel'.

Adolf Galland again:

"Experience showed that a pilot in difficulty over the Channel had more chance of surviving if he ditched his aircraft than if he came down by parachute. It took 40 – 60 seconds for the

– 113 –

THE BATTLE OF BRITAIN IN COLOUR

Above For bomber crews, the stresses of operational flights over the sea were also considerable. This was especially the case for the Heinkel 111 crews of KG26 who flew long flights across the North Sea when based in Norway.

aircraft to sink. Time enough to get out. And our air-sea rescue services were good. Also, thanks to the initiative of General Udet, we had rescue buoys anchored in the Channel in the hope that pilots who got in trouble could swim to them. Inside was bedding, food, first aid kits, books and games and a radio transmitter. The idea was good, but I never heard of a single instance of one ever being used by a downed pilot. Also, the British sank them whenever they found them."

But whatever Galland's positive views on a fighter pilot's survival chances in the English Channel, it didn't allay the fears.

Channel Sickness

Indeed, such was the concern of Luftwaffe fighter pilots in 1940, that a psychological affliction soon became apparent: Kanalkrankheit, or Channel Sickness. This was a form of combat fatigue and many fighter pilots reported stomach cramps or were unable to eat. As combat wore on, the number of aircraft turning back to France owing to overheating engines, low oil pressure or instrument failure steadily increased. Pilots suffered mysterious bouts of illness, finding various reasons to make their way to the sick bay.

These medical ailments and 'equipment failures' were all symptoms of chronic stress, caused by extreme fatigue. There was no policy of 'R&R' for the German fighter pilot who was expected to keep flying until he was captured, killed, or promoted out of the front-line.

Another fighter pilot, Oberleutnant Ulrich Steinhilper of JG52, recalled:

"Although most of us were still not outwardly showing major signs of nerves, arguments were becoming more frequent, tempers frayed quicker and the strain of unrelenting front-line flying was beginning to show. And a number reported symptoms of appendicitis. In the end, the medics realised what the problem was and admitted pilots to hospital for appendix operations they didn't need. But it was a way of getting pilots out of the front-line for a while. One CO was sent back to Germany to run a training unit because of a 'grumbling appendix'. You've no idea how many Luftwaffe fighter pilots on the Channel coast in 1940 got appendicitis!"

Another fighter pilot, Unteroffizier Werner Karl of JG53, wrote:

"There was no talk about fear or of being taken prisoner. At least, nobody admitted if he was scared. All around us, we saw heroes both in the newspaper and on the radio. I think that everybody thought he was the only one who was afraid. For example, our briefings were always held outside in the open air. Immediately after it finished, and before we went to our 'planes, we all ran to the latrines and sat on the toilet. It was an all-pervading fear."

Werner Karl ended up being shot down and taken prisoner on 2 September 1940. It was an event to which he had resigned himself as ultimately inevitable:

"After all, one could not go on playing Russian Roulette and win forever."

But it was not just the Messerschmitt 109 fighter pilots who were suffering. The Messerschmitt 110 crews also took punishing losses. Of these, Galland noted:

"As to the Messerschmitt 110 in 1940, when units had originally been formed it was intended they should be used to escort bombers. The 110 was unable to

LUFTWAFFE AIRCREW DAY

SURVIVAL KIT

For a Luftwaffe airman coming down in the Channel, his lifejacket and his dinghy would hopefully keep him alive until rescue came. And according to Adolf Galland, he stood a fair chance of survival and rescue.

Two types of lifejacket were issued to Luftwaffe fighter or bomber aircrew in 1940. These were the kapok lifejacket **(1)** or the inflatable version **(2)** which could be blown-up by a CO2 cylinder. The latter became popular 'trophies' for RAF pilots, who often preferred them to the British issue lifejackets.

Dinghies of different sizes were provided for aircrew, either for a single man, two men or for bomber crews. This example, in an official photograph, **(3)** shows the two-man dinghy which would have been used by Messerschmitt 110 crews. The dinghy was equipped with survival equipment, first aid kit, rations and flares etc.

A downed German airman stood a good chance of being picked up by one of the Luftwaffe's Heinkel 59 rescue seaplanes **(4)** which were often painted white with Red Cross markings – albeit that the RAF were instructed not to recognise any protected status and to shoot them down as being non-compliant with the Geneva Convention. Additionally, an airman in the sea had a dye marker packet which coloured the water around him to make him more visible.

If he was not picked up by a seaplane, then a rescue launch might well come to his aid. **(5)** This bomber crew of KG55 are being rescued from the English Channel by a German launch on 26 August 1940. A trace of marker dye can be seen swirling near the dinghy.

As a last resort, ditched German airmen might be lucky enough to get to one of the 'Udet' rescue buoys. These rescue aids were painted bright yellow with red cross markings. **(6)** Not in place until later in 1940, Adolf Galland was not aware of a single pilot ever making use of one.

Overall, the Luftwaffe airman was well equipped in terms of survival aids. He also had a signal pistol and flare cartridges in the dinghy to attract attention.

Often, airmen carried side-arms, although one fighter leader banned his men from carrying them in case they came down in the sea and were tempted to use the pistol on themselves when despairing of rescue.

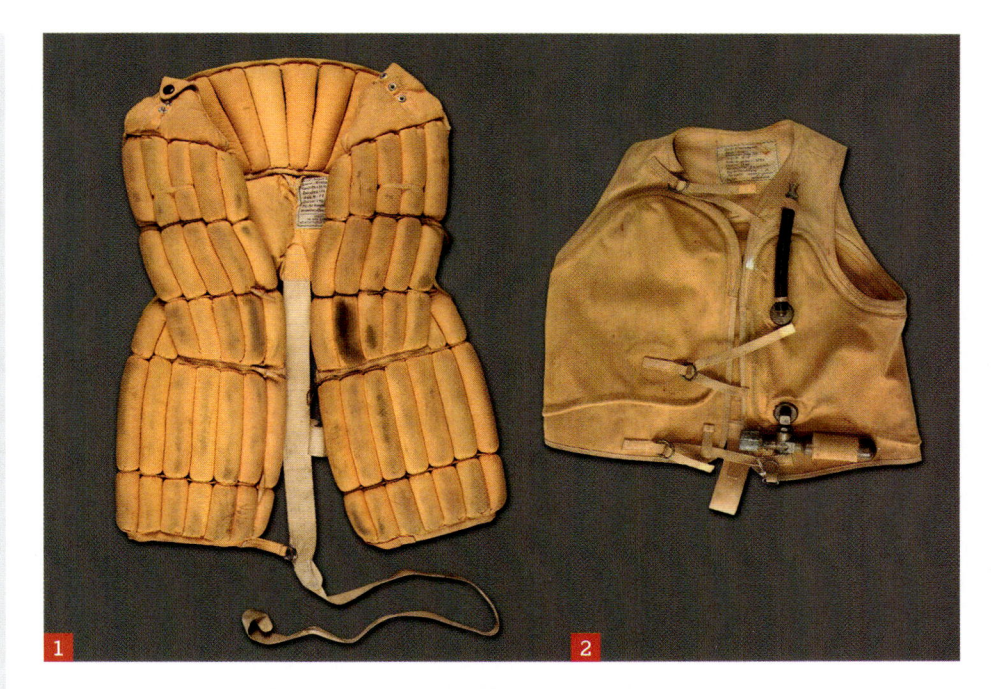

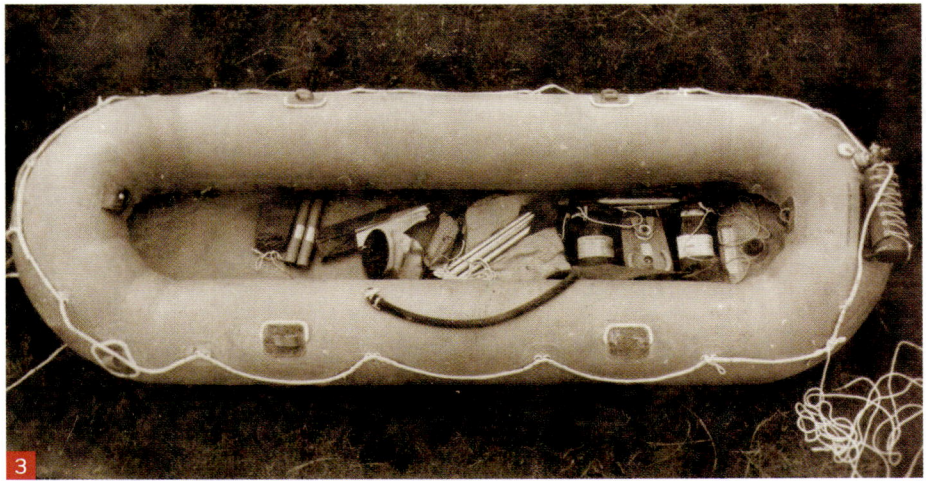

THE BATTLE OF BRITAIN IN COLOUR

Above A Luftwaffe crew member of KG26 counts the bullet holes in a Heinkel 111 which managed to get home.
Right Scrambling out before the aircraft sinks, these two crewmen of a Messerschmitt 110 brought down in the English Channel during the Battle of Britain must get in their dinghy quickly and wait for rescue which will hopefully come.
Far right Sight of the northern French coast was a relief for all Luftwaffe airmen returning from operations over Britain

give a good account of itself in combat with British fighters, and the enemy singled them out for attack. When they were attacked, they were obliged to make a series of very tight turns, an 'Abwehrkreis', or defensive circle. Though nobody was willing to admit it, this was a defensive measure and they had to rely on Messerschmitt 109s coming to their assistance. Otherwise, they had to escape as best they could and suffered heavy losses. Whatever the value of the 110 in combat, they were of little use. The men who flew them, knew so. But they had to keep going."

However, it was not just Luftwaffe fighter pilots and crews who were under strain in 1940.

Anxious Despair

Tensions and nerves in the bomber force were also near breaking point. Every day, fewer familiar faces appeared in the mess or at briefings. Each bomber failing to come home resulted in four or five men no longer there.

Unteroffizier Peter Stahl, a Junkers 88 pilot with II/KG30, was regularly over London. Often for three nights running. His Staffel also struggled with inexperienced new crews. On 16 October, during a night attack on London, four crews failed to return and two crashed on landing, although the men escaped alive. But six aircraft out of nine was a terrible night of losses. In the crew bus back to their quarters afterwards they discussed what point there was in sending out hundreds of men every night and without hope of any reasonable results. He noted:

"And tomorrow, the communiqué of the OKW will state that our brave aircrews have flown another major operation. Despite bad weather conditions, they have inflicted devastating blows on various vital targets. Our own losses, of course, were only 'minimal'!"

Earlier in the Battle of Britain, on 25 August, he wrote in his diary:

"It is being said that the British are already on their last legs, but when you hear what the operational pilots have to report, then the overall losses being suffered by our bomber crews must be terrible."

LUFTWAFFE AIRCREW DAY

Above At least a third of these Messerschmitt 110 crew members of 1/ZG26 would not survive the Battle of Britain. Here, they pose in front of one of their aircraft marked with the unit badge: a German crocodile chasing a British minnow.

Another Luftwaffe bomber crew member was 18-year-old Unteroffizier Robert Götz, an air gunner in Heinkel 111s of KG55, who kept a diary recording his 39 sorties over Britain. In it, youthful optimism gradually turned to a degree of anxious despair. On 26 September, he wrote:

"Still no news of our missing comrades. Have they had it? We all know that this can happen to any of us. This would be very painful for me, but only because of my mother and my little brother."

Another crew member on KG55, Gefreiter Hans Pawlik, suffered the same fears. On 8 October, briefed to carry out a low-level sortie to attack RAF airfields, Pawlik confided to another member of the unit, Feldwebel Fritz Pons, that he did not want to go. He had a bad premonition. *"Well, it's my birthday, and I don't want to go either!"* said Pons, trying to reassure his friend. But Pawlik would not be consoled, staying with Pons right up until it was time to board their aircraft. As it turned out, Pons would never see his friend again.

Certainly, there was no glamour in flying and fighting in the Battle of Britain. For either side. ■

Above Unteroffizier Robert Götz was just 18 years old when he took part in his first operational flight over Britain.
Left Often, Luftwaffe bombers would return home carrying wounded, dead or dying crew members. Unteroffizier Paul Schüll was killed in his KG55 Heinkel 111 over Portland on 15 September 1940.

THE BATTLE OF BRITAIN IN COLOUR

Ursula's Demise

An account from one Luftwaffe pilot of his experiences during the Battle of Britain is accompanied by a series of rare photographs of the period - all the more remarkable because they are taken using colour film, and during the height of the battle.

Enemy air activity over the British Isles on 16 August 1940 showed every sign of increasing its already quickening pace, and it was a day that would see significant raids against a wide range of targets through the daylight hours. Principally, this activity was confined to south-east England and the part of the action with which this account is concerned is perhaps best summarised in the official RAF report on the day's activities:

"Whilst activity was ongoing further to the east between 16.00 and 18.30 hours, the Germans had been engaged on an even larger operation further west.

The forces that had originally been located off the Normandy coast between 16.33 and 16.40 hours came steadily across the Channel and the first of them was near the Isle of Wight by 16.50 hours. But the period of warning had been sufficient for a considerable defending force to take to the air and by that same time eight squadrons were covering various points between Portland and Worthing.

Nevertheless, it would appear that three German forces were able to make their landfall without being intercepted. The enemy force was deployed in four formations; one crossed the Isle of Wight at about 17.00 hours, turned east near Winchester and operated towards Godalming and Haslemere. Another came up to Selsey Bill and turned towards the Isle of Wight; the third crossed just east of Tangmere and flew north-eastwards; and the fourth crossed near Worthing. Only this last force was intercepted as it crossed the coast. It was described as a large formation of He 111s and Me 110s flying at a height of 15,000 to 18,000 ft."

Almost certainly, these were the Heinkel 111s of KG55 with their Messerschmitt 110 escort provided by aircraft of ZG76. With several RAF squadrons intercepting as the formations traversed Sussex, and then attacking again as the formations turned about to retire, it is difficult to pin down with certainty who it was that downed one of the Messerschmitt 110s that was destroyed over the South Downs of West Sussex, falling to earth at Droke, near Upwaltham. However, a "claim" by Spitfire pilot Squadron Leader "Sandy" Johnstone, the CO of Westhampnett based 602 Squadron, might perhaps fit the bill. However, the details later

- 118 -

GERMAN CAMERA COLOUR

Far Left Messerschmitt 110s of ZG 76's III Gruppe roar fast and low over the English Channel during the summer of 1940. Clearly visible is the emblem of ZG 76's III Gruppe, depicting three wasps above a cloud.

Left Snatching a moment to snap a photograph of III./ZG 76 Messerschmitt 110s as they cross the Dorset coast, Lt Marchfelder catches two aircraft in formation off his port wing. One of them, 2N + AN, carries three white victory tabs on its tailfin.

Below Left At low level and crossing the coast, this photo was captioned as taken from the aircraft of Lt Dieter Nülle, 2N + BC.

Below Right This stunning shot shows Marchfelder's aeroplane, 2N + CC, Werke Nummer 3278, up on trestles for firing at the gun butts. This is the aircraft in which Marchfelder and Jentzsch were shot down over Sussex on 16 August 1940.

relayed by the Messerschmitt 110 pilot do not entirely fit the facts as described by Johnstone, although he was certainly involved in that same action which also saw the downing of Marchfelder's Messerschmitt.

The RAF pilot later wrote of his experiences that day:

"The air was a kaleidoscope of aeroplanes swooping and diving around us, and for a moment I felt like pulling the blankets over my head and pretending I wasn't there! I had no idea it could be as chaotic as this! Selected a gaggle of Me 110s and dived to attack. Out of the corner of my eye I caught sight of another Spitfire having a go and blowing the canopy clean off an Me 110. A Hurricane on fire flashed by, and I was momentarily taken aback when the pilot of the aircraft in front of me baled-out - until I realised he had come from the Me 110 I had been firing at! Then it was all over. No one else was about."

'Spitfire!'

Johnstone had set fire to the starboard engine of the Me 110 in question, crippling it fatally, and causing the crew to bale out into captivity – drifting down to land near Cucumber Farm, Upwaltham. The German crew in question were Leutnant Richard Marchfelder (Gruppen Technical Officer) and Obergefreiter Herbert Jentzsch of Stab III/ZG76. Years later, Marchfelder told his own fascinating story, in which he calls his aircraft *Ursula*.

"We were on our way back from a raid to London, cruising at an altitude of 7,000 metres, the superchargers whining with revved-up power to feed *Ursula*'s hungry twin engines with oxygen. It was peaceful up here. Relaxed, Herbert had his feet propped against the bulkhead, his bottom slumped in the seat and secured by his harness. He was watching the vapour trails streaming out behind and forming a fluffy railroad track between the double rudders. They were expanding like dreams which vanished off into the distance.

"A little bit bored, I called to my radio operator: 'Get us some nice music, Herbert, French or English. I don't care as long as it's pleasant'. After some ear-piercing shrieks at full volume as he slid along the receiver scale, he finally found a station playing music. From the way it faded in and out, I think it came from Ireland. A woman's voice was sobbing her heart out. She was singing about peace and love...eternal love...that she would wait for him for ever and ever. Then, a voice came over the music: 'We have a visitor....' There was a scramble of British voices, and then: 'Watch out, Tony. It's a bloody Messerschmitt 110. Not a Heinkel'.

"Right then, a single aircraft appeared at eleven o'clock! It popped out of the clouds into the sky like a cork from a Champagne bottle. As it ignored the Heinkels it was obviously a Messerschmitt 109 – like us, guarding the bombers, or perhaps it had lost its way. Relieved that someone else was keeping a watch on the bombers, there was no reason to hand around any longer, I thought.

"I changed or course five degrees to the right, to beam in on our home run to Lannion via Portsmouth. The other 'plane must have seen us because he too changed direction and turned away from the Heinkels. Now facing us, as he banked into position, so he exposed for a moment his elliptical wings. Spitfire!"

Hail of Bullets

"In response, I pushed both throttles forward to increase speed, at the same time diving head-on towards the Spitfire which was climbing to reach our altitude. 'If that cowboy thinks he can engage us in a dogfight, he has a surprise coming!'

"He realised that I was coming straight at him, and, as anticipated, he showed signs of trepidation! His only chance now was to try passing us, but in the heat of the moment he miscalculated and opened fire first. Bit too early! Fiery spots bounced along his wings. Seconds later, he appeared in my gunsight to be greeted by Ursula with a hail of bullets and cannon fire.

"Something went wrong. We both pulled away, unfortunately in the same direction. There was a thud and Urusla shuddered like a car hitting its wheel

THE BATTLE OF BRITAIN IN COLOUR

"A Hurricane on fire flashed by, and I was momentarily taken aback when the pilot of the aircraft in front of me baled-out - until I realised he had come from the Me 110 I had been firing at! Then it was all over. No one else was about."

Squadron Leader 'Sandy' Johnstone, 602 Squadron.

against a large stone. Nothing happened, except that Herbert landed on the floor together with his harness. 'He's baling out!' shouted Herbert. I hardly registered what he said, because for some inexplicable reason Ursula was shifting to the right and demanded all my attention to get her under control. What a pity that it was not possible to trim the rudder from the cockpit, so as to relieve the pressure on my left foot.

"With great effort I tried to keep Ursula on her course praying that I didn't get cramp in my left leg! Only after I managed to move my right leg over to the left rudder pedal to help reduce the pressure was it possible to keep Ursula on her course.

"Then, unexpectedly, the Messerschmitt's starboard engine burst into flames, its propeller paddling in a ball of fire. Closing the fuel line had no noticeable effect. Then, as I was about to cross the coast heading back for France, flames began to eat into the cockpit. At first, they nibbled gently at my legs and then with increased appetite they began to devour whatever was consumable."

Ball of Fire

Marchfelder ordered Jentzsch to bale-out, but the canopy cover would not budge. Fumes from burning rubber and other material in the cockpit began to overwhelm Marchfelder and he became light-headed but tried to turn *Ursula* onto her back to help Jentzsch escape, although suddenly realised he was turning to starboard over the burning engine. Quickly, he jerked the aircraft back and, in doing so, the cockpit canopy cover was flipped off, flinging Jentzsch out into the sky. Now, he had to save himself.

"I tried to lift myself out of the cockpit, but my parachute pack got caught in the canopy frame. It was impossible to move any further – let alone jump! I was trapped. Desperately, I struggled. It was a struggle amplified by the potential agony of being roasted alive and I finally managed to wrench the parachute clear of the frame and jumped. I was free. But not before passing through a ball of fire. What a relief to then be greeted by the soothing cold air at seven thousand metres.

"Now began the highlight of the whole drama. At the beginning, my body somersaulted with the world spinning around like an out of control gypsy merry-go-round. Now, I panicked again. Would the parachute open? Or am I at the end of my terrestrial pilgrimage? Perhaps a prayer would help? But instead of any divine intervention, a nagging thought was in my head. 'Seven thousand metres, and without oxygen!' At this altitude, hypoxia would start within a few minutes. This was like falling from the frying pan into the fire, but the will to live made me let myself just fall until I had reached a denser atmosphere. Debris of all kinds and of different sizes was falling around me and racing me on the way downwards. Lighter objects, which were dislodged from the aircraft by the slipstream, floated upwards. Among them was my logbook and two photographs of Michelle in the company of some pictures of spicy

GERMAN CAMERA COLOUR

Left Lt Marchfelder photographs his Messerschmitt 110 having its guns aligned at the firing butts. White tracer streaks away from the Messerschmitt's nose.
Right Leutnant Richard Marchfelder, wearing a red silk scarf, is photographed from the rear cockpit by his gunner/radio operator, Ogefr Herbert Jentzsch.
Below Post war, Richard Marchfelder drew cartoons depicting his adventures over England. The scenes included his bale-out and capture.

young French ladies which were hidden between the pages. They were all waving at me! I reached out to catch them, but they swerved elegantly out of reach as I continued to somersault.

"It was the parachute pack, though, which would stop me somersaulting. I pulled the cord. Then followed seconds of unbearable tension which almost turned to panic as the auxiliary drogue 'chute unfolded between my legs, instead of above my head. Before I was able to figure out the reason why, so my body was brutally jerked around into a normal head-up and feet down position. But tragedy also had its comical moments, and I suddenly realised I was still holding onto my control column like the rolled-up umbrella of an English bank manager. How it had become dislodged from its socket, and how I was still holding onto it, was completely beyond my comprehension."

Rhapsody of Machine Guns

"At last, I was falling gently under the spread of my parachute and into layers of cloud. It was very quiet, except for the rhapsody of machine guns in the distance. This was occasionally interrupted by the huskier bark of cannons. The battle was raging on. I couldn't see where my burning aeroplane had gone, but a little distance away there were four Hurricanes peacefully minding their own business.

"Viewed from seven thousand metres, it had appeared that the cumuli below were resting on a blanket of tightly-knitted altostrati. But getting closer they proved to be separated from each other. I was now passing through a fat cumulus which embraced me with her moist softness of expanded vapour and produced the strange sensation of floating through a boiler house with leaking steam pipes. Slowly, the blanket unfolded. Then, my face was washed with condensed vapour which smelt like stale gasoline. Fuel must have spilled into the cloud from my Ursula on her way down before I had arrived there.

"Passing through the next layer of cloud, it became darker and more saturated with moisture. The obvious reason for this was that there must be sea below. Damn it! That was all I needed now. I was afraid of falling into the English Channel, without anyone around to rescue me. The horror of floating around for days, slowly dying of dehydration, made my blood run cold. My state of mind was further poisoned by the overwhelming smell of burning rubber. Maybe the parachute was on fire? I tried to look up, but the clouds were so dense that I couldn't see anything above my harness. Going to wipe my eyes, I discovered to my amazement that my rubber oxygen mask was still over my face. Hastily, I ripped it off. Contemplating what to do with the mask for a moment, I decided to let it fall. With my helmet, it tumbled a few times and then fell straight down with the hose trailing behind like a tail. The mask, helmet and goggles resembled some sort of predatory monster stalking its prey. But now...
LAND!"

— 121 —

THE BATTLE OF BRITAIN IN COLOUR

Spasms of Pain
"My worries turned to joy when I left the clouds and discovered land below! It came rapidly closer. In my elation, I was talking to myself: 'Remember to turn against the wind. Don't forget to bend your knees. Above all: relax!' Unfortunately, the heat had affected my eyes and they were constantly filled with tears. Just as I prepared to land, my eyes got blurred and I misjudged the distance and twisted my right leg badly on impact.

The terrible pain almost made me jump back up again. But, I couldn't. For a few minutes, I was unable to move. Terrible pain prevented me from thinking straight, let alone make plans about what I should do next. Gently massaging my kneecap to help circulate the blood was all I could think to do. After a few minutes, the pain began to subside. But it still prevented me from moving about.

"Behind me, was my parachute. It was spread out across a patch of grass advertising my hideout. Interrupted by spasms of pain, my somewhat dented senses began to return. At that moment, I was preoccupied with the wonderful sensation of being alive. I was reasonably intact, and I was also relieved from immediate duty. 'You don't have to fight anymore, nor spend half the night repairing aircraft and the rest of it writing stupid reports!' As I lay there, the sun was peeping out through the clouds. Just as it did at home. Even the grass and the bushes looked the same. It was so peaceful, but I mused that the grass here was lusher and richer than in France, though. Then, air raid sirens wailed in the distance – spoiling my daydreams.

"A few minutes later they were joined by the rumble of multi-engine aeroplanes. Nearby, anti-aircraft batteries began to bark like a watchdog, plotting the course of the raiders as they went and passing them along from one battery to the next. This dramatic spectacle must have lasted the best part of an hour before it was finally terminated by the 'all clear' signal. Then peace was reinstalled again. At least, for the moment."

In Distress
"Nagging thoughts began to invade my mind, probing in all directions to find a solution to my current predicament. I was sitting here as if waiting for a train or a bus to get me back. But where? And how? To run away was impossible. My leg would not allow it. As if to answer my question, there was somebody approaching.

"Turning my head, I was confronted by a big cow! She seemed surprised to see me sitting there, and initially started away from me as I moved. Her curiosity, though, was directed at the large blanket of my parachute. She sniffed at the fabric which smelled faintly of gasoline. Disappointed, she turned around, but before leaving she lifted her tail and deposited her stamp of disapproval on the 'chute. Then, she turned her soulful eyes back towards me and regarded me for a while, as if making up her mind what to do next. From her expression, it seemed to me that she knew I was in distress. I almost imagined that her face radiated with sympathy. Motherly, she then started to wash my face – missing no part of it with her

- 122 -

GERMAN CAMERA COLOUR

soggy tongue. Or perhaps she just liked the taste of burnt rubber? Finished, she stepped back to admire her work. Now, her mouth moved to chew the cud. Just like a teenager chewing bubble gum. As she came at me again, all I could do was to protect my face with my hands. This presented a new challenge for her, and she now attacked my neck. Now, more cows appeared, wanting to investigate what all the commotion was about. Expecting something edible, they turned away. Disappointed, they examined the spread-out parachute."

'Hands Up!'

"Was it my imagination, or did I now hear footsteps? Looking in the direction from which the noise came, I saw a strange figure groping its way through the cows towards me. It was a man holding a rifle with both hands and puffing like a weightlifter. Unable to move, let alone stand up, I watched helplessly as the strange apparition came closer and put the barrel of the gun under my nose. Afraid of his trepidation, I was scared he may accidentally pull the trigger! 'Hands-up!', he shouted. His face was purple. Dear God, don't let him have a heart attack. They will blame me for it, I thought.

"Carefully, I pushed the barrel away from my face with two fingers as I gave him a frozen smile. 'Are you hurt?' he demanded. Holding my knee, I nodded. 'I twisted my leg on impact. It's my knee which hurts.' Suddenly, he relaxed a bit. 'Ah! You speak English!' he cheerfully responded. So, I took off my flying boot and unzipped the leg of my combination flying suit and carefully peeled back my trouser leg. 'Whew! That looks bad. It's all swollen' he remarked.

"He now knelt down next to me to investigate the bruise. This gave me an opportunity to have a closer look at him. I guessed he must have been around 50, quite handsome in appearance, and with a greyish moustache sprouting below his prominent nose. He had friendly blue eyes, with a host of lines fanning out from their corners. His appearance was certainly distinctive, his body stuffed into a boiler suit which partly covered a red-striped shirt. He had a well-worn Derby hat lobbed rakishly over one ear. It was a size too large, the front of the brim shiny from being frequently handled by greasy fingers. Fortunately, his ears stuck out like ping-pong bats and prevented the hat falling over his face. In this get-up, he resembled the ringmaster at a provincial circus. But it was his bow-tie which gave his appearance an altogether artistic flair. Decorated with red dots on white fabric, it had clearly been selected to match his shirt. Perhaps it was a gift from his wife? If he had one.

Above Left Taken by Richard Marchfelder the day before he was shot down, this image was captioned as showing the aircraft of Hptm Dickore (2N + BC) displaying four victory tabs and leading a formation in across Weymouth. It was in this aircraft that Dickore was lost on this very operation.

Below Left Obergefreiter Herbert Jentzsch was the radio operator/air gunner to Lt Marchfelder when the pair were shot down and taken POW on 16 August 1940.

Above One of the III/ZG 76 Messerschmitt 110s on approach to land. This is 2N + AC, the aircraft usually flown by the Gruppe Kommandeur, Hptm Dickore.

"Apart from the cows, we were alone. There was not a soul in sight – unless you include the dog which now came bounding up. Its tail wagging, it sniffed my swollen leg and then started to lick it. When I tried to push him away, he started on my face which was still gummy from the cow's attention. 'Cut it out, Shorty!' shouted my host, before asking me my name. I told him. 'That's too difficult for me to pronounce. I shall call you Blondie.' For a moment, he regarded me to see if I approved the name and then helped me get my boot back on again. 'By the way, my name is Mr Bradshaw. I own all the land around here' he said with a circular movement of his hand to expansively indicate the extent of his property."

THE BATTLE OF BRITAIN IN COLOUR

Top Low level over France, aircraft of the unit prepare to climb to operational altitude as they head out to the English Channel.
Above Left High in the summer sky, the Messerschmitts of III/ZG 76 hold formation as they approach the south coast of England in a scene that must have been identical to Marchfelder's last operational flight.
Above Centre Although not in colour, this close up shows the emblem of III/ZG 76, depicting three wasps above a cloud. The reverse of this original photograph shows that it was developed and printed by 'Star Snaps' of Charing Cross, Jersey.
Above Right An aircraft of the unit on finals as it prepares to land – a picture snapped by Herbert Jentzsch.

'Hide the Parachute!'

"Mr Bradshaw helped me get onto my feet, encouraged by barks from 'Shorty'. Standing on one leg, I had to lean on him to keep my balance and I apologised for my clumsiness. Still, I saw no other way to walk by myself. 'My house is over there'. He pointed to some bushes. The house must be behind them. Out of sight. I didn't remember seeing it from the air, but my eyes were in no condition to properly scan the landscape. Now, Mr Bradshaw asked me to put my arm over his shoulders, but it didn't work. 'It would be easier if you carried the rifle. And why are you laughing?' he remarked. 'Well, you certainly make an excellent guard, Mr Bradshaw, giving your prisoner your gun!'

"Suddenly, I realised 'Shorty' was missing as we limped and staggered along, taking a rest now and again. I asked where the dog had gone. 'He went home to tell my wife we are coming. He always goes home first when I've finished work in the fields.' Sure enough, 'Shorty' returned in the company of an elderly woman, together with three girls. 'My missus' explained Bradshaw. 'With my daughter Audrey and her two friends.' He then explained: 'Blondie here is a Luftwaffe pilot. He's hurt his leg and can't walk.' They all said Hello. I said Hello. Then they asked where I came from, and I told them. 'Go and collect his parachute!' he demanded.

GERMAN CAMERA COLOUR

Above Aircrew members of III/ZG 76 practice dinghy drill in a French river – although this looks suspiciously like fun-and-games rather than serious practice!

Left Sightseeing! Returning from an operational flight, Marchfelder and Jentzsch take a close look at Mont St Michel on the Normandy coast.

"Right then, an Army truck was racing towards us and the girls mentioned it to Mr Bradshaw as he couldn't see it because the Derby hat had fallen down over his eyes. 'Jesus! Hey, run and tell Betsy to hide the parachute!' he shouted, just as the truck pulled up in front of us. From its front seat disembarked a young Army officer, and from the back emerged two soldiers armed with rifles and with bayonets blinking dangerously in the sunlight. Facing the officer, whose toothbrush moustache quivered with excitement, they jumped to attention as the officer barked some orders and pointed his bamboo stick at us. Both shouted 'Yes, Sirrr!' and marched menacingly towards us.

"Confusion! Now, to my utter astonishment, the two soldiers grabbed Mr Bradshaw and pulled him away from me. He was shouting in vain, just as his wife arrived in the middle of this peculiar comedy act. Swiftly, she kicked at one of the soldiers' shins and yelled: 'Let him go! He's my husband'. Meanwhile, I stood there unsteadily, still holding the rifle. In all the excitement, the soldiers had assumed that the man holding the rifle was the farmer guarding the German prisoner. 'But he's carrying a gun!', they exclaimed. Sheepishly, I handed it over and the girls started to laugh loudly. Then, the soldiers laughed. We all laughed."

'For me, the War was Over'

"As they went to put me in the Army truck, Mr Bradshaw remarked: 'Wait a minute! Let's all have a drink. I've saved a good Scotch for a special occasion. And this is that occasion." At first, the Army officer was having none of it. But he was persuaded by Mr Bradshaw. 'That poor chap' he said, pointing at me, 'That poor chap, Blondie, he will be in the slammer for God knows how long. He's slightly injured, but nevertheless he's alive. Which is worth celebrating.' Very soon, the bottle was produced, and the drinks were duly poured all round.

"Although I had made an effort to disconnect the radio lead when I baled-out, it must have been caught around my throat when I jumped. What with that, and having inhaled molten rubber and fumes, the Scotch burned the back of my throat when it hit it, making me gasp and splutter for air. 'I told you it was a good Scotch!' exclaimed Mr Bradshaw, laughingly slapping my back.

"Before too long, it was time to say goodbye. The soldiers helped me into the back of the truck, and we were off. Now, I was a Prisoner of War and I sat opposite the two soldiers, guarding me with rifles. Both soldiers stared at me. I stared at them. Both seemed uneasy as I scanned them and examined what they wore. As I looked at them again, I tried to read their minds. No doubt they were doing the same. Nobody spoke, and I realised I was no longer in control of anything. I was a prisoner. I could no longer make any decisions. From now on, they were being made for me. For me, the war was over."

As to the "claim" by Johnstone, it will be seen that not all the facts fit the circumstances he describes. And it was certainly not the case that Johnstone's Spitfire collided with the Messerschmitt as Marchfelder supposed. However, Johnstone had seen a man bale-out of the aircraft he attacked, and this must have been from Marchfelder's aircraft. Most likely, the impact felt by the German pilot was simply a fusillade of bullets hitting the aircraft. Either that, or he hit another Messerschmitt which survived the impact and returned home. There are no RAF aircraft, either, which were either lost or damaged through a mid-air collision.

Herbert Jentzsch and Richard Marchfelder had both landed, some distance apart, at Cucumber Farm, Upwaltham. Both went on to spend the next six years in captivity. Jentzsch ultimately returned to Zittau, East Germany, where he worked as a textile engineer until his death in 1999.

Marchfelder, meanwhile, emigrate to the United States where he became an architect. He died in Greenwich, Connecticut, on 12 May 1989, leaving a unique legacy in the form of this series of colour photographs from the Battle of Britain. ■

THE BATTLE OF BRITAIN IN COLOUR

Men of the Battle

A total of 2,946 pilots and aircrew participated in the air war over the British Isles during 1940. Over five hundred of them lost their lives. We look at who the Battle of Britain airman was and pay tribute to the valour of this small band of men.

To qualify for the accolade of being a Battle of Britain fighter pilot (or aircrew member in the case of those who flew in Defiant, Blenheim or Beaufighter aircraft) it was necessary to have served with an accredited Battle of Britain squadron or unit and to have flown the requisite minimum of one operational flight during the period 10 July to 31 October 1940. Such a qualification entitled the airman to the award of the Battle of Britain clasp which was worn on the ribbon of the 1939 – 45 Star. It also entitled the airman to prestige post-war membership of the Battle of Britain Fighter Association, an association which was necessarily an exclusive 'club'.

Merely serving as an operational pilot on an accredited squadron was not sufficient qualification alone to be considered for Battle of Britain aircrew status. In fact, there were considerably more than 2,946 pilots and aircrew on the establishment of RAF Fighter Command during the official Battle of Britain period. However, unless those pilots or aircrew flew on an operational flight during that time, then they were not deemed Battle of Britain participants. Equally, if they became casualties during the 10 July to 31 October period, but had not flown on at least one operational flight, they would not be included on any official Roll of Honour. A case in point is that of Sgt Sydney Ireland, a Spitfire pilot with 610 Squadron, who was killed in a flying accident whilst carrying out dogfighting practice from Biggin Hill on 12 July 1940. Whilst his death came within the qualifying period, and he was serving on an accredited squadron, he had not yet flown the required single operational flight when he was killed. Consequently, he is not regarded as a Battle of Britain participant or casualty.

- 126 -

THE FEW

Facing page Some of Churchill's 'Few'. Pilots of 310 (Czech) Squadron pose for the press photographer during the summer of 1940.

Right The North American Harvard was the advanced training aircraft in which the pupil fighter pilot could expect to gain flying hours before eventually being transferred to an Operational Training Unit, and then on to his first front-line fighter squadron.

Above There were frequently mishaps during the flying training of Battle of Britain pilots-to-be. This Tiger Moth came a cropper when being flown by Pilot Officer Roy Marchand, who later went on to fly in the Battle of France. He was killed in action during the Battle of Britain on 15 September 1940.

Surprisingly, no formal official list of Battle of Britain participants is maintained by either the RAF or MOD, the accepted roll of participants being based largely on investigations carried out across many years by researchers, enthusiasts, family members or the Battle of Britain Fighter Association. Consequently, that list has varied up and down in its total across the decades as various previously unrecognised participants came forward to claim their Battle of Britain status, or family members discover previously overlooked evidence which make it clear that their relative participated. Equally, others on the roll have been removed when it became apparent that they did not, after all, meet the qualifying criteria.

In many cases, original squadron Operations Record Books were unclear about whether personnel qualified. In some cases, those record books failed to properly identify exactly who that airman was. For example, it can be difficult to be sure who an individual is when, in some cases, they are referred to as just, say, Sgt

FLYING TRAINING

Before recruits selected for aircrew training got anywhere near an aircraft, they first endured the rigours of an Initial Training Wing. For many Battle of Britain aircrew, this began with No 4 ITW (Bexhill on Sea) or No 5 ITW (Hastings). Here, hapless recruits were put through the paces of basic training; drill, PE, rifle practice and learning about service life generally. Both Initial Training Wings were accommodated in seafront hotels, flats and large houses commandeered for the duration. Drill, PE and route marches were frequently conducted up and down the deserted and often windswept promenades, along a coastline over which many would shortly be doing battle. From here, their 'square bashing' done, recruits were posted out to Elementary Flying Training Schools.

At the EFTS, pupil pilots were taught the theory of flight and given initial flying instruction. This was usually on the Tiger Moth or Blackburn B-2. The trainee pilot would make his first solo flight after around eight hours tuition. From here, he moved to a Flying Training School and progressed to the Miles Master and North American Harvard: aircraft with performances a little closer to the Spitfires or Hurricanes they might expect to fly operationally should they be posted to Fighter Command.

On satisfactory completion of their stint at FTS, the trainee was awarded his coveted 'wings', officially called the Flying Brevet, and be posted to an Operational Training Unit (OTU) for final training on Spitfires or Hurricanes. There were no dual control Spitfires or Hurricanes, the novice pilot simply reading the pilots notes, be shown around the cockpit controls and then making his first flight. Attrition rates for trainee and novice pilots killed whilst undergoing flying training was significant, as RAF Flying Training Command worked to keep up a supply of replacement pilots. There was undoubtedly a diminution in the performance of newly trained pilots as corners were cut to get them to the front-line to replace operational losses impacting on the operational capabilities of squadrons.

On posting to a squadron, the pilot would first be sent out on 'Sector Reconnaissance Sorties' to familiarise him with the airfield, the area of operations and the squadron's aircraft. When the Squadron Leader was satisfied that a pilot was combat-ready he would be placed on the roster for duty and thereafter be expected to take his place on scrambles and operational patrols. It was, quite literally, a baptism of fire. Most new pilots came to their first squadron with very few solo hours and not much flying experience. Some did not even survive their first operational sortie.

THE BATTLE OF BRITAIN IN COLOUR

MEN OF MANY NATIONS
Some fifteen national groups were involved as participants in the Battle of Britain, made up as follows:

Great Britain	2,346
Australia	32
Barbados	1
Belgium	28
Canada	112
Czechoslovakia	88
France	13
Ireland	10
Jamaica	1
Newfoundland	1
New Zealand	127
Poland	145
Rhodesia	3
South Africa	25
United States	9
Stateless	1

THE FEW

Facing page Squadron Leader Johnny Kent, with a group of Polish pilots of 303 Squadron at RAF Northolt, leads his men away from a Hurricane in October 1940.
Facing page below Other nations represented amongst the fighter pilots of 1940 were the Canadians of 1 (RCAF) Squadron. One of the squadron's pilots is seen here in his Hurricane, preparing to take-off.
Below One of the 2,946 airmen who comprised the 'Few', Flying Officer Anthony Eyre, DFC, 'B' Flight, 615 (County of Surrey) Squadron, Royal Auxiliary Air Force, briefs his squadron's Intelligence Officer having just shot down two enemy aircraft on 15 August 1940.

VIA DEBORAH SCARFE

Smith. With no identifying initials or service number there can be no clarity. However, if an individual or family could present evidence in the form of logbooks or some other official record then they were awarded the clasp and added to the roll of participants.

In total, some 535 of those who were Battle of Britain accredited pilots and aircrew became casualties during the qualifying period.

Across the following pages, we look at a selection of those men of RAF Fighter Command who served in the Battle of Britain, including many who lost their lives during that period. ∎

Note: At the time of going to press with this publication on 22 May 2020, there was only one living survivor of the Battle of Britain: Group Caption John 'Paddy' Hemingway, DFC, a Hurricane pilot with 85 Squadron during the Battle of Britain.

Left Squadron Leader Geoffrey Wellum, DFC, flew Spitfires with 92 Squadron from Biggin Hill during the Battle of Britain. He is seen here with HRH Prince Charles after a Battle of Britain commemorative event. In 2002, Geoffrey Wellum wrote his autobiography 'First Light', which achieved critical acclaim. He died in 2018, aged 96.
Below left The medals of Battle of Britain veteran, Arthur Charles Leigh, who served as a Sergeant pilot flying Spitfires with 64 and 72 Squadron during the Battle of Britain. He was later promoted to Flight Lieutenant. Left to right: Distinguished Flying Cross, Distinguished Flying Medal, 1939-45 Star with Battle of Britain clasp, Aircrew Europe Star with France & Germany clasp, Defence Medal, War Medal and Air Efficiency Medal. The clasp to the 1939-45 Star marked out the recipient as an accredited Battle of Britain pilot.

THE BATTLE OF BRITAIN IN COLOUR

BOMBER COMMAND

The role played by RAF Bomber Command during the Battle of Britain is an important one to pay tribute to, especially given the fact that Bomber Command suffered heavier casualties than any other RAF Command during the Battle of Britain, with 718 personnel lost. It is also important to look carefully at the "Never in the field of human conflict..." speech by Prime Minister Winston Churchill in which he referred to the "few".

In this context, it is often seen that this was a specific reference to the pilots and aircrew of RAF Fighter Command. However, his speech of 20 August 1940 singled out the bomber crews for special praise.

However, the content of that speech and reference to 'the few' arose from a visit the Prime Minister made to HQ 11 Group, RAF Fighter Command, at Uxbridge when he watched the battle being played out in front of him on the general situation map.

Afterwards, he told his Chief of Staff, General Ismay: "Don't speak to me. I have never been so moved." Then, he leaned across to Ismay and said: "Never in the field of human conflict has so much been owed by so many to so few." There can thus be no doubt that Churchill's inspiration for his momentous speech must have been from witnessing, first hand, the work of RAF Fighter Command, even if he ultimately reserved the greatest specific praise for the work of Bomber Command.

However, the post-war context of his speech is generally regarded as specifically marking the heroic defence of Britain by pilots of RAF Fighter Command.

RAF Bomber Command, poorly equipped and lacking sufficient technology to bomb accurately, continually assaulted German military and industrial targets. Nevertheless, the appearance of taking the fight to the enemy was as important in raising the morale of the British population as any damage inflicted on the enemy.

Whilst questionable as to how effective the bombing attacks against German targets actually were, the campaign waged by RAF bombers against German airfields, and especially the invasion ports, barges and vessels in France, Belgium and Holland, helped place a check on German invasion plans.

Thus, the part played by RAF Bomber Command should not be overlooked, and its Order of Battle showed an average of around forty operational squadrons during the Battle of Britain.

The squadrons of RAF Coastal Command cannot be overlooked, either, in terms of participation during the Battle of Britain, its aircraft carrying out coastal patrols and also attacking enemy shipping and ports.

However, neither the pilots or aircrew of Bomber and Coastal Commands are officially recognised as Battle of Britain participants.

THE FEW

Facing page The crew of an Armstrong-Whitworth Whitley bomber board their aircraft prior to a sortie during the summer of 1940. Over 700 aircrew from RAF Bomber Command were lost during the period of the Battle of Britain.

Above right Aircraft of Bomber Command were frequently tasked during the Battle of Britain to attack ports along the French coast where barges and other craft were being assembled by the Germans for the planned invasion of the British Isles. These are vessels at Boulogne being readied for that proposed invasion.

Right Although the airmen of RAF Bomber Command who served or were lost during the Battle of Britain are not commemorated specifically on any memorial, they are collectively remembered at the Bomber Command Memorial in Green Park, London.

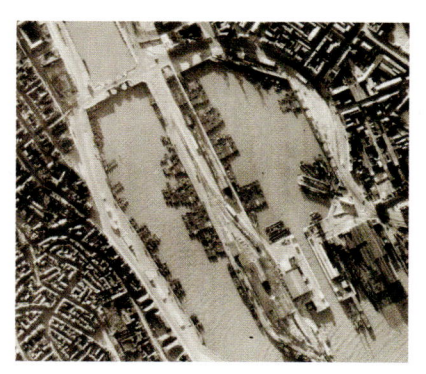

Left Pilot Officer Michael Homer had earned a DFC as a bomber pilot with 44 Squadron in April 1940, but volunteered as a fighter pilot in August 1940. After a brief conversion course onto Hurricanes, he was posted to 242 Squadron on 2 September. He was shot down and killed over Sittingbourne, Kent, on 27 September 1940.

MAKING UP THE NUMBERS

A considerable number of other pilots volunteered or were seconded from different Coastal, Bomber, Army Co-operation and Training Commands to make up the shortages of pilots and aircrew.

Also, two Fleet Air Arm squadrons (Nos. 804 and 808) were placed under Dowding's command to help bolster his fighter force. Additionally, a total of 56 Fleet Air Arm pilots found themselves posted to RAF Fighter Command squadrons.

In these instances, a brief course at an Operational Training Unit to familiarise the pilot on the type of aircraft he would fly operationally preceded his posting to an RAF fighter squadron.

Right Desperately short of pilots during the Battle of Britain, RAF Fighter Command drew in pilots from other commands, along with 56 Royal Navy pilots from the Fleet Air Arm. This is Sub Lieutenant Arthur Blake who flew Spitfires with 19 Squadron from RAF Duxford during the battle. He was shot down and killed over Chelmsford on 29 October 1940.

BATTLE OF BRITAIN IN COLOUR

The 'Big Name' Aces

Names like Bader, Stanford Tuck and Malan are synonymous with the Battle of Britain. That these men survived the war with impressive 'kill' scores, tales of derring-do and chests full of medals has resulted in enduring fame, while countless books and accounts about their deeds adds much colour to their individual stories. Later, they became iconic figures. Despite a rather unbalanced focus on individual achievements, their stories do much to foster wider interest in the Battle of Britain and no publication of this nature would be complete without paying homage.

Group Captain Adolph 'Sailor' Malan
DSO & Bar, DFC & Bar, Croix de Guerre (Belg), War Cross (Czech), Legion d'honneur (Fra), Croix de Guerre (Fra)

A South African, he was better known as 'Sailor' Malan, the squadron commander who led 74 Squadron during the Battle of Britain.

Malan had been a naval cadet during the 1920s, and this led to his nickname of 'Sailor'. In 1935 he signed-up with the RAF and joined 74 Squadron in 1936, where he rose through the ranks to eventually command the squadron on Spitfires in 1940.

Malan was an aggressive fighter pilot and acknowledged tactician, writing a guide for fighter pilots: 'Ten of my Rules for Air Fighting'.

He finished his fighter career in 1941 with 27 destroyed, 7 shared destroyed and 2 unconfirmed, 3 'probables' and 16 damaged. At the time, he was the RAF's leading ace.

He died on 17 September 1963.

NOTE: The ranks given are those which these officers held at retirement, not ranks held during the Battle of Britain.

Group Captain Sir Douglas Bader
CBE, DSO & Bar, DFC & Bar

Arguably the best-known of all Battle of Britain pilots, Bader lost his legs in a flying accident during low-level aerobatics in 1931. Invalided out, and fitted with artificial legs, Bader pestered to re-join the RAF on the declaration of war and was eventually granted a flying test, which he passed.

Initially flying Spitfires on 19 and then 222 Squadrons at Duxford, Bader was eventually promoted to Squadron Leader and given command of 242 Squadron, a Hurricane unit mostly comprising Canadian pilots.

Douglas Bader became a controversial figure but was promoted to lead the Tangmere Wing in 1941, but was brought down over France and captured in August 1941. He claimed this was the result of colliding with a Messerschmitt 109, but subsequent research indicates that friendly fire was more likely the cause. After capture, escape attempts eventually resulted in incarceration in Colditz Castle.

His biography 'Reach for the Sky' by Paul Brickhill became a best seller, and it was followed by a film of the same name with Kenneth More playing lead.

His final score was 20 destroyed, 4 shared, 6 and 1 shared 'probables' and 11 damaged.

After the war, Douglas Bader did a great deal of work for the disabled and was conferred a Knighthood for this work in 1976.

He died on 5 September 1982.

Wing Commander Robert 'Bob' Stanford Tuck*
DSO, DFC & Two Bars, AFC, DFC (United States)

Like Malan, Tuck had started out as a naval cadet and entered the RAF in 1935, joining his first fighter squadron in 1936.

Flying Spitfires with 92 Squadron, Tuck saw action over Dunkirk and later, with the same squadron, during the early part of the Battle of Britain. However, in September he was posted to command 257 Squadron flying Hurricanes.

He led the squadron until the summer of 1941, when he was promoted to lead the Duxford Wing, although by late that year he commanded the Biggin Hill Wing. Unfortunately, that leadership ended on 28 January 1942 when he was hit by anti-aircraft fire and had to crash-land near Boulogne.

After many adventures as POW, and subsequently, he arrived back in Britain in 1945, retiring from the RAF in 1949.

His final score was 27 destroyed, 1 and 1 shared unconfirmed destroyed, 6 'probables' and 6 and 1 shared damaged.

His biography by Larry Forrester, 'Fly for your Life', is a colourful account of his many escapes and escapades.

He died on 5 May 1987.

*Officially Robert Roland Stanford Tuck, with Tuck as his family name and Stanford as one of his given names, he later changed his family name to Stanford Tuck, the name by which he is better known.

THE FEW

A few of the 'Few'

In contrast to the well-known pilots from the Battle of Britain, the 'glamour boys', there were those who never became household names. These were men who fought in the summer of 1940, but who often did not survive to see either the resultant success they helped achieve in the Battle of Britain, or ultimate victory in the Second World War.

In death came virtual anonymity, and none of the laurels and adulation subsequently heaped on the more famous survivors. But all played their part.

The men shown here were among those who never lived to tell their tales.

"Marvellous Machines"

Sergeant Dennis Noble was an ordinary boy from Retford, Nottinghamshire, who had long been fascinated by aircraft and flying, although an apprenticeship and training led him to ultimately become the chief radio engineer for a company called Masto Ltd of Watford before he was 20. However, a member of the RAFVR pre-war, he was already learning to fly when war broke out and he was called up. Completing his training, he was posted to 43 Squadron on 3 August 1940. On 13 August, his Hurricane was hit and damaged and he had to make an emergency landing at Tangmere. On 19 August he wrote to his sister, telling her of the incident, but saying:

"I still fly the Hurricane and would not change for anything. I think that they are marvellous machines and would tackle anything in one."

Less than a month after joining his squadron, Dennis Noble was shot down over Hove, East Sussex, by a Messerschmitt 109. His Hurricane dived vertically into the ground, crashing into a street. (Note: This portrait photograph is one the family had colour tinted in 1940.)

Lost On First Sortie

Born in Concepcion, Chile, 21-year-old Flying Officer Arthur Rose-Price, the brother of actor Dennis Price, joined the RAF in 1937. A flying instructor, he transferred to RAF Fighter Command in August 1940, joining 501 Squadron at Kenley on 2 September, and flying a Hurricane to Gravesend for his first operational sortie that afternoon.

Over Dungeness, Arthur was shot down and no trace of him was found. His operational life as a fighter pilot had lasted much less than an hour. Fellow pilots recalled his unpacked sports car parked outside the Officer's Mess, complete with squash racquets. They did not even get to know his name. (Note: From a portrait painting commissioned by the family.)

Captured Pole

Pilot Officer Witold Glowacki arrived in Britain in January 1940. After training, he served on two other fighter squadrons before joining 605 Squadron on 31 August. He saw action throughout early September and shot down one Messerschmitt 110 and damaged another. On 24 September, he chased a Dornier 17-Z from Beachy Head to the French coast with Flight Lieutenant Ian Muirhead, but they were 'bounced' by Messerschmitt 109s and Glowacki was shot down.

Pictures were taken of the captured pilot, wounded, sitting on the wing of his wrecked Hurricane. The 26-year-old died later that day after receiving a tetanus injection from his captors.

"For A Moment In Time"

Flight Lieutenant Hugh Beresford, the son of a Leicestershire rector, was a pre-war officer in the RAF who had seen a variety of postings and appointments since joining the service in 1935. By May 1940, he had been posted to the Hurricane-equipped 257 Squadron as commander of 'A' Flight. He had seen action throughout the Battle of Britain, claiming one aircraft probably shot down, one shared victory and a Messerschmitt 110 destroyed on 31 August.

On 7 September, he was involved in the interception of the heavy attacks on London and was shot down and posted 'missing'. He was discovered in the wreck of his Hurricane on the Isle of Sheppey in 1979. At his military funeral, Air Chief Marshal Sir Christopher Foxley-Norris said:

"For a moment in time, he held the whole future of civilisation in his two sweaty palms and he did not let it go."

Hugh Beresford is pictured here on his wedding day, along with his bride, Pat.

THE BATTLE OF BRITAIN IN COLOUR

The Sergeant Pilots

The Sergeant pilots of RAF Fighter Command have often been described as the backbone of the fighter force in 1940. In many ways, they were. Very often, they were pre-war 'regular' pilots and, typically, were some of the most experienced pilots on the squadron. It was not unusual for many to achieve quite high 'kill' scores, to be decorated for gallantry or to eventually be commissioned as officers. Many of those who survived, later went on to become senior officers in the RAF.

Here, we look at the stories of just a handful of those sergeant pilots of 1940. The RAF's Battle of Britain was certainly not fought by just an officer elite.

Upside-down and well Alight

A Sergeant pilot who had joined 41 Squadron in June 1940, John McAdam was already one of its more experienced pilots when the battle began.

On 7 September 1940, John McAdam claimed one Dornier 17-Z and another 'probable' - along with a Messerschmitt 109 probably destroyed. After attacking the Messerschmitt 109, another attacked him, putting several cannon shells into his Spitfire and setting it on fire.

John explained what happened in a letter home:

"I tried to land in a field 150 yards long, but smoke and flames made it difficult.

"I side-slipped and went into a slight dive from 50 ft. I pulled my knees up and put my head between them and at 10 ft or 5 ft from the ground I pulled the stick back. The machine came down tail first, the hood shut tight, and the aircraft finished upside-down. I was unhurt, but how to get out? The machine was well alight and was extremely uncomfortable. I was about to pull out my pistol to shoot myself when a civilian came along. I told him to get an axe and release me. He brought a chopper and stripped the side of the cockpit for me to get out. Two minutes later, the aircraft exploded."

He was shot down again on 23 September. Baling out over Dover, he was rescued from the sea unhurt but had another escape on 12 October when his engine cut on take-off and he crashed between some houses.

His luck finally ran out when he was shot down of Dover and killed on 20 February 1941.

Above Sergeant John McAdam sits astride the engine cowling of his 41 Squadron Spitfire in the autumn of 1940. He survived two close calls when flying Spitfires, but was eventually shot down and killed over the English Channel in February 1941.
Below Sergeant Cyril Babbage was lucky to escape unharmed when he made an emergency landing on the South Downs on 12 October 1940, his Spitfire overturning.

THE FEW

Finding 'Cock Sparrow'

Sergeant Hugh Ellis, like Sergeant Scott (see over) was another of those sergeant pilots who achieved much in a short career as a fighter pilot, but then disappeared. Literally.

Serving in Squadron Leader Peter Townsend's 85 Squadron, and flying Hurricanes, Townsend remarked on Ellis' cheerful nature and disposition – calling him 'Cock Sparrow'.

Already on the way to probably becoming an 'ace', this skilful fighter pilot had downed at least two enemy aircraft, probably destroyed a Messerschmitt 109 and damaged a Messerschmitt 110 by the time he was shot down over Battle, East Sussex, on 29 August. Baling out, he survived this episode and almost immediately returned to operations.

Just days later, Sergeant Ellis was shot down in the Kenley area, during an air battle on 1 September, and was posted as missing in action. Then, in 1992, his remains were uncovered in the wreck of a Hurricane at Chelsfield, Kent. He was buried with full military honours at Brookwood Military Cemetery the following year.

At his funeral, Group Captain Peter Townsend, his CO, sent a wreath of blue, yellow and white flowers: blue for the sky he loved, yellow for his shock of blonde hair and white for the flying overalls he wore. Indeed, as the white-overalled fighter pilot of 1940, wearing a Mae-West with its distinctive 'Saint' emblem, Sergeant Ellis' face had graced newspapers and magazines during 1940. Forgotten, he was remembered again by the news media in 1992 and 1993.

Top right Sergeant Hugh Ellis, a Hurricane pilot with 85 Squadron based at RAF Croydon, disappeared on 1 September 1940. No trace of him was found until 1992.
Above Sergeant Cyril Babbage of 602 Squadron is welcomed ashore on the beach at Bognor Regis on 26 August 1940 after being shot down by a Messerschmitt 109 and rescued from the sea by rowing boat. Here, he is having a cigarette lit for him by the local constabulary - his own cigarettes having turned into a soggy mush in his uniform jacket! The 'glare' was introduced on the original photograph to hide the fact that the pier has had its central section removed as an anti-invasion measure.

Double Trouble

On 26 August 1940, Spitfire pilot Sergeant Cyril Babbage, flying with 602 Squadron from RAF Westhampnett, was involved in a late afternoon battle over the English Channel near Bognor Regis. Having shot down one Messerschmitt 109 and attacked a German bomber, when he experienced heavy crossfire, his aircraft was then hit by a cannon shell from another Messerschmitt and set on fire. Forced to bale-out, he landed 300 yards from the shore and was rescued by rowing boat.

Later, on 12 October, his Spitfire was hit by return fire from a Junkers 88 off Beachy Head and he attempted a landing, wheels down, in a field at Iford, East Sussex. However, the aircraft ran through a hedge and overturned, although Sergeant Babbage was unharmed. As a consolation, though, he was awarded the Distinguished Flying Medal that same day. He ended the war with a tally of seven aircraft destroyed and one claim shared.

Cyril Babbage remained in the RAF, retiring in 1964 as a Wing Commander. He died in 1977.

THE BATTLE OF BRITAIN IN COLOUR

Above This was the Hurricane in which Sergeant 'Jim' Hallowes made an emergency landing at Amberley, West Sussex, after an 'unexplained' engine failure when taking-off from RAF Tangmere on 20 July 1940.
Left Sergeant Ernest Scott of 222 Squadron standing by his Commanding Officer's Spitfire during the Battle of Britain. The aircraft is showing signs of battle fatigue and considerable wear-and-tear. The pennant on the fuselage side denotes this as the CO's aircraft. Sergeant Scott was posted as missing on 27 September 1940, but was found with his aircraft in 1990.

No Longer 'Missing'

Sergeant Pilot Ernest Scott from Mansfield, Nottinghamshire, a pre-war regular NCO airman, was posted to 222 Squadron, flying Spitfires, in July 1940. He went on to become one of the sergeant pilots of the Battle of Britain who achieved 'ace' status – in other words, five victory claims or more. His first victory score was over a Dornier 17-Z on 3 September, and his last of at least five claims was on the morning of 27 September 1940.

Later that same day, Ernest Scott was shot down over Maidstone by Major Werner Mölders of JG51, becoming the German ace's 41st victim. Initially posted as missing in action, and with no known grave, evidence came to light during the 1970s indicating that his Spitfire had crashed at Hollingbourne in Kent, and that the wreckage was deeply buried in a farmer's field with Sergeant Scott entombed inside.

Appeals to HRH Prince Charles by the pilot's sister in 1990 resulted in an RAF team excavating the crash site and recovering the Spitfire, along with the mortal remains of Ernest Scott.

When Sergeant Scott had shot down a Messerschmitt 109 on the morning of 27 September, it is noted in the squadron records at The National Archives, Kew, that this pilot had not had time to complete a combat report before being killed later that day. When the RAF found his body in 1990, that Combat Report was found tucked inside Ernest's flying boot.

Sergeant Scott was buried with full military honours at Manston in 1991, the station commander of RAF Manston remarking:

"Sergeant Scott did not want or seek to lose his life. But he was willing to risk it for things that matter. It was taken from him at the threshold of achievement. But in his short span he did more than most of us. It is our honour to recognise that today.

Sergeant Pilot Ernest Scott is no longer missing."

Bomber 'Killer'

Sometimes, the enemy was not only the Luftwaffe. Sometimes, it was the weather. Sometimes, it was pilot error. And other times it could be mechanical failure. And for Sergeant Herbert 'Jim' Hallowes, a Hurricane pilot with 43 Squadron, it was almost a mechanical failure which was his undoing.

Hallowes, a pre-war pilot, had already seen action in France where he had earned a DFM but with the onset of the Battle of Britain, there was no let-up in the pace of things. Mostly, throughout July, it was the odd skirmish or engagement with lone bombers, but on 20 July, Hallowes had taken-off from RAF Tangmere at 07.40 hours for a patrol when, almost immediately, the oil pressure dropped and the engine seized. With a stationary propeller, little altitude to play with no chance of baling-out so low, he selected a field at Amberley, near Arundel in West Sussex, and executed a near-perfect belly landing in a meadow – the landing only marred by smashing off his tail wheel on an obstacle. Things could well have had a more serious outcome.

The aircraft had previously flown on a night patrol between 04.25 and 06.15 that day, and it transpired much later that the aircraft had simply not been topped up with oil. Essential on the Rolls-Royce Merlin.

That morning, the NCO in charge of the flight line, 'Chiefy' Savage, took a party out to the crashed Hurricane with a drum of used oil and announced to the Army guard that he needed to put some oil in the tank to prevent the engine corroding! Later, the engineer officer was mystified as to why the engine had seized. Nobody was any the wiser. Not even 'Jim' Hallowes.

Many years later, long after 'Jim' Hallowes had passed away in 1987, one of the ground party owned-up. When asked why he had never told him, he replied: "I was too scared to!"

Sergeant Hallowes was the second highest scorer against Lufwaffe bombers during the Battle of Britain, achieving 9 ½ victories over bomber aircraft. He retired from the RAF as a Wing Commander, holding the DFC and DFM and with a total score of 17 victories, plus two shared.

Brothers in Arms

One of the enduring tragedies of the Battle of Britain: the story of two brothers who flew side-by-side as Hurricane pilots in the same squadron during the battle.

For any family, the loss of loved ones during war is always a terrible blow. And during the Battle of Britain, that was not any more so than it was at any other point of the war. But for Battle of Britain pilot Antony Fisher, the loss of his brother, Basil, was the most shattering personal tragedy imaginable. Not least of all because Basil was Antony's only close family, but also that they flew Hurricanes, together, and on the same squadron.

Antony Fisher, and his younger brother Basil, were born in 1915 and 1917 respectively. Their father, George, had been killed by a Turkish sniper in Palestine just after Basil's birth. Thus, they never knew their father.

The boys went on to be educated at Eton College where Basil excelled at sports. As captain of the Eton College cricket first eleven, he played against the rival public school, Harrow, at Lords. Later, the brothers graduated from Trinity College, Cambridge, where they had joined the University Air Squadron and learned to fly. Both were commissioned into the RAFVR in 1938.

In the immediate pre-war years, Basil and Antony regularly flew their own private aircraft around Europe. Sadly, their Mother Janet died just before the war and this event doubtless drew the brothers ever closer together. From a family perspective, they just had each other.

The 'Shooting War'

On the outbreak of war, the brothers were called to full-time service, completing mandatory training before joining an operational squadron. Both were posted to 111 Squadron: Antony in March 1940 as a Pilot Officer and Basil in May as a Flying Officer. Up until now, war had not really come to the squadron in any sense of it being a 'shooting war', but by May 1940 the squadron was operating from RAF Croydon.

Now, things were getting hot for the BEF on the other side of the

Above Basil Fisher (left) and his brother Antony, 1940. They served together as Hurricane pilots on 111 Squadron during the Battle of Britain.

THE BATTLE OF BRITAIN IN COLOUR

English Channel, and for RAF fighter squadrons valiantly trying to provide some protection for the troops on the ground.

Although 111 Squadron were not based in France, its aircraft sometimes operated from French airfields and also participated in patrols covering the Dunkirk evacuations. Often, the squadron flew down from Croydon to operate from RAF Hawkinge. And it was from here, flying over France, that the brothers first had a real taste of battle.

On 6 June, Basil was credited with probably destroying a Messerschmitt 109 near Abbeville while the squadron escorted Blenheims on a bombing raid. Although 111 Squadron had thus seen success, five of the Blenheims were shot down. Also, one of 111 Squadron's pilots baled-out, returning to Croydon wounded in the thigh.

Antony and Basil, though, had returned unscathed from the action, albeit 'blooded' in battle. The war was now a real 'shooting war', and although the evacuation from Dunkirk had since seen a slackening of pace, the fury of the Battle of Britain was about to break.

Head on Attacks

Still based at Croydon, the squadron regularly patrolled the English Channel providing fighter cover for merchant shipping which was increasingly being singled out for attention by the Luftwaffe. And it was over the Channel on 10 July – the day deemed to have seen the start of the Battle of Britain – that 111 Squadron saw frantic action.

In the early afternoon, the squadron engaged 24 Dornier 17s attacking Convoy 'Bread' in an action which cost the squadron its first fatality when Flying Officer Thomas Higgs collided head-on with a Dornier 17-Z of 3/KG2 off Dungeness. The tragic accident was an inevitable consequence of the squadron's terrifying tactic of attacking enemy formations head-on to 'scatter' the aircraft and put the bombers off their aim. Two other Hurricanes returned to Croydon damaged, one of them piloted by Flying Officer Michael Ferriss who would later that evening be joined by Basil when the pair were sent to investigate 'unidentified aircraft' as the squadron patrolled over Hawkinge.

Finding the 'unidentified aircraft' were Spitfires, Basil and Michael turned to fly back and re-join 111 Squadron to resume the patrol. Unfortunately, the Spitfires misidentified the Hurricanes as hostile and, unseen, they crept up behind Basil's Hurricane and opened fire, sending bullets through both wings and the petrol tank and ripping holes in the tail plane. With a damaged Hurricane, and considerably shaken, Basil limped home with his bullet scarred fighter.

Held his Fire

Throughout July, the pace quickened for 111 Squadron, but it was on the 28th that Basil was engaged in another action over the Channel. The Intelligence Report of 111 Squadron takes up the story:

'Squadron were ordered to patrol Maidstone at 20,000 ft and afterwards diverted to mid-channel.

At 15.15 hours, Sgt Robinson, followed Plt Off Wilson in a steep dive towards an enemy aircraft which he identified as a Heinkel 59 seaplane. Plt Off Wilson circled the enemy as he perceived a red cross on the fin, a large red cross on the fuselage and another red cross the position of which he did not note.

THE FEW

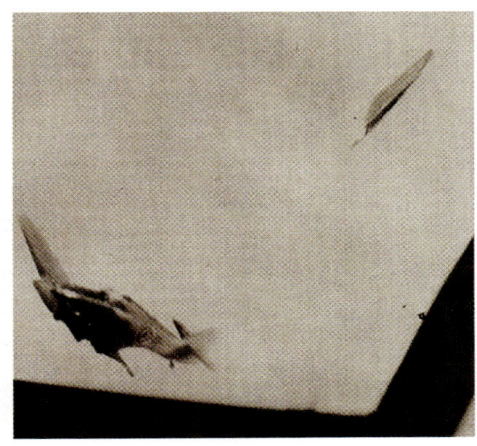

Top This Junkers 88 was brought down by 111 Squadron at Earnley in the air battle over Selsey on 15 August 1940, just a very short distance from where Basil met his death.
Left Flying Officer Michael Ferriss standing by the caravan which served as 111 Squadron's dispersal office. His Hurricane is parked beyond, along with one of the squadron pilot's cars behind the caravan.
Above left Basil Fisher's well cared-for grave at St John's Church Cemetery, Eton.
Above right This grainy photograph supposedly depicts the aftermath of the collision between Pilot Officer Higgs' Hurricane and a Dornier 17-Z on 10 July 1940. However, it is likely that it is a photograph which was faked by the German Propaganda Kompanie.

The enemy aircraft was coloured silver, but Sgt Robinson only noticed a black swastika on a red roundel on the fin and gave a five second burst on half deflection at 200 yards. Enemy aircraft dived, burst into flames and struck the sea sending up a large column of smoke 10 miles north-west of Boulogne.

At about 15.20 hours, Fg Off Ferriss and Fg Off Fisher observed a silver coloured aircraft when patrolling over ships west of Boulogne. The pair dived on this aircraft which was riding on the water and Fg Off Ferriss riddled it with bullets from 800 yds closing to point blank range. No return fire was noticed.

Fg Off Fisher, after a short burst, held his fire as he saw red cross markings on the fuselage of the aircraft which was a Heinkel 59.'

The Heinkel 59 Basil spared had landed to assist the other downed seaplane, although two of the crew were wounded.

Parachute on Fire

Into August, battle continued apace for the Fisher brothers. And with little respite. Although the squadron was gradually building a tally of victories, it was also taking casualties. By now, every pilot in RAF Fighter Command was essentially living on borrowed time. On 15 August, that time ran out for Basil. And, to an extent, it did for Antony, too.

Scrambled in the late afternoon to patrol Shoreham, the squadron were then sent off to engage a formation approaching Selsey Bill. Here, the Hurricanes found a mass of Junkers 88s, escorted by Messerschmitt 109s and 110s. Together, Basil and Antony, attacked and destroyed a Junkers 88 in a unique victory for RAF Fighter Command: an enemy aircraft shot down by two brothers. But it was something of a pyrrhic victory. In the melee, Basil's Hurricane was hit and set on fire.

Baling-out of the burning fighter, Basil fell away, but his parachute was on fire; the horrifying spectacle seen by the whole squadron, including Antony. As the blazing Hurricane slammed into farm cowsheds at Selsey, Basil fell to his death nearby. Making matters worse for the squadron, on return to Croydon they found it badly bombed and ground crew members killed and injured. The personal belongings of Basil and Antony had also been destroyed.

Shattered by witnessing the awful death of his brother, the squadron diary noted:

'Combat report for Pilot Officer Fisher is not available as he is now on sick leave suffering from a nervous breakdown'

The very next day, 16 August, Basil's friend, Flying Officer Michael Ferriss, was killed over Kent after colliding head-on with a Dornier 17-Z.

Basil was laid to rest in Eton on 20 August 1940, just as Prime Minister Winston Churchill was delivering his *Never in the field of human conflict* speech in the Commons.

Eton was where Basil had been happiest, and it was the only place Antony could think to have him buried. Today, his grave is maintained by Eton College staff and pupils.

Unable to return to operations, Antony invented a device to train fighter pilots in gunnery (the 'Fisher Trainer') and was awarded the AFC. A successful businessman, he was knighted for his work defending freedom just four weeks before his death in 1988. ■

THE BATTLE OF BRITAIN IN COLOUR

An RAF airman inspects the severed wingtip of Pilot Officer 'Mac' MacKenzie's Hurricane after he had made a force landing near Folkestone on 7 October 1940. The damage had been caused by MacKenzie deliberately knocking the tail off a Messerschmitt 109 in close combat.

BRITISH AIRCRAFT LOSSES

Incident Report

Date .... 7 October 1940
Location .... Folkestone, Kent
Aircraft .... Hurricane, 501 Squadron
Pilot: . Pilot Officer K W 'Mac' MacKenzie

"I spotted about eight Messerschmitt 109s coming across the coast from the east about 1,000 ft above me. With ample speed in hand, I pulled up into a loop under them and half rolled off onto the last three when a fourth came into sight a little ahead and slightly above me. Obviously, they had not seen me. He was so close that I gave him a quick burst in the belly from about 200 yards, noting many strikes around the radiator and under the cockpit.

"He took violent evasive action and half rolled into a dive and nearly hit me in doing so. It took me a few seconds to recover and dive after him, by which time he had drawn away to about 800 or 900 yards with glycol streaming from his radiator. I pulled maximum boost and began to catch him as he dived towards Folkestone.

"Passing close to the harbour, I closed right up and opened fire at 100 yards. I could not see any direct result and my guns went silent after two or three seconds. What to do? He was down to about 180 knots and losing height but flying straight and level with no evasive action whatsoever. We got to within about 80 or 100 ft of the sea and were watched – as I later discovered – by AA gunners and others around Folkestone.

"I was determined that he shouldn't get away and having got him to this state he had to be finished off quickly and before we were too close to France. It was as if we were doing formation practice. But with a difference!

"I flew alongside him, round him, signalled him to ditch; he never looked up but seemed slumped over the control column. I lowered my undercarriage, thinking to knock his tail off with it. But it slowed me so much that I lost ground. Raising it, I got along his port side and, in an impulse, smacked my starboard wing down onto his port tail plane. It broke off, and he plunged into the sea as I pulled up to the left as three or four feet of my wing tip flew up into the air. He partially sank without opening the canopy.

"The pair of Messerschmitts with him were now onto me. A persistent pair, who hit me in the radiator and the armour plate behind me.

"As I approached Folkestone, they broke off and I managed to pull up and crash land on the hill immediately north of the town. Foolishly, I had undone my harness for a quick exit and on landing I was jerked forward onto the gunsight, splitting my jaw and smashing some front teeth.

"I was taken to naval sick quarters in the town, where I found I could put my tongue out through the hole in my face.

A Navy doctor stitched me up, although he had been called from a lunchtime session and was…well… quite nicely, thank you! He approached me with a large curved needle and a wicked gleam in his eye. I watched his wobbly hand with great trepidation, but he did a magnificent job and pierced my chin four or five times in quick succession. Three plain and two purl, I thought!" ■

Kenneth 'Mac' MacKenzie, DFC, AFC

'SPITFIRE SNOBBERY'?

Just before Pilot Officer 'Mac' MacKenzie sent the German fighter into the Channel by knocking off its tail plane with his Hurricane's wingtip, he shot down another Messerschmitt 109 which fell into the sea:

"We took off in squadron strength, Squadron Leader Hogan leading, to patrol Sevenoaks in company with 605 Squadron at 20,000 ft. First, we were vectored south and then east. When flying east, the CO saw two Messerschmitt 109s in front of us and below and going south east. These two split up as we broke to attack them and we also got ready to have a go at another larger formation which appeared below us to the east.

"In the ensuing dogfights, I was attacked but got clear and followed the CO down as he attacked a Messerschmitt 109 which entered cloud. I broke above the cloud at 6,000 to 6,500 ft, being sure he would come out on a reciprocal course, or certainly not straight ahead!

"In fact, he came out at right angles and turned towards the sea. With superb height advantage, I half rolled after him giving the Hurricane everything it had got.

"Closing fast from astern, I hit him in the radiator and under the engine from 150 yards. He slowed rapidly, lost height, and ditched off Hythe.

"I watched the aircraft sink and the pilot get out. With activity high above me, and some ammunition left, I climbed to 23,000 ft. Hearing the controller reporting enemy positions, I decided to patrol between Dover and Folkestone, but keeping a good watch on my own tail."

The pilot who 'Mac' had seen get out of his sinking Messerschmitt was Leutnant Erich Meyer of 2/JG51 who had been escorting bomb-carrying Messerschmitt 109s to London. On interrogation, Meyer insisted he had been shot down by a Spitfire.

In fact, he had certainly been engaged by Hurricanes. Meyer's insistence that he had been brought down by a Spitfire was perhaps a case of 'Spitfire snobbery', where Luftwaffe pilots perceived the Spitfire as far superior to the Hurricane. Thus, if shot down, they often maintained their victor had been the 'better' Spitfire!

Many years later, though, both 'Mac' and Erich were re-acquainted with the events of 7 October 1940, events which had so nearly claimed both their lives.

In July 1976, a team of divers working for the Brenzett Aeronautical Museum in Kent, managed to raise the wreck of a Messerschmitt 109 from the English Channel off Hythe. This turned out to be the aircraft ditched by Leutnant Meyer on 7 October 1940.

Photo: Leutnant Erich Meyer being carried shoulder-high after an earlier victory during the Battle of Britain.

THE BATTLE OF BRITAIN IN COLOUR

Last Letter Home

Letters from loved ones away on active service were always welcome, but were inevitably read with huge elements of worry for the safety of the sender. Such letters would sometimes gain added degrees of poignancy.

David Stewart Harrison was typical of the majority of pilots making up RAF Fighter Command during the Battle of Britain. From a middle-class family, David initially joined the RAFVR as a trainee pilot on 16 January 1939; a part time airman, keen to fly and to 'do his bit'.

As war loomed, Volunteer Reserve airmen were called-up on 1 September 1939, with David undertaking his training before a posting to 238 Squadron, flying Hurricanes, at RAF Middle Wallop on 12 September. In between, he had found time to marry Ruth Sharpe, a widow.

In the short time he was with 238 Squadron, David wrote home to his wife (whom he called Judy) regularly. On 26 September he wrote:

"Dear Judy

I have been away for a day as I had to force land with a bullet in the engine. Managed to land in a field with three haystacks and some logs in it but all was well, machine undamaged. The whole squadron dived into a formation of 27 Heinkel 111s and 20 110s. I had one Heinkel in my sights and fired a long burst with no apparent effect. It lagged behind and was shot down by another Hurricane as my cockpit was full of smoke and steam, but the engine kept turning although getting hotter and hotter. It was very exciting missing the haystacks!

"A farmer's wife gave me lunch and introduced me to the family. It was a cheddar cheese making farm, there were whole rows of cheeses in a loft, and real butter and fresh milk for tea. Why wasn't I a farmer?

The squadron attacked the formation for miles and shot down 8. No one was hurt at all. Not even me!"

David ended his letter saying:

"I must finish now as we are called to readiness soon and I must catch the post. Think of me, won't you, and be sure I am thinking of you all the time.

Your loving husband,
David"

It was his last letter home.

Two days later, on 28 September, Pilot Officer David Harrison was shot down over The Solent, his Hurricane crashing into the sea. On 9 October, his body was washed ashore on Brighton beach. He was later buried in St Andrew's Churchyard, Tangmere.

His life on the front line lasted just two weeks. ■

Above Pilot Officer David Stewart Harrison, 238 Squadron, 1940.
Top David Harrison's poignant last letter home along with his wallet and identity disc which were found on his body when he was washed ashore on Brighton beach – a sad reminder of a life cut short. The wallet and its contents show signs of water damage, his body having been in the sea for nearly two weeks.

THE FEW

Unconquerable of Spirit

Without the men and women of the RAF who served on the ground, the pilots and aircrew would never have got into the air. And yet their part in the Battle of Britain, their heroism and their sacrifice, is largely eclipsed by the deeds of the fliers they served.

Without exception, those who flew and fought in the Battle of Britain heaped nothing but praise on the men who kept them in the air: the fitters who dealt with the engines, the riggers on the airframes and the armourers on guns and ammunition. Alongside these men, of course, there were the other myriad trades keeping a fighter squadron going: the clerks, drivers, parachute packers, cooks, telephonists, medical orderlies and scores of other occupations. All of them integral and essential to the effective running of fighter squadrons and aerodromes. And all of them equally exposed to the risk of air attack. However, it was the fitter, the rigger and the armourer with whom individual pilots established particular close familiarities. For it was these men who looked after the pilots' aircraft, keeping them in tip-top condition, and helping keep 'their' pilot safe. It was a unique bond.

The fitters, riggers and armourers, then, were key ground personnel on fighter squadrons, and one man from each category would be assigned to an individual aircraft and pilot. The fitter would have been responsible for issues relating to the engine and its maintenance, as well as looking after ancillary equipment, re-fuelling, re-oiling etc. Meanwhile, the Rigger would have responsibility for the airframe including basic running repairs, replacing oxygen cylinders, ensuring the tyres were in good order and properly inflated, keeping the canopy and windscreen spotlessly clean, patching the doped canvas patches over the gun ports and helping the pilot strap in etc.

As might be expected, the armourer was responsible for both the maintenance of the aircraft weapons and for re-arming between sorties. He would also be responsible for the Gun Camera (if fitted) and the removal and replacement of exposed film cassettes.

Issues relating to the wireless equipment, or other electrical systems, would be dealt with by a specialist electrical tradesman, or 'Sparks', although there would not be a dedicated wireless specialist per aircraft. Between them, the three key airmen formed a team that revolved around 'their' aircraft and 'their' pilot.

However, it is important to recognise that it was not just NCOs and 'other ranks' who took the brunt on the ground, or that non-flying personnel among the officer cadre were not in harm's way, too.

Above Although taken just after the official period of the Battle of Britain, this original colour photograph encapsulates the scene repeated countless times during 1940 as the fitter, rigger and armourer swarm over a Spitfire at RAF Hornchurch after it returned from a sortie. Pilots discuss the action they have just been involved in, as a wireless mechanic deals with the wireless in the fuselage hatch.

THE BATTLE OF BRITAIN IN COLOUR

Right An armourer serving with 19 Squadron at RAF Duxford feeds belted rounds into the wing ammunition boxes of one of the squadron Spitfires. Empty boxes were taken out of the wings and replaced with replenished boxes between sorties.

Bitter and Relentless Attacks

At RAF Hornuchurch in Essex, right alongside the River Thames and beneath the eastern air approaches to London, the Station Commander was Group Captain Cecil 'Boy' Bouchier, KBE, CB, DFC, who was a fighter pilot veteran of the First World War, but now occupied a ground posting.

In February 1941, Bouchier made a BBC wireless broadcast about his experiences at Hornchurch. For security reasons, his identity, the name of his fighter station or any mention of casualties was not revealed:

"With the 4th June, the Dunkirk days were over. What a difference the complete collapse of France, which followed, meant to us. Now we were faced with the enemy a few miles across the water, and rapidly occupying aerodromes all along the French and Belgian coasts.

"From these bases—from June to the beginning of August—he concentrated his attacks on our shipping. Often my squadrons were engaging odds of anything up to ten to one, and rarely less than five to one. But in six weeks, fighters from my station added a further one hundred and thirty-five enemy aircraft destroyed, together with another sixty 'probables' to their score.

"And then, suddenly, in mid-August, the Hun - for about a month - launched bitter and relentless attacks against our fighter aerodromes. During this short period, we added another one hundred and twenty-five destroyed, and, from the air, the Thames Estuary and Kent could be seen strewn with his wreckage.

"I hope I'm not giving you the impression that all this was "just too easy"—it wasn't. Here and there, we had to "take a bit" ourselves. I well remember the days when his bombers got through . . . and fairly blew blazes out of my station—on one occasion twice in one day, until the whole place was rocking. I remember thinking after each attack how incredible it was that so many bombs could fall all together—produce such an inferno of noise—blot out the station and aerodrome with their black and yellow smoke, in so short a space of time . . . and yet, when the smoke cleared, do so little real damage. But then, we were always a lucky station.

"I remember every man and woman turning to and filling in the hundreds of craters, rushing round in circles organising the labour—rounding up steam rollers from near and far. I remember, too, the fabulous bills that came to me afterwards for the free beer which I had promised . . . but it was well worth it. We were never out of action for a single day.

"I like to remember with a grateful heart what a privilege it has been to serve and live amongst the people of my station. Of the happy spirit that permeates my station—and all those unsung airmen and airwomen who have worked so unceasingly—so uncomplainingly, day and night to keep the airscrews turning - their loyalty and confidence in me made my work such a joy.

"They, along with the pilots, were unconquerable of spirit."

Although Bouchier's words were very

'Royal Air Force bravery during the Battle of Britain was not exclusively the domain of pilots and aircrew.'

much aimed at boosting public morale, they nevertheless painted a worthy picture of the 'forgotten many' on the ground.

Risk of Air Attack

For the most part, the ground crew were up and at work in the open air, long before the pilots arrived at the dispersal points, to ready the aircraft and hand them over to their pilots. Then, their role became key in getting the aircraft started and quickly away in the event of any call to action – whether that be a patrol or

THE FEW

Above Aircraftman E S Mulholland, a fitter with 615 Squadron, admires his handiwork of hastily applied red-doped canvas repair patches on the bullet-holed fuselage of 'his' Hurricane, P2801, KW -T. This aircraft would eventually carry Sergeant Derek Halton to his death during an air battle on 15 August 1940. Mulholland described the damaged Hurricane as: "...like a patchwork quilt!"

Left The fighter pilot's trusty trio: fitter, rigger and armourer. The aircraft and men are of 609 Squadron, RAF Middle Wallop.

Above left The waiting game; the Battle of Britain involved much anxious waiting by both pilots and ground crew. Here, a pilot of 609 Squadron discusses technical points with a group of ground personnel in a dispersal 'E' pen which protected aircraft from air attack. An example of a pen under attack can be seen on page 69. The banked sides held air raid shelters for the ground crew.

a scramble. And while the aircraft were away, there would be an anxious wait; would their pilot come back safely, would he have shot anything down and what state would the aircraft be in? It was an anxious wait which would sometimes be filled with a game of cricket or football, but with ears permanently attuned for the distant sound of returning aircraft.

On return from sorties, the ground crew would anxiously enquire of their pilot if there had been any snags and would seek to rectify them during the turn-around. He would also be excitedly asking: "Any joy sir?" – keen to know if 'his' pilot and 'his' aircraft had scored any victories. They were, after all, a team.

If an aircraft were to be declared unserviceable due to a fault, or because of damage, the Flight Sergeant (colloquially called 'Chiefy') in charge would make any decision as to whether to pull the aircraft from the flight line, but major decisions regarding more serious repairs and rectifications resting with the squadron Engineering Officer. Ordinarily, though, the aircraft was quickly turned around so that it was ready for immediate action once more. Almost before the propeller had stopped turning, and before the pilot had unstrapped, the ground crews were swarming over the fighter, unbuttoning panels and replenishing fuel and ammunition. There was not a second to be wasted. And all the while, there was the risk of air attack. On occasions, the scramble take-offs or turn-arounds were carried out in the face of enemy action, with the ground personnel working in tin helmets and eschewing the air raid shelters - when everyone else had taken cover – just to get their pilots into the air.

Inevitably, there were sometimes casualties during such attacks and at RAF Biggin Hill on 30 August 1940, 30 ground personnel were killed and 13 wounded while at RAF Hornchurch and RAF Debden a total of six were killed and 12 wounded. All four stations were front-line RAF fighter airfields.

But not all of them were fighter ground crew. And some of them were women

Remarkable Heroism

The RAF's ground personnel who were killed during the Battle of Britain includes three WAAF personnel, and one NAAFI lady, along with several others who were wounded on the ground. Despite perceptions to the contrary, however, which was possibly engendered by the post-bombing airfield scene from the 1969 film 'Battle of Britain', the number of WAAFs killed in air attacks was low. However, the script writer for that film might be forgiven, bearing in mind that in a 1942 HMSO publication, an anonymous WAAF Officer talked of an air

- 145 -

THE BATTLE OF BRITAIN IN COLOUR

A HURRICANE 'ERK' REMEMBERS

As with the pilots who flew them, the men on the ground who serviced Spitfires and Hurricanes became very much attached to 'their' type of aircraft:

"I was an Airman Fitter IIE in 1940, just what we called an 'Erk', serving with 145 Squadron and their Hurricanes at RAF Westhampnett near Chichester – now Goodwood Aerodrome. I was with 'B' Flight.

I hadn't really seen a Spitfire close-up, or had anything to do with them, until 602 Squadron arrived with their aircraft in August. And I wasn't at all impressed.

With considerable reluctance, and a degree of distaste, I had to work on them once because our squadron numbers had been depleted to such an extent there weren't enough Hurricanes to work on.

And I think if we'd had just Spitfires in 1940, we'd have lost!

Do you know, the turn-around time on the ground for Spitfires was so poor that 'Jerry' could not have failed to get us on the deck? The Spitfire I and II took 26 minutes to turn around. That is, a complete service to re-fuel, re-arm, oil, oxygen etc. With the Hurricane, it took us just nine minutes. And that was when we didn't hurry!

No. I was very much a 'Hurricane boy'. Through-and-through."

Eric Marsden (Fitter IIE), 145 Squadron, RAF Westhampnett, 1940.

Above Airmen at RAF Middle Wallop examine bomb craters after an air raid on 14 August 1940. The attack killed three airmen who were killed when the heavy hangar door was blasted onto them as they struggled to close it to protect the aircraft inside. Another airman was injured and three civilians were killed with two injured.
Above left Aircraftman Eric Marsden, left, acquired an impressive trophy for the pilots of 145 Squadron with this tail section of a Heinkel 111 shot down at Selsey on 11 July 1940. The ground crew shared the pride of the pilots in squadron successes.
Left Group Captain Cecil 'Boy' Bouchier, the station commander at RAF Hornchurch in the Battle of Britain. The oil painting was by Thomas Cantrell Dugdale.

raid on a fighter station, is quoted thus:

"*All was now deathly silent. I climbed through debris and round craters back towards the WAAF guardroom. As I drew nearer, there was a smell of escaping gas. The mains had been hit. Another bomb had fallen on the airwomen's trench, burying the women who were sheltering inside.*"

Almost certainly, this must refer to an attack on RAF Biggin Hill during August 1940, in which 39-year-old Aircraftwoman Edna Button of Tasmania and NAAFI lady Mary Cremin were both killed. And there were also instances of remarkable heroism shown by WAAF personnel on RAF airfields and establishments under attack during the Battle of Britain, too.

As we have already seen on page 71, Sergeant Elizabeth Mortimer was awarded the Military Medal for bravery following an attack on RAF Biggin Hill, while at RAF Detling two more WAAFs were awarded the Military Medal for their conduct during an air raid on 13 August 1940. In that instance, Sgt Jean Youle and Corporal Josephine Robins were the recipients. Another WAAF, Corporal Hearn-Davis, was awarded the Military Medal for staying at her post at the Poling Chain Home radar station during a heavy air attack on 18 August 1940. The citation for the WAAF Corporal's MM stating: 'This airwoman displayed courage and devotion to duty of the highest order.'

In addition to the WAAFs, however, Military Medals were also awarded to other airmen on the ground during the Battle of Britain, including two RAF medical orderlies during an air attack at RAF Tangmere on 16 August 1940, to rescue a pilot from his burning Hurricane. In that instance, Corporal George Jones and AC2 Cyril Faulkner were the worthy recipients of the award, the *London Gazette* recording:

-146-

THE FEW

Above right Corporal Josephine Robins, MM. (By Laura Knight)
Above Smoke rises from RAF Tangmere on 16 August 1940 after a devastating attack by Junkers 87 Stukas. It was an attack which resulted in considerable damage and loss of life, as well as the award of two Military Medals and a Military Cross.

'During a heavy attack on an aerodrome, a burning British fighter aircraft landed. Despite heavy bombs which were falling, and enemy machine gunning, Corporal Jones and Aircraftman 2nd Class Faulkner took their ambulance across to the burning aircraft, assisted the pilot from it, extinguished his burning clothing and rendered First Aid treatment. Both airmen displayed calm courage and devotion to duty.'

Meanwhile, at the same airfield during the same attack, ten other ground crew personnel were killed and seven injured, along with three civilians killed. Also at Tangmere, Flying Officer Courtney Willey, the Medical Officer of 601 Squadron, was buried up to his waist in the rubble of the bombed sick bay but carried on with his duties – an act for which he was awarded the Military Cross. Royal Air Force bravery during the Battle of Britain was not exclusively the domain of pilots and aircrew.

Away from RAF Fighter Command airfields, though, other non-flying RAF personnel were either killed or injured and the RAF's Marine Craft branch had two fatalities off the Isle of Wight on 8 August 1940, while Air Sea Rescue Launch HSL 121, operating out of Newhaven, was badly shot-up by German fighters off Brighton on 4 September 1940, when Pilot Officer G L Bateman was hit in the right arm by a bullet.

Later, as another example, 16-year-old Aircraftsman Harry Clack, serving with a Maintenance Unit, was electrocuted at Eaton Socon in Bedfordshire on 25 October 1940, when the crane he was operating to recover a shot down Dornier 215 touched an overhead electric cable.

A Sobering Tally

During the Battle of Britain, a total of 312 RAF ground personnel died and another 451 were wounded in air attacks against airfields, radar installations and other sites.

However, this total did not comprise entirely fighter ground crew, nor was that total made up exclusively of personnel from RAF Fighter Command. Most of them, though, were front-line casualties of the Luftwaffe's assault on RAF or other targets – whether directly or indirectly caused by enemy air action.

Overall, the total of ground personnel casualties presents a sobering tally, especially when compared against combatant aircrew who suffered 535 fatal casualties across the same period, with those killed on the ground being roughly 58% of the total of flying casualties.

Those serving on the ground, or other

COURAGE AND COOLNESS

Bravery in the face of the enemy was frequently exhibited by RAF ground personnel during the Battle of Britain, and a number of officers, NCOs and airmen, as well as WAAF personnel, were decorated for gallantry. Among them was Corporal Josephine Robins:

'Corporal Robins was in a dug-out which received a direct hit during an intense enemy bombing raid. A number of men were killed and two seriously injured. Though dust and fumes filled the shelter, Corporal Robins immediately went to the assistance of the wounded and rendered First Aid. While they were being removed from the demolished dug-out, she fetched a stretcher and stayed with the wounded until they were evacuated. She displayed courage and coolness of a very high order in a position of extreme danger.'
(Citation for the award of Military Medal to Corporal Robins for her bravery at RAF Detling on 13 August 1940. Published in the London Gazette, 20 December 1940.)

in non-flying capacities with the RAF, were equally combatants in the Battle of Britain, their role a key one in ensuring the overall operation of the air defence system. They received no 'Battle of Britain' clasp to their 1939 – 45 Stars, and no special medal. Nevertheless, they deserve recognition echoing the accolades heaped upon them by the pilots and aircrew whom they worked tirelessly to support. ∎

THE BATTLE OF BRITAIN IN COLOUR

Victoria Cross Hero

Only one Victoria Cross was awarded to RAF Fighter Command during the whole of the Second World War. It went to Hurricane pilot Flight Lieutenant James Brindley Nicolson for extraordinary heroism during the Battle of Britain.

In December 1940, the BBC broadcast an anonymous RAF fighter pilot talking about his experiences during the Battle of Britain. That un-named pilot was Flt Lt James Brindley Nicolson who had flown Hurricanes with 249 Squadron from RAF Boscombe Down, and by the time of the broadcast, an announcement had been made in the London Gazette promulgating the award of a Victoria Cross to Nicolson. But for those listening to him telling his story, no connection was made to the recent announcement, or his VC award.

By the middle of August 1940, the Battle of Britain was in full swing and many of the RAF's fighter squadrons had already seen action. Number 249 Squadron, though, had been in the relative backwater of RAF Leconfield, Lincolnshire, before the unit was posted south to Boscombe Down on 14 August. Two days later, over Southampton, the squadron had its first taste of battle.

In the space of a couple of minutes, two Hurricanes were shot down: Pilot Officer Martyn King was killed, Nicolson severely wounded and another Hurricane was damaged. On the 'credit' side, Nicolson claimed one Messerschmitt 110 'probably destroyed', albeit 'inconclusive'.

'Four Big Bangs'

Exactly what happened in that brief engagement, though, has subsequently been subject to some confusion. However, let us look at the transcript of James Nicolson's BBC broadcast:

"That was a glorious day. The sun was shining from a cloudless sky, with hardly a breath of wind anywhere. My squadron was going towards Southampton on patrol at 15,000 ft when I saw three Ju 88 bombers about four miles away flying across our bows.

"I reported this to our squadron leader and he replied, 'Go after them with your section'. I led my section of aircraft round and towards the bombers. We chased hard after them, but when we were about a mile behind, we saw the 88s fly straight into a squadron of Spitfires. I used to fly a Spitfire myself and guessed it was curtains for the three Junkers. I was right. They were all shot down in quick time with no pickings for us. I must confess I was very disappointed for I had never fired at a Hun in my life and was dying to have a crack at them.

"So, we swung round again and started to climb up to 18,000 feet over Southampton to re-join our squadron when suddenly, very close in rapid

BATTLE OF BRITAIN GALLANTRY

Facing page The pilots of 249 Squadron pictured during the Battle of Britain. At this point, James Nicolson was recovering in hospital. The squadron's CO, Squadron Leader John Grandy, is third from right wearing the hat. James Nicolson dictated his combat report to Grandy when in hospital after being shot down.
Right Flight Lieutenant James Brindley Nicolson, VC.

succession, I heard four big bangs. They were the loudest noises I'd ever heard, and they had been made by four cannon shells from a Messerschmitt 110 hitting my machine.

"The first shell tore through the hood over my cockpit and sent splinters into my left eye. One splinter nearly severed my eyelid. I couldn't see through that eye for blood. The second cannon shell struck my spare petrol tank and set it on fire. The third crashed into the cockpit and tore off my tight trouser leg. The fourth shell struck the back of my left shoe, shattering the heel of the shoe and making a mess of my left foot, but I didn't know anything about that until later. Anyway, the effect of these four shells was to make me dive away to the right. Then I started cursing myself for my carelessness. 'What a fool I'd been', I thought. 'What a fool'. "

'Right in my Gun Sight'

Nicolson continued his report with a dramatic account of what happened next:

"I was thinking about jumping when suddenly a Messerschmitt 110 whizzed underneath and got right in my gun sight. Fortunately, no damage had been done to my windscreen or sights and when I was chasing the Junkers, I'd switched everything on, so everything was set for a fight. I pressed the gun button for the Messerschmitt was in nice range.

"He was going like mad, twisting and turning as he tried to get away from my fire, so I pushed the throttle wide open. Both of us went down in a dive. First, he turned left then right, then left and right again. He did three turns to the right and finally a fourth turn to the left. I remember shouting out loud at him: 'I'll teach you some manners, you Hun'. I shouted other things as well. I knew I was getting him nearly all the time I was firing.

"By this time, it was pretty hot from the burst petrol tank. I couldn't see much flame, but reckoned it was there alright. I remember looking at my left hand, which was keeping the throttle open, and seemed to be in the fire itself. I could see the skin peeling off yet had little pain. Unconsciously, too, I'd drawn my feet up under my parachute on the seat - to escape the heat, I suppose.

"Well, I gave the Hun all I had and the last I saw, he was going down with his right wing lower than the left. I gave him a parting burst, and as he disappeared started thinking about saving myself."

From this dramatic account of a desperate action, with the pilot overwhelmed by 'red mist' and exacting retribution on his erstwhile attacker, there is little wonder he was recommended for a Victoria Cross.

However, Nicolson left another testimony: his personal Combat Report. In it, having described the combat, he goes on:

"I then abandoned aircraft with difficulty and after dropping some 5,000ft pulled cord – I was shot in buttocks by an LDV just before landing".

Censored for public consumption, this wasn't mentioned in the BBC broadcast. However, the combat report, dictated to his CO, Sqn Ldr John Grandy, whilst Nicolson was in hospital, also added:

"I cannot swear whether firing button was at 'safe' or 'fire' "

This is completely at odds with definitive statements made in his broadcast, and rather strangely it contradicts what he later said in his BBC broadcast about having 'everything switched on'.

'Intent on Harm'

That aside, there is no doubt that Nicolson stayed with his burning fighter trying to turn the tables on his attacker. And there is no doubting he was fired on from the ground in his parachute.

A local Southampton man, Robert Stanley, took up the story:

"In 1940 I served in the LDV. On 16

- 149 -

THE BATTLE OF BRITAIN IN COLOUR

Right James Nicolson's attacker is often portrayed as a Messerschmitt 110. In fact, he was engaged with Messerschmitt 109s of JG53 'Pik As' and was shot down by Oberleutnant Heinz Bretnütz. Aircraft of JG53 are depicted in this original 1940 period colour photograph.

August I saw a Hurricane descending with a trail of smoke. The pilot baled-out and I decided to follow him to be on hand if help was required.

"I set off in hot pursuit of the airman, now drifting westwards. Keeping him in sight, I was horrified to see tracer bullets winging towards him from the ground. Arriving where he landed, I helped release him from his parachute.

"At this point a group of Royal Engineers came yelling into the field - clearly intent on harm. I ran towards them shouting: 'No! He's one of ours!', and with a Policeman managed to calm things. Clearly, they'd been responsible for the shooting as the gunfire came from their nearby HQ.

"Later, I found eleven recently fired .303 cases in a field near their base. The LDV got the blame for it, but I know it was the REs - because we in the LDV had .300 rifles, not .303."

Nicolson, peppered in the buttocks, had heard the shooting and concluded these wounds to be shotgun pellets. In fact, they were probably splinters which came from cannon shells as they exploded around him – this being borne out by examination of his tunic, trousers and Mae West displayed at Tangmere Military Aviation Museum. Luckily, the soldiers were poor shots, else the outcome might have been very different.

Another pilot on the squadron, Pilot Officer 'Ginger' Neil, related the tale:

"It appeared he had had shot at the Hun who had set him on fire. Stout fellow. The account which John Grandy received was very factual and not at all in the manner of 'Nick', who could be quite imaginative at times. We were all especially amused when we learned than an LDV had shot him in the backside before he landed in his parachute. In the bum, for heaven's sake! Everything happened to 'Nick'."

Acquitted Himself Bravely

As to the Messerschmitt 110 'probably destroyed' by Nicolson, there is yet more confusion. His attacker was reportedly the same aircraft, but there were no Messerschmitt 110s in combat in that area, no Messerschmitt 110s are shown in Luftwaffe records as lost or damaged and no Messerschmitt 110 pilot made any victory claims. There was, however, a Messerschmitt 109 pilot who *did* make victory claims over two Hurricanes in exactly the right place and time: Oberleutnant Heinz Bretnütz of 6./JG 53 who claimed his 13th and 14th aerial victories – clearly, Nicolson and King.

The involvement of 249 Squadron with Me 109s is confirmed in a report by Squadron Leader Grandy, dated 19 August 1940, stating Nicolson was involved with an 'unknown number of Me 109s.' Nevertheless, confusion by Nicolson and in official reports has clearly led to the accepted version of events involving Messerschmitt 110s.

Whatever the facts, one thing is certain; James Brindley Nicolson acquitted himself bravely in combat and endured terrible injury in efforts to down the enemy.

Fully recovered by September 1941, Nicolson was posted to India in 1942. Between August 1943 and August 1944, as

Left A representation of the markings carried on the Hurricane of 249 Squadron which was flown by Flight Lieutenant Nicolson during his VC action on 16 August 1940. (MOD)
Inset The little red devil emblem carried on James Nicolson's Hurricane. (MOD)

BATTLE OF BRITAIN GALLANTRY

Squadron Leader and CO of 27 Squadron, he flew Beaufighters over Burma, earning the DFC.

As a Wing Commander, Nicolson was killed on 2 May 1945, when the 355 Squadron B-24 Liberator in which he was flying as supernumerary, caught fire and crashed in the Bay of Bengal. No trace of him was ever found.

His medal group was sold at auction by his widow in 1983 for £110,000, then a record for a Victoria Cross, and was purchased by the RAF Museum, Hendon.

LONDON GAZETTE
15th November 1940

The citation for the award of Nicolson's Victoria Cross, "in recognition of most conspicuous bravery", was published in a supplement to *The London Gazette* on 15 November 1940:

"During an engagement with the enemy near Southampton on 16th August 1940, Flight Lieutenant Nicolson's aircraft was hit by four cannon shells, two of which wounded him whilst another set fire to the gravity tank. When about to abandon his aircraft owing to flames in the cockpit, he sighted an enemy fighter. This he attacked and shot down, although as a result of staying in his burning aircraft he sustained serious burns to his hands, face, neck and legs.

"Flight Lieutenant Nicolson has always displayed great enthusiasm for air fighting and this incident shows that he possesses courage and determination of a high order. By continuing to engage the enemy after he had been wounded and his aircraft set on fire, he displayed exceptional gallantry and disregard for the safety of his own life." ■

Top Flight Lieutenant James Nicolson (centre) seen at the RAF Hospital, Torquay, with fellow patients after learning he had been awarded the Victoria Cross.

Above right Pilot Officer Tom 'Ginger' Neil of 249 Squadron was a pal of James Nicolson and recalled the day when Nicolson was shot down. He is shown here, posing for the camera in front of Hurricane GN -A. Nicolson was shot down in a Hurricane marked GN – A, but it is likely the aircraft seen here replaced the one lost on 16 August 1940.

TYPHOON TRIBUTE

To mark the 75th anniversary of the Battle of Britain, the RAF painted one of its 29 Squadron Typhoon fighters to represent the aircraft flown by James Nicolson during his VC action on 16 August 1940. The aircraft wore 1940 period camouflage, carried the squadron and individual aircraft code letters GN – A and the red devil emblem painted on Nicolson's Hurricane. The aircraft also carried the name 'Flight Lieutenant James Nicolson VC' below the cockpit. The typhoon was flown as the air RAF's Typhoon display aircraft at air shows during the 2015 season.

– 151 –

THE BATTLE OF BRITAIN IN COLOUR

A Victoria Cross Earned?

Although only one Victoria Cross was awarded to a fighter pilot during the Battle of Britain, evidence exists that suggests another such award was initially recommended for an act of gallantry but not actually promulgated.

During the morning of 27 September 1940, at Mayfield in East Sussex, a young Home Guard Messenger, George Tuke, stood riveted to the spot in the roadway outside his home as a Messerschmitt 110 screamed towards him. A Hurricane was in hot pursuit, and in George's words "...it was almost attached to the German's tail".

As it zipped past, the Messerschmitt's rear gunner was firing continuously at his pursuer, the Hurricane blazing away with return fire. Empty bullet cases pinged and clattered off the tarmac around George, as rounds seared through branches of the trees which swayed in the slipstream as the aeroplanes flashed past, virtually at ground level. Then, as suddenly as they had burst upon the scene, they were gone.

What George had witnessed was a duel to the death between the Austrian CO of V./(Z)LG1, Hauptmann Horst Liensberger, his crewman Albert Kopge and a young South African, Flying Officer Percy Burton of 249 Squadron.

Near Horam, Phyllis Pitcher shouted to her husband, Robert, who was standing atop a pile of hay in their farmyard as the two aircraft flashed by. She called him to come down to avoid the bullets lashing around them. However, rooted to the spot, the danger had passed before he could join his wife behind the safety of farm buildings. Matter-of-factly, Robert recorded in his diary: "An exciting time with 'planes today. One down at Horam. Two more at Hailsham."

'A Blazing Inferno'

Seconds after they had passed the Pitchers, the aircraft were over Hailsham where the guns of both aircraft fell silent and watchers on the ground just heard the roar of engines, with brief glimpses of the wildly twisting aircraft.

One of the best views was had by farm worker Doug Weller. Approaching him, head-on, he could see both aircraft as they cleared the town centre and curved round towards him. What happened next was so sudden and so unexpected that Doug could scarcely believe his eyes:

- 152 -

BATTLE OF BRITAIN GALLANTRY

Left Hauptmann Horst Liensberger prepares to take off in his Messerschmitt 110 at Ligescourt, France, 6 September 1940.
Right Flying Officer P R-F 'Percy' Burton, 249 Squadron, 1940.
Far Right Hauptmann Horst Liensberger, Commanding Officer, V./(Z)LG1, 1940.

"I was working in the fields when the siren sounded so I stopped the tractor and settled down near a deep ditch - in case bombs started dropping - to have my mid-morning snack. The air raid warning had provided a convenient break. Then, I saw a Messerschmitt 110 approaching at great speed with the German insignia clearly visible in the morning sunlight. At the same time, I saw a Hurricane flying in a wide sweep, turning to come into the flight path of the Messerschmitt. I was expecting there to be a burst of gunfire, but nothing happened. He just kept coming, and as he passed below and beneath the Messerschmitt, he banked so that the tip of his wing hit the tail of the Messerschmitt. The timing was perfect, and the tail broke off the German 'plane - but so did part of the Hurricane's wing. The Messerschmitt dived into the ground, and then a column of black smoke rose from the next field where the Hurricane was a blazing inferno. The pilot was laying some 20-30ft away from the wreck. His parachute was extended, but not fully open, and we used it to cover his body until he was taken away."

The stricken Messerschmitt disintegrated on hitting the ground, the Hurricane briefly roaring on before slamming into a massive oak tree.

'A Very Deliberate Ramming'

Horst Liensberger, Albert Kopge and Percy Burton all lay dead, their broken bodies just a stones-throw apart; Liensberger strapped into his seat as if still at the controls, with his crewman, Kopge, laying on his back nearby, lifelessly staring into the sky that had recently been his battleground.

Like his adversaries, Percy was a long way from South Africa and could not be sent home for burial. Instead, he was interred at St Andrews Church near RAF Tangmere, West Sussex. The two German airmen, meanwhile, were buried at Hailsham with military honours.

In the aftermath of the incident, there was consensus that Percy Burton's actions had been a deliberate act. Out of ammunition, he severed the Messerschmitt's tail but was too low to recover or escape by parachute.

Sergeant Pilot George Palliser, of 249 Squadron, was flying not far distant from Percy at the fateful moment and later recalled:

"Percy was about 400 yards from me in what was quite a melee. It was as though someone had given him a punch on the nose, and he went for him. It was a very deliberate ramming"

George Palliser was in no doubt as to Percy Burton's bravery.

Publicly, though, the first recognition of Percy's action came in in a local newspaper report:

"British Pilot Rams a Messerschmitt"

"On Friday, residents in a market town in the south-east saw an enemy aeroplane and an attacking British fighter crash on the outskirts of the town. The RAF pilot appeared to ram his opponent deliberately. Spectators of the incident heard fierce machine gun fire overhead before the two aircraft – the Nazi one a Me 110 – dived steeply from the clouds almost down to the housetops. The Nazi pilot attempted to make off when his opponent, after circling part of the town, appeared to ram the Messerschmitt deliberately. The Me 110 crashed into an overhead sewer carried on tall brick pillars and parts of the machine were scattered over a wide area in fields near a sewage works. In the collision the British aircraft lost a wing and went on to hit a tree before catching fire."

It was almost the stuff of Victoria Cross citations!

'Recommendation For An Award'

Journalistic input aside, rather more telling is correspondence in local ARP archives sent to RAF Fighter Command:

"I beg to report that Pilot Officer P R F Burton [sic.]was killed in action when his 'plane crashed in Wellers Field, Station Road, Hailsham, on 27 September 1940. He had been taking part in an air battle over Hailsham and was first seen engaging an enemy bomber which he was forcing down.

I confirm that it is the general opinion of all who witnessed the occurrence that the act of gallantry performed by Pilot Officer Burton should be suitably rewarded. In saying that, I should state that the evidence of all eyewitnesses is quite spontaneous and has not been canvassed.

I should add that whilst the enemy bomber had ample ammunition, Pilot Officer Burton's had none. I trust that the

> **"I should add that whilst the enemy bomber had ample ammunition, Pilot Officer Burton's had none. I trust that the act of Pilot Officer Burton in ramming the enemy will be reported to the appropriate authority with a recommendation for an award."**
>
> Mr A Carr, ARP Sub-Controller, Hailsham, East Sussex, 1 October 1940.

THE BATTLE OF BRITAIN IN COLOUR

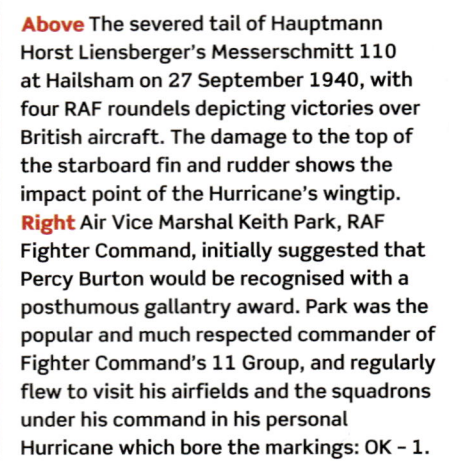

Above The severed tail of Hauptmann Horst Liensberger's Messerschmitt 110 at Hailsham on 27 September 1940, with four RAF roundels depicting victories over British aircraft. The damage to the top of the starboard fin and rudder shows the impact point of the Hurricane's wingtip.
Right Air Vice Marshal Keith Park, RAF Fighter Command, initially suggested that Percy Burton would be recognised with a posthumous gallantry award. Park was the popular and much respected commander of Fighter Command's 11 Group, and regularly flew to visit his airfields and the squadrons under his command in his personal Hurricane which bore the markings: OK – 1.

act of Pilot Officer Burton in ramming the enemy will be reported to the appropriate authority with a recommendation for an award."

That Percy Burton was out of bullets is a factor that cannot be ignored when considering the circumstances of this incident.

In a reply on behalf of Air Vice Marshal Keith Park, the AOC of 11 Group RAF Fighter Command, dated 23 October 1940, Squadron Leader A C H MacLean wrote:

"I thought you would like to know that I have recommended this pilot for a posthumous decoration and I very much hope that this will be awarded in due course."

Significantly, the only decoration available for a posthumous award is the Victoria Cross. No other gallantry decoration may be awarded posthumously.

On 17 March 1941, Percy Burton was Mentioned in Despatches in *The London Gazette*, although in the absence of any detail, it is impossible to say if this was related to the action on 27 September 1940.

On the face of it, a Mention in Despatches is a poor substitute for a Victoria Cross – the supreme award for valour. Maybe, though, the authorities had some difficulty with the idea of a VC award to two pilots on the same squadron within a matter of weeks.

However, it could be that no definite proof existed to establish whether this was anything other than an accident instead of an act of the most incredible bravery.

Those on the ground, as well as Sergeant Pilot Palliser, were in no doubt. To all of them, this was a supreme act of valour: a Victoria Cross earned but not awarded. ■

Flying Officer Percival Ross-Frames Burton, RAFVR, No. 74348

Percy Burton was born in Cape Province, South Africa, on 6 June 1917. His father was the Rt. Hon. Henry Burton, P.C., K.C., LL.B. (a South African lawyer and Minister of Finance who died in 1935), and his mother was Helen Marie Kannemeyer. Percy was their youngest son and was educated at Diocesan College, Rondebosch, Cape Town, and matriculated in 1938, going to Oxford to read Jurisprudence. He was reserve cox for the University Boat in 1938 and learnt to fly with the Oxford University Air Squadron.

He was called up in October 1939 as a member of the Royal Air Force Volunteer Reserve. After completing his training he was posted to 6 Operational Training Unit, RAF Sutton Bridge, on 22 June 1940, to convert to the Hawker Hurricane, joining 249 (Gold Coast) Squadron, RAF Church Fenton, on 21 July 1940.

He was promoted to Flying Officer on 26 September 1940, the day before his death.

He is seen above (right) with Pilot Officer Bryan Meaker of 249 Squadron who was also shot down and killed on 27 September 1940.

Note: His brother, Flight Lieutenant William Westbrooke Burton, was lost in action with RAF Bomber Command. On the night of 20 August 1941, flying a Wellington of 104 Squadron, he was killed during a bombing raid on Cologne. He was reported missing and is commemorated on the CWGC Runnymede Memorial.

WWW.EPICMILITARIA.COM

Secured by sage|pay

Over 6000+ WW2 & Military Products

Worldwide Shipping

UK First Class or Next Day Delivery

Secure Checkout

📞 0800 772 3448
✉ contact@epicmilitaria.com

Europe's largest collection of military re-enactment clothing and equipment

SOLDIER OF FORTUNE

WWW.SOFMILITARY.CO.UK

RAF Battle of Britain Volunteer Reserve

WAAF Uniform and Accessories

Browse our 1000's of militaria products via our website online Now

RAF Battle of Britain Pilot

Battle of Britain Flight Sergeant

Soldier of Fortune, 13 Tyn-Y-Llidiart Ind Est, Corwen, Denbighshire, North Wales, LL21 9QX
Email: sales@sofmilitary.co.uk   Tel: 01490 412225

THE BATTLE OF BRITAIN IN COLOUR

'Their Finest Hour'

As Prime Minister, Winston Churchill led the nation throughout the Battle of Britain. It was his galvanizing and inspirational leadership which rightly ensured he would be remembered as the architect of victory while prevailing against the odds.

In the early hours of 10 May, German forces invaded Belgium, Luxembourg and the Netherlands as a prelude to their assault on France. It was to be a momentous day – both on the war front and on the home front.

Following The defeat and evacuation of the Allied Expeditionary Force from Norway in early May, Prime Minister Neville Chamberlain had suffered a vote of no confidence, leading to his resignation just hours before Hilter's Blitzkrieg was unleashed on France and the Low Countries.

With Great Britain now facing its greatest crisis of modern times, the Conservative Party's favourite, Foreign Minister Edward Wood, 1st Earl of Halifax, and architect of Chamberlain's earlier failed appeasement policy with Hitler, declined to become prime minister, thus leaving Churchill as the country's last hope. Halifax stated that he felt Churchill would make a more suitable war leader, and Chamberlain duly advised His Majesty King George VI to ask Churchill to form a government and become Prime Minister.

Of his appointment, Churchill later wrote: *"I felt as if I were walking with destiny, and that all my past life had been but a preparation for this hour and for this trial."*

Today, he is rightly remembered as Britain's inspirational wartime leader who played an important role in the defence of democracy in Europe against Nazism. More importantly, he galvanized and inspired a nation during its darkest hour, leading it on to its finest hour.

'So Few'

Renowned for his stirring speeches, it was Churchill who first used the phrase 'Battle of Britain' in a speech on 18 June 1940, when he said:

"What General Weygand has called the

- 156 -

WINSTON CHURCHILL

"The gratitude of every home in our Island, in our Empire, and indeed throughout the world, except in the abodes of the guilty, goes out to the British airmen who, undaunted by odds, unwearied in their constant challenge and mortal danger, are turning the tide of the World War by their prowess and by their devotion. Never in the field of human conflict was so much owed by so many to so few."

Prime Minister Winston Churchill, House of Commons, 20 August 1940

Battle of France is over...the Battle of Britain is about to begin. Upon this battle depends the survival of Christian civilisation. Upon it depends our own British way of life, and the long continuity of our institutions and our Empire."

From that moment, the term Battle of Britain was established and enshrined in Britain's history, entering the English lexicon. Later, in that same speech, he went on to say:

"Let us therefore brace ourselves to our duties, and so bear ourselves, that if the British Empire and its Commonwealth last for a thousand years, men will still say, 'This was their finest hour.' "

Not only did Churchill lead Britain through the dark days of Dunkirk, the Battle of Britain and the Blitz – and then on to an ultimate Allied victory – but he also established the deep national reverence for the pilots and aircrew of the Battle of Britain. It is a reverence which endures to this day. Not only that, but it was another of Churchill's speeches which further established, henceforth, that this gallant group of airmen should become known as the 'Few'. This arose from his speech to the House of Commons on 20 August 1940 (part of which appears above on this page) in which he referred to them as: '...so few'.

It is tempting, perhaps, to think that Churchill's inspiration was drawn from the St Crispin's Day Speech in Shakespeare's play, Henry V:

"We few, we happy few, we band of brothers."

However, such was the oratory skill of Churchill that he doubtless needed no inspiration, save for the inspiration which had so moved him when he visited the underground HQ of 11 Group, RAF Fighter Command, at Uxbridge on 16 August 1940, and watched the battles unfold before him on the general situation map.

The name of Winston Churchill is as synonymous today with the victory achieved during the Battle of Britain as are the men he lauded as the 'Few'. ■

"DEAR GOD, I HOPE IT ISN'T A BRITISH 'PLANE..."

On 28 August 1940, Prime Minister Winston Churchill was touring defences around Dover when an air battle developed, and a German fighter was shot down. With Churchill was his bodyguard, Inspector Walter Thompson, who later took up the story:

"It was while we were at Dover, that we saw the approaching German bombers and just a short distance away they were met by British fighters. Mr Churchill seemed mesmerised as the air battle took place almost overhead. We saw maybe two German bombers crash into the sea and some fighters with smoke trailing from them as they spiralled away from the main dogfight. Later that afternoon, we had to drive to Ramsgate and on the way saw a smouldering aircraft in a field. Churchill asked the driver to pull off the road and get as close to the wreckage as he could. There were firemen, soldiers and ARP men standing around and I walked with the Prime Minister towards the aircraft. I warned Mr Churchill about the dangers of being out in the open during an air raid, but he said that he must have a look. When he saw the tangled mess, he said: "Dear God, I hope it isn't a British 'plane." He was reassured it was not."

The aircraft was a Messerschmitt 109 of Stab.I/JG3 which had been hit and set on fire by a Spitfire. The pilot, Leutnant Hans-Herbert Landry, baled out but was seriously burned. He died of his injuries in the Royal Military Hospital, Woolwich, on 23 September 1940.

Above Prime Minister Winston Churchill walks away from the crash site of the Messerschmitt 109 at Church Farm, Whitfield, on 28 August 1940. On his left is his bodyguard, Inspector Thompson. Clutched in his right hand, with his stick, he holds a bullet case – a souvenir he picked up from the wreckage which still smoulders behind him.

Left Firemen and ARP workers hold up the wing of the Messerschmitt 109 to show the Prime Minister, who was greatly relieved to discover that it was a German aircraft.

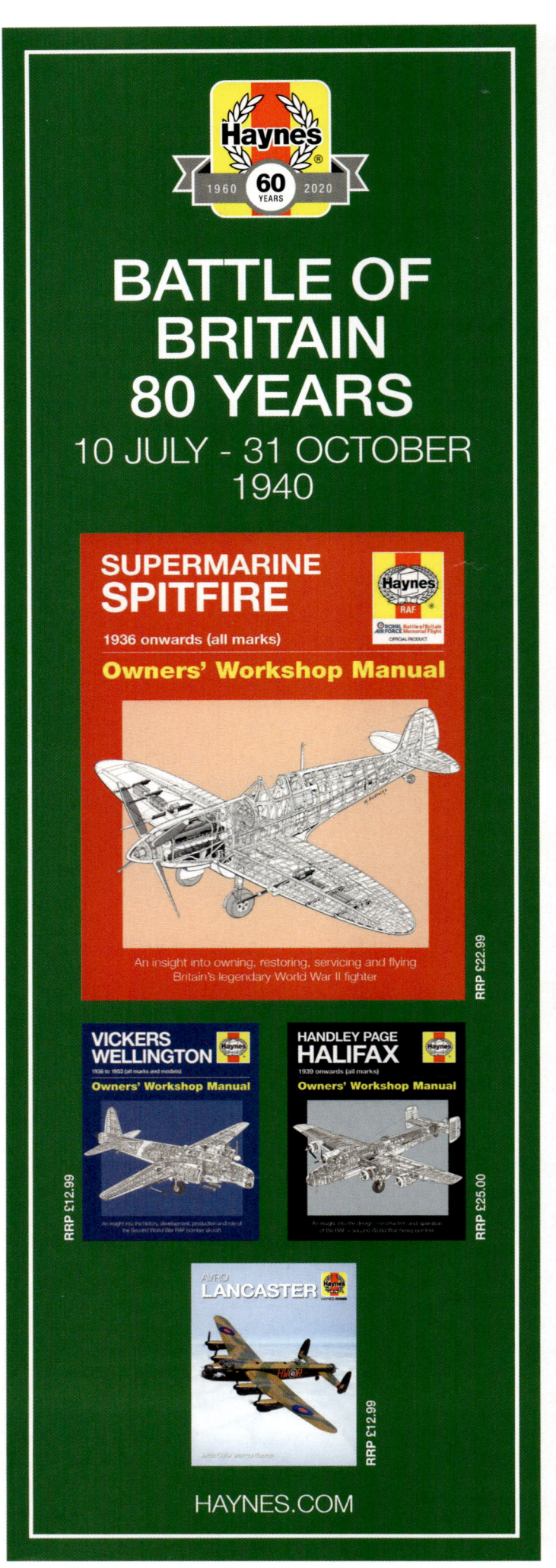

Haynes
60 YEARS 1960-2020

BATTLE OF BRITAIN 80 YEARS
10 JULY – 31 OCTOBER 1940

SUPERMARINE SPITFIRE
1936 onwards (all marks)
Owners' Workshop Manual
An insight into owning, restoring, servicing and flying Britain's legendary World War II fighter
RRP £22.99

VICKERS WELLINGTON
1936 to 1953 (all marks and models)
Owners' Workshop Manual
An insight into the design, construction, operation and role of the Second World War RAF bomber aircraft
RRP £12.99

HANDLEY PAGE HALIFAX
1939 onwards (all marks)
Owners' Workshop Manual
An insight into the design, construction and operation of the RAF's second World War heavy bomber
RRP £25.00

AVRO LANCASTER
RRP £12.99

HAYNES.COM

LONDON MEDAL COMPANY
No. 13 Cecil Court
London WC2N 4AN

We are a leading British War Medal dealership based in the heart of London.

We specialise in British and World Orders, Decorations and Medals and carry an extensive range of general militaria from both Great Britain and around the world.

www.london-medals.co.uk
020 7836 8877

BUY & SELL WAR MEDALS • BUY & SELL MILITARIA
VALUATIONS • PART EXCHANGE WELCOME • MEDAL MOUNTING SERVICES
BUY MEDAL RIBBON • DISCREET SERVICE • NEXT DAY DELIVERY
• BUY & VIEW ALL AVAILBLE STOCK ONLINE

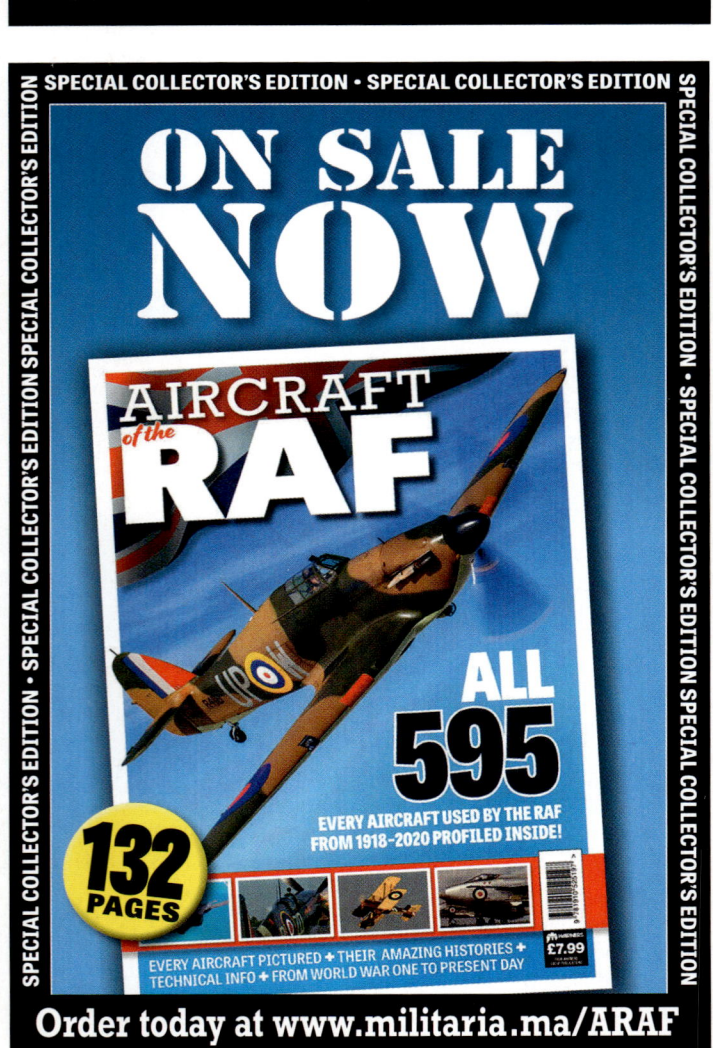

SPECIAL COLLECTOR'S EDITION

ON SALE NOW

AIRCRAFT of the RAF

ALL 595
EVERY AIRCRAFT USED BY THE RAF FROM 1918–2020 PROFILED INSIDE!

132 PAGES

EVERY AIRCRAFT PICTURED + THEIR AMAZING HISTORIES + TECHNICAL INFO + FROM WORLD WAR ONE TO PRESENT DAY

£7.99

Order today at www.militaria.ma/ARAF

The Balance Sheet

The casualty list and the tally of aircraft losses for both the RAF and the Luftwaffe during the four months of the Battle of Britain make for sobering reading. The cost to both sides, both in terms of men and machines, was a very considerable one.

Officially, the Battle of Britain drew to its conclusion on 31 October 1940. The RAF had held the line against a numerically superior enemy, and whilst no outright victory in terms of an irrevocable defeat of the Luftwaffe had been achieved, the important fact of the matter was that Germany had failed to wrest air superiority from the British. The cost to both sides, however, had been high.

Here, we take a look at the final tally of losses sustained by both the RAF and the Luftwaffe between 10 July and 31 October 1940:

RAF Fighter Command
Number of Pilots Avaliable:
1 July......................................1,200
1 August..................................1,434
1 September 1,381
1 October................................1,703
1 November............................1,796 *

*Despite attrition rates, RAF Fighter Command had more fighter pilots available than the Luftwaffe and the number never decreased throughout the battle.

Number of Pilots Killed, POW or Missing*
July 74
August 148
September............................... 159
October 100
Total..**431**

*NB: These figures are based on immediate post war data from the Air Ministry, although subsequent research has shown the total number to have actually been 535, a discrepancy of nearly 100 against the originally quoted figure. Ten pilots were later confirmed to be POWs. A full one-third of the total number of fatalities (ie, 179) were reported as 'missing' and have no known grave.

Number of Pilots Wounded and Injured*
July 49
August 156
September............................... 152
October 65
Total: 422

*NB: A number of these men succumbed to their injuries some time later, and at least in a few cases after the end of the Battle of Britain itself. To an extent, therefore, these subsequent deaths will have slightly skewed the casualty totals ..

Total Numbers of Fighter Aircraft Available for Operations*
(The bracketed figure represents the total number of aircraft losses)
July ....644.................(115)
August ....708.................(294)
September..................746.................(389)
October ....734 ....(251)

*NB: Despite these aircraft losses, the attrition rate was always adequately coped with by production output from the aircraft factories and replacements from storage at RAF Maintenance Units.

Above RAF casualties were buried with full military honours in all cases where their bodies were recovered. Here, Flying Officer John Hardacre of 504 Squadron, shot down off the South Coast on 25 September 1940, is laid to rest at Fawley, Hampshire. His family follow the flag-draped coffin, which is borne by RAF personnel.

THE BATTLE OF BRITAIN IN COLOUR

The Luftwaffe

In considering the losses of the Luftwaffe, it is impossible to do so using exactly the same criteria as that applied to the RAF losses above and no direct comparison can be made. Instead, we can look at approximate totals of losses sustained by the Luftwaffe during this period:

Aircraft and Aircrew Losses

July
Aircraft 185
Aircrew..................................... 348
(Of the above, 56 aircraft were fighters and 52 of the personnel losses were fighter aircrew)

August
Aircraft 694
Aircrew..................................... 993
(Of the above, 330 aircraft were fighters and 233 of the personnel losses were fighter aircrew)

September
Aircraft 629
Aircrew..................................... 829
(Of the above, 321 aircraft were fighters and 191 of the personnel losses were fighter aircrew)

October
Aircraft 379
Aircrew..................................... 492
(Of the above, 166 aircraft were fighters and 75 of the personnel losses were fighter aircrew)
Total Aircraft Losses........................ 1,887
Total Aircrew Losses........................ 2,662

In looking at the Luftwaffe casualties above it is important to also take into account that several hundred Luftwaffe aircrew were taken POW over this same period. These men were, operationally, total losses so far the Germans were concerned. The exact figure is uncertain and is not included in the loss figures quoted.

Approximately 85 Junkers 87 'Stuka' crew members were killed in action.

In terms of available aircraft, the Luftwaffe had available at the commencement of the battle some 1,500 bomber aircraft. That figure stood at around 1,393 on 31 October. Thus, re-supply had not kept pace with losses and of approximately 1,050 front line fighters available to the Luftwaffe at the commencement of the battle a little under 850 were available at the conclusion of the period.

The Other 'Few'

RAF Fighter Command is remembered in terms of fighting the air battle over Britain in 1940, but Bomber Command was also fighting back, particularly in bombardment of the invasion ports. During the period of the Battle of Britain, Bomber Command lost 718 personnel, not including those taken POW.

In conclusion, we must not forget RAF ground personnel who were often very much in the front line during the Battle of Britain, especially during the course of Luftwaffe attacks on RAF airfields and other establishments. The Luftwaffe did not restrict its attacks to airfields of Fighter Command, and so the total number of airmen killed on the ground between 10 July and 31 October 1940 includes many from other Commands. It also includes three WAAF personnel. Astonishingly, the total number of ground casualties stands at 312 and with another 467 wounded, many seriously.

Speaking before the Battle of Britain commenced, Prime Minister Winston Churchill had said:

'If the British Empire and its Commonwealth last for a thousand years, men will still say, "This was their finest hour" '.

Surely, it was Britain's 'finest hour'.

It had, however, taken a terrible toll.

NB: The figures of all losses quoted here are, in many cases, only approximate totals and are based upon the best information available. They are figures, however, which are frequently subject to minor adjustments, up or down, with historical research often turning up fresh information which sheds new light on losses, British and German. ∎

Top When Flying Officer Richard 'Dick' Plummer of 46 Squadron was shot down and badly burned over Essex on 4 September 1940, his family received the ever-dreaded telegram, bluntly informing them of his predicament. Sadly, he succumbed to his injuries on 14 September 1940. His family were later sent his identity discs with a horseshoe lucky charm attached.

Above Leutnant Hans-Herbert Landry, a Messerschmitt 109 pilot with Stab./I JG3, was shot down and badly wounded north of Dover on 28 August 1940. He died in hospital from his injuries some four weeks later.

THE BALANCE SHEET

Below On August 31 1940, the popular weekly Picture Post carried an image of Pilot Officer Keith 'Colt' Gillman, a Hurricane pilot of 32 Squadron, on its front cover. He was the very epitome of the archetypal Battle of Britain pilot, one of 'The Few', who were adulated through the British press of the time. But by the time the magazine had gone on sale, Keith Gillman was already dead having been shot down into the sea south of Dover – his hometown. No trace of him was ever found.

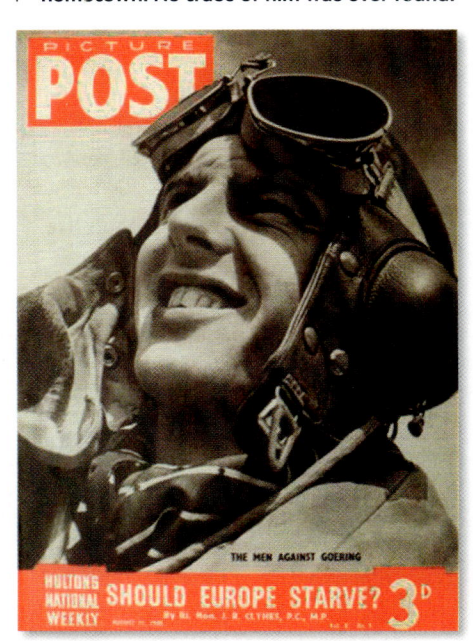

Above More RAF Bomber Command losses were suffered during the Battle of Britain than in RAF Fighter Command, with 718 killed and many taken POW. This is the wreckage of a Fairey Battle of 103 Squadron, shot down near Calais on 9 September 1940 whilst attacking barges and shipping being assembled for the projected invasion of Britain. (Note the uncompleted long-range German gun emplacement behind the aircraft.) The three crew, Squadron Leader De Sanoul-Servier, Pilot Officer W A Cooper and Sergeant F Drinkwater were all killed but have no known grave and are thus still 'missing in action'. It is presumed that they were buried in field graves which have subsequently been lost.

Left & Above Left Pilot Officer William 'Scotty' Gordon was a twenty-year-old Spitfire pilot serving with 234 Squadron at RAF Middle Wallop and was shot down and killed over Hadlow Down, East Sussex, on 6 September 1940. He was taken home to be laid to rest in his hometown of Mortlach, Banff.

'Scotty' Gordon had been with his squadron since November 1939, so was already an 'old hand'. On 12 July 1940, he shared in the probable destruction of a Junkers 88 and on 24 August 1940 he was involved in an air battle over the Isle of Wight with his squadron when he shot down a Messerschmitt 109.

– 161 –

THE BATTLE OF BRITAIN IN COLOUR

Left Burial of Luftwaffe airmen by the RAF was commonplace during the Battle of Britain, always with full military honours and with coffins draped with swastika flags. Here, crew members of a Dornier 17 shot down off Brancaster, Norfolk, on 21 August 1940, are buried at Catton, near Norwich. Respect to enemy dead was generally a given on both sides.

German personnel who were buried at cemeteries in the UK were re-interred at the German Military Cemetery, Cannock Chase, during the 1960s, unless they were buried in cemeteries or churchyards where there was already a CWGC plot. Around 5,000 now lie at Cannock Chase.

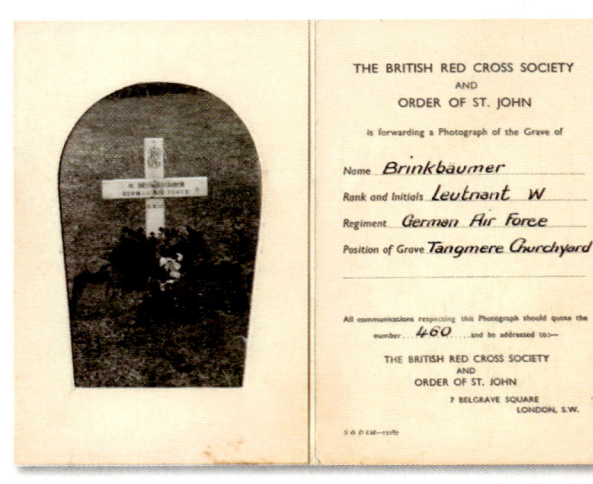

Left German airmen shot down over Britain were also buried with full military honours by the British military and their families later sent photographs of their burial locations by the Order of St. John, via the International Red Cross. Leutnant zur See Karl-Wilhelm Brinkbäumer was attached to the Luftwaffe and was shot down in a Junkers 88 near Sidlesham, West Sussex, on 13 August 1940.

Right One of the bronze relief panels of the Battle of Britain Monument at Victoria Embankment, London, which commemorates those who served during the battle. Further details may be found here: https://bbm.org.uk/

This memorial is one of two national monuments to the Battle of Britain in the UK, the other being symbolically situated atop the White Cliffs at Capel-le-Ferne, Kent.

BREAKFAST

His place was laid,
The Messroom clock struck eight,
The sun shone through the window
On his chair...
No one commented on his fate,
Save for a headshake here and there;
Only old George, who'd seen him die,
Spinning down against the Autumn sky,
Leaned forward and turned down his plate.

And, as he did, the sunlight fled,
As though the sky he loved so
Mourned her dead.

Hannah Hunt, 1940

THIS PUBLICATION IS DEDICATED TO THE PERSONNEL OF THE ROYAL AIR FORCE WHO SERVED IN THE AIR AND ON THE GROUND DURING THE BATTLE OF BRITAIN IN 1940.